To Catch the Su...

CAROLINE CASS

Anthony Eyre

MOUNT ORLEANS PRESS

Published in Great Britain in 2024
by Anthony Eyre, Mount Orleans Press
23 High Street, Cricklade SN6 6AP
https://anthonyeyre.com

ISBN 978-1-912945-47-4

A CIP record for this book is available
from the British Library

Set in 11/14pt Rongel

Printed in Malta by
Gutenberg Press

Also by Caroline Cass:

GRAND ILLUSIONS—CONTEMPORARY INTERIOR MURALS
Phaidon, 1988

JOY ADAMSON—BEHIND THE MASK
Weidenfeld & Nicolson, 1992

ELTON JOHN'S FLOWER FANTASIES
Weidenfeld & Nicolson, 1997

THE PLANT HUNTER'S TALE
Quartet, 2012

FARU THE LITTLE RHINO
Troika Children's Books, 2016

TO CATCH THE SUN

Let's enjoy it while we can
Won't you help me share my load
From the dark side of the street
To the bright side of the road

Van Morrison, 1979

For my daughters Tara and Tasmin

and

Cal, Jago, Zac and Fin

Contents

Kenya

KAJIADO — LIFE IN THE BUSH

IT SEEMED THAT a generosity of spirit permeated the land where I lived. Under a larkspur sky which gave the impression of being the largest on earth, lay a place of great natural beauty and variety—untouched forests and wild deserts, a snow-peaked mountain and flawless white beaches. I grew up immersed in the steady rhythm of Africa in Kenya, and the sense of limitless freedom and adventure it offered is the strongest memory of my childhood. Sunshine taken for granted; the smell of the earth soothed by rain; early morning mists blowing off Mount Kilimanjaro which stood like a sentinel on the Tanganyika border a few hours from our house in Kajiado; these were amongst the elements that nourished me.

In the midst of this bucolic existence something happened to me as a child that to some degree affected the rest of my life. On a day seared into my mind I remember lying on the cool earthen floor of an African hut newly plastered with mud and cow dung. Moments before I had swum up from the watery depths of unconsciousness, and as my eyes slowly adjusted to the dark interior I could see rows of bright, shiny beads hanging round the necks of the Maasai women bending anxiously over me. A group of grey-haired elders with long pierced earlobes and red blankets slung over their shoulders, huddled round the entrance and peered in. Filtering through the men's low murmuring I could hear far away the unsettling sound of the wind racing across the grassy plains.

A short time earlier our neighbour, Mr Jacobs, an amiable Afrikaner farmer, had brought me seemingly lifeless into the hut after giving me a ride on his brand new tractor. He left me there before rushing back to our house and announcing to my mother that he had, most regrettably, killed me. My young father, the District Commissioner in charge of this vast expanse of Maasai land, was off on safari. The farmer's children, Otto and Anita, who were my own age and at boarding school with me in Nairobi, were my friends and the only other white children in Kajiado. I was eight years old.

It was a breezy morning when their father suggested as a treat he take us all for a ride along the dusty dirt road leading to the only *duka* in the region, a small ramshackle Indian shop a mile away. In the casual manner of a man who lives a hard life in the bush Mr. Jacobs placed four excited young children on the metal mudguards covering the huge back wheels. As the tractor bounced over the railway track which snaked its way to the soda-rich lake of Magadi, my four year old sister Susie lost her balance and was about to fall off. In grabbing her to safety, I slipped and fell backwards over the side into the black space between the mudguard and the wheel. As I slid round, the fat tyre gripped my right leg and three quarters of my calf muscles were severed before Mr Jacobs realised what had happened.

When my distraught mother arrived at the hut with the farmer and rushed to my side to find me still breathing, she knelt down and gently wiped the matted hair and dirt from my face. Mr. Jacobs picked me up and hurried over to our blue humped-back 1950s Ford where he lay me on the back seat. Within seconds my mother jumped in the car, put her foot flat down on the accelerator and we tore off down the bumpy corrugated road to Gertrude's Garden, the children's hospital in Nairobi, fifty miles away.

My earliest recollection is only a tiny fragment of my life but however small, I have always held on to it. I still have a small scar to prove the first episode and don't feel I have distorted the second. I was three and we were living at Kwale, a village south of Mombasa where Dad was the District Officer. Our simple house was surrounded by an untamed garden full of coconut palms, mango trees and white flowering frangipanis. A seedbed of images crowd my memory and I tend to find the smells of childhood emotionally charged. Lifting a freshly cut lime and inhaling its bitter-sweet scent, instantly transports me back.

During one rainy season my six year old cousin Christopher came from upcountry Gilgil to stay with us and he and I were sitting outside on the grass below the verandah. The earth smelled new after a morning burst of tropical rain and we were playing with my small mongoose Riki. Perhaps we were suffocating the creature with childish love but he suddenly turned and bit me hard with his sharp pointy teeth down to the knuckle of my right middle finger. In tears I rushed up the stone steps to be consoled by my mother who bandaged me up with a plaster and a kiss.

Later my cousin and I meandered down to the bottom of our garden near a coconut grove where we took turns pushing each other on the swing. I was waiting for my push when something suddenly made me look up into the dark interior of the grove. A strange flickering movement. I jumped off and grabbed Christopher, whispering,

"Look, look, what's that?" as I pointed in its direction.

He froze and we stood there together unable to tear our gaze away, both as frightened as each other. It was a white and wispy apparition, tied securely round its flimsy middle to the trunk of a coconut tree. The flailing creature seemed to be trying to wrench itself free. It made no sound but we felt we were looking at something quite terrifying which would suddenly come for us if we didn't get away. In slow motion, similar to being in a nightmare in which you try to run but your feet are treading through treacle, the two of us managed to burst out of our momentary paralysis and scuttle back to the house to the safety of my mother for the second time that day. I have thought about that strange apparition over the years but long ago decided that it must have been the troubled ghost of an African who had died in his village behind the kai-apple hedge on the other side of the grove.

My father, Leslie Pritchard, inherited our large rambling house in Kajiado in 1950, not long after one of his fellow District Commissioners, Hugh Murray Grant, had been speared to death by a Maasai warrior in a bitter argument over a cattle dispute. The local Narok tribesmen had been deeply resentful of the compulsory purchase of their cows by the British and a young *moran*, Karambu ole Sendeu, came home one afternoon to find that his cherished pet bullock had been confiscated, along with nine cows. Maasai imbue their cattle with a near-spiritual significance and Ole Sendeu had nursed the bullock ever since its mother died. Having rushed to the collecting pen and pleaded for his animal's release, he offered to replace it with another. He was refused. Twenty minutes later as the DC was supervising the cattle auction, a spear suddenly whizzed past the animals with the force of a rocket, tearing through the back of Hugh Murray Grant and pinning him in the dirt. Ole Sendeu leapt forward, picked up his weapon and sprinted away. He was later hanged for murder.

Deep in the African bush south of Nairobi our home had many rooms and was originally built for White Hunters and their rich clients to spend a restful night or two on their long safaris. When that quixotic venture failed, the house was given to the incumbent District Commissioner. Until we moved to Kajiado we had lived in places with names that sounded magical to a child—besides Kwale there was Mombasa, where a confused stingray leapt over the sea-wall and landed with a noisy splash in the Club pool while my astonished father was swimming; Kiambu, homeland of the Kikuyu—it was there that Jomo Kenyatta came to tea and, according to Mum, sat me on his knee. By then the magnetic young future leader of the country had changed his name from Johnston Mathau to the Swahili word for 'burning spear'.

Soon after my father returned to London from the Far East at the end of the Second World War, he and my mother decided they wanted a more exciting and fulfilling life than their battered country could offer. Pa immediately joined the Colonial Service and at the age of twenty-five, swaddling me in their arms, off they went to Kenya, a land full of hope and purpose.

Rows of tall eucalyptus trees lined the driveway of our house in Kajiado and beyond them thorny acacias punctuated the plains all the way to distant blue hills. The air was alive with the camphor smell of *leleshwa* leaves and the soothing call of the Cape Turtle doves, a sound I still love. A tangle of bouganvillea and golden shower grew untamed up the cream-painted walls of the house and cascaded down the side of the windows. Inside, the main rooms of the house were high-ceilinged and panelled in dark, polished Indian teak; herringbone floors were laid throughout. Practical wooden furniture made by Indian craftsmen in Nairobi filled each room. Sunlight flooded an expansive interior courtyard full of earthenware pots spilling over with red geraniums and a favourite pastime of Susie's and mine was to ride our bikes, trailed by our younger sister Anne, whom we called Pods, in and around the open space.

Night falls abruptly on the equator. One moment the sun is on fire, like a large molten orange sitting on the edge of the world; within minutes it's curiosity has got the better of it. It slips over the horizon to see what lies beyond and melts swiftly into the night. We had no electricity in our house and as soon as twilight fell our African servants (the term 'staff' was unknown in households at that time), wearing crisp white *kanzus* and red baize fezes on their heads, filled each room with the soft glow of hurricane lamps. As the temperature dropped quickly on the equator, a fire was lit in the drawing room before dinner each night. At bedtime I carried my own smaller paraffin lamp to my room, with its tall dark cupboard where I stashed my weekly pocket money and sweets on the very top, far away from sibling fingers. Bear-With-One-Eye, my comforting, lifelong companion, was sitting against the pillow on my narrow bed waiting for me. I read until Mum came in and kissed me goodnight.

Mine was mainly a life of simple pleasures. Until I was unhappily torn away at seven to go to boarding school, I had been taught over the radio and by correspondence course under my devoted mother's surprisingly disciplined tutelage. My parents' wireless seemed permanently frozen on the BBC World Service and I found listening to the sound of the jaunty tune and the hourly bong of Big Ben a reassuring ritual. Once my leg mended I was left with a permanent dent in the back of my calf, though it didn't impede me in any way. Barefoot and curious, I could go off anywhere within reason on my bike. In those days bush parents seldom worried about the freedom afforded their offspring unless a lion had been spotted prowling round the area. As we were surrounded by Maasai, in time I got to say 'Sopa'—'hello' —and a few halting words in their language of Maa to some of the young children who lived with their families in *manyattas*, small circular villages of huts surrounded by prickly thorn bushes to protect their cattle and goats at night from marauding animals. The Maasai are semi-nomadic pastoralists and follow the growing of the grass for the grazing of their cattle as the rains fall. But on hot, hazy afternoons the wives and mothers sat in the shade of a tall yellow fever tree near our house, with branches spreading out like a crocheted umbrella. Naked children ran around them, their eyes and faces covered in flies which never seemed to bother them. I was a shy child but on particularly lucky days the women invited me to sit with them and taught me how to thread the colourful African beads for their intricate necklaces.

With the help of the young African gardeners, my mother managed to scrabble flower beds and vegetable plots out of the arid earth into what we children thought of as a botanical gem. Blue plumbago, zinnias and yellow dahlias added small splashes of colour. The tennis court, on the far side of the garden, was surrounded by tall chicken wire to keep out wild animals; grazing zebra and Thompson's gazelles seemed quite naturally part of our extended family. I have always hated the sound of the wind tearing through wire, probably subconsciously something to do with my accident. We also inherited a much used squash court which nestled among the jacaranda and red pepper trees.

After the long rainy season when the small tufts of new grass sprung up through the parched plains as though the land was reborn, a field near our house was filled with a thousand small white lilies. As the annual mass of pale yellow butterflies rose in the air like spring, I collected bunches of these white flowers as a present for my mother. It remains a poignant memory for me but when I asked her years later,

"Do you remember all those lilies I used to pick for you in Kajiado?"

"No darling, what lilies?" she replied vaguely.

I remember feeling rather hurt but it made me realise how fragile memories of a simple shared event can be. Although I seldom visit now I have retained a deep sentimental attachment to Kajiado. Of everywhere I have lived it is the place I loved the most.

NAIROBI

Four years later, just before I turned eleven, we moved to Nairobi. At first I missed the wide open plains and my tribal companions but in town I could pursue new interests, one of which was ballet. My family has long had a tendency for what we termed our 'Kikuyu' sense of humour—laughing at the unintended mishaps of others—which seems to have been passed down to my children and grandchildren. However inappropriate at times, we still find it totally irresistible. My first public display of this questionable trait was as a keen young ballet student. Our studio was next to the Nairobi National Theatre and we were on stage dancing a short, simplified version of *Sleeping Beauty* under the gimlet eye of Madame Zerchovich, our exacting and frightening old Russian ballet teacher. I was the Lilac Fairy and our principal dancer, a new, very pretty friend named Angela Pringle, played the main role of Princess Aurora. Many years later when she became too tall to be a fully-fledged ballerina she married an heir to Marks and Spencer which I have always thought was a pretty decent trade off.

In one scene I was standing on stage minding my own balletic business and looking pretty lilacy on tip-toes with my arms poised gracefully above my head. Just as Tchaichovsky's dreamy music picked up tempo Angela soared out of the wings in a dramatic *grande jeté* right past me, slid on a couple of leaves inadvertently left over from the previous woodland scene, and shot off into the orchestra pit. She landed on top of the middle-aged bassoonist who looked more than a little surprised as he and his precious instrument unceremoniously hit the floor. It was so unexpected, happening in a split second, and although the poor girl was unhurt, I lost all control. Most of the young dancers on stage were stunned into an embarrassed silence but my own fairy composure disintegrated on the spot and, arms still akimbo, I could clearly be seen shaking with laughter.

Old settlers down from the Kenya highlands, happily sipping their sundowners on the verandah of the Norfolk Hotel opposite, remained oblivious to the commotion coming from the stage, the orchestra pit and the concerned audience as parents rushed forward to help. I was obviously in deep disgrace and Madame Zerchovich, appalled at my lack of control, later dashed all hope of my being the new Pavlova.

"Caroline, perhaps it would be best if you left the company and found somewhere more suited to giggling than the stage." I had expected the ticking-off, but expulsion seemed a bit harsh. Not a complete disaster though as I was mad about horses and enjoyed nothing more than riding to hounds on Giselle, a nippy little hunter to whom I devoted many of my teenage years.

In the early days of 1899, Nairobi was a small bustling town. Its roads and alleyways had been haphazardly snatched from a windswept papyrus swamp inhabited by lion and mosquitoes. The Wild West atmosphere of this frontier town was augmented by a broad main street, which ran in a straight line from the station to the Norfolk. It was from here that the man who became the leader and political guru of the settlers, the diminutive, eccentric Lord Delamere, with long titian hair cascading down to his shoulders, developed a penchant for galloping on his horse from one end of town to the other and shooting out as many street lights as possible. The Norfolk had a certain cachet as a playground for licentious members of the aristocracy. It was also renowned as the departure point for the first hunting safaris, when rich sportsmen, complete with a large retinue of African porters, set forth into an untamed land teeming with trophies. The supremely confident Delamere had been the first to buy land in the Highlands and together with another aristocrat, Lord Francis Scott, proved to be a remarkable man who toiled hard to shape Kenya's future, eventually becoming an integral part of the fledgling colony.

The Baron was also a passionate champion of the Maasai and had been initiated as a blood brother. They continually stole Lord Delamere's cattle and each time he forgave them. One by one those who lived near his house filed up to his verandah each morning, their superb painted bodies barely covered by a small red shuka—a rectangular strip of cloth. As the Baron chomped his way through a full English breakfast, the Maasai looked on with anticipatory giggles of delight. To start the day off he always wound up his old phonograph and, with unusual care, placed his only record on the turntable. Every day of the week the extraordinary sounds of *All Aboard for Margate* rippled through the Highland air.

By the time we moved to the capital, its heart was the New Stanley Hotel and its popular open air café The Thorn Tree. This was named after the original tree at its centre, once used by travellers to pin up messages for others onto the long sharp thorns. Film stars, authors Ernest Hemingway and Robert Ruark, white hunters, upcountry farmers, good-looking Kenya cowboys and glamorous visitors from around the world loved to gather round their favourite watering hole, though none more so than us young teenagers with our warm Coca-Colas. On the opposite corner stood Woolworths, the only shop I have ever pinched anything from—a wooden pencil when I was twelve. It was a silly rite of passage for many kids my age but the guilt has obviously stayed with me.

Our first house was high on a slope in front of the house belonging to the legendary paleoanthropologists Louis and Mary Leakey and their three sons Jonathan, Richard and Phillip. Both our families lived next to the Coryndon Museum, now the National Nairobi Museum, where Dr. Leakey was Curator. It was a natural history treasure trove for a child and I was allowed to roam around at will when I came back from day school. I could also slip outside into the pen that enclosed the giant tortoises from the Seychelles where I would sit on their backs and chat to them. Sitting there contentedly, with small lizards scurrying across the warm earth beneath my bare feet, I watched jewel-coloured birds flitting through the sunlit trees—chittering weavers and sunbirds, kites and an occasional lilac-breasted roller.

At the bottom of our garden was a stream of cold clear water surrounded by bamboo, flame trees and trees of the forest. Lying in bed at night I could hear the tiny tree frogs calling, the rhythmic pulse of their warbling voices lulling me to sleep.

Jonathan Leakey had a young frog which he was training to become a world champion frog leaper. I was full of wonder that such a thing was possible. He was two years older than me and didn't seem to mind when I skippped up the dirt road between our houses where he did his training.

"Hello, Jonathan," I said shyly, all skinny legs and heart beating faster. "Can I crouch down and watch you?"

"Alright, as long as you don't disturb my froggy friend here," he replied nonchantly. In time 'Vesta', his Sharp-Nosed frog—not much of a looker in the handsome prince department—surpassed all expectations and in 1958 Jonathan decided to enter him for the Frog Olympics in South Africa. Kenyans were not allowed to enter the country due to 'Apartheid' but Jonathan somehow persuaded the powers that be to give his frog a passport and a visa in order to compete. A few days after nervously waving him off, 'Vesta', amid great excitement, completed three consecutive jumps of seventeen feet and won the Championship. Jonathan was given a huge silver trophy, a cardboard copy of which he still has. 'Vesta' went on to further glory and was sent off to America for another championship, without Jonathan again who this time could not afford the fare. Somebody stole 'Vesta', put him under his own name and went on to win the race. Frog and forlorn former master never saw each other again.

Outside the perimeters of Nairobi, the herds of wildebeest and gazelle kept a silent vigil as dusk settled in. The Ngong Hills, which lay south-west of the town, had four uneven, rounded peaks that rippled across the top of the grassy ridge, like knuckles of soapstone worn smooth by the forces of time. The Kikuyu tribe believed they were molded by the hand of God as he shaped the earth. In the changing light of day, there was a mysterious quality to the Ngongs, drawing the eye down to the dark creases of forest below the peaks, where the buffalo hid. After the rainy season the slopes were coated in a fragile mantle of green and where the hills arched their narrow backs, thick rainforest inhabited by fauna and woodland flowers crept down the grassy banks. On the far side, where the roots of the hills grew deep into the Rift Valley, the winds of a thousand years blew gently over the earth.

It was one of my favourite places. My sisters and I never tired of going up there for a family picnic but best of all we loved running through the long grass and rolling down at the top of the hill until we were worn out.

THE SHEIKH'S DHOW

The siren call of the coast often bubbled below the surface of those who lived upcountry. How we longed to see the graceful lanteen sails of ancient dhows, wooden seafaring vessels that, through the centuries, had plied the waters between Persia and Zanzibar; to watch them cut through the horizon into the deep blue waters of Mombasa Harbour, their vast holds filled with spices and sweet dates. It was on one of these boats that the first of two seminal encounters I had amongst Arabs occurred; it remains one of my most enchanting experiences.

Mombasa has always managed to retain the raffish charm of its past. The old town of narrow streets sprawled down to the sea, forever dominated by the brooding presence of Fort Jesus, built by the invading Portuguese in the 15th century. We spent hours exploring the labyrinth of alleyways linking the Arab shops and Swahili houses, cut out of rough coral. Elaborate doorways, carved on the nearby islands of Lamu and Zanzibar opened onto courtyards filled with chickens and barefoot children with rings in their noses. Later, in the cool of the early evening, at the time of day when the noise of the crows became most persistent and the muezzins called the faithful to prayer, Indian families in silks and saris strolled along the seafront. Scarlet flowers of coastal Flamboyant trees swayed in the sea breeze and the silver filigree branches of baobabs guarded the secrets of the island's mysterious past.

When aged thirty-five my father became Private Secretary to Sir Evelyn Baring, then Governor of Kenya. It was part of his job to travel down to the coast to meet various high-ranking sheikhs who sailed down from Arabia on the monsoon wind. One afternoon as we were sitting on the verandah of Government House in Mombasa where we were staying, he casually said to me, "Tupps", (short for Tuppence), "how would you like to come with me tomorrow and meet an Arab sheikh on his dhow?"

Naturally I jumped at the chance. That night I fell asleep listening to the ceiling fan whirring round in a whisper and awoke early the following morning, looking out to sea with mounting excitement. A thin line of foaming white horses rippled along the edge of the reef where a magnificent dhow was pulling proudly into the harbour. A few hours later Dad and I were rowed out to it in a sizeable dugout canoe, an *ingalao*, carved from a single tree trunk. An African stood at the bow blowing on a large conch shell and sung Swahili songs of love and adventure with the other men during the short ride.

Once on board I was briefly introduced to the sheikh, a bearded, dark-eyed twin of the 'Ali Baba' of my imagination, before he led my father away to sit at the far end of the deck and discuss matters of trade and state. I was invited to sit alone on an old carpet where I listened to the soft lilt of Arabic and the lapping of the waves against the wooden hull. The smell of jasmine oil lay heavily on the creaking bows as I watched skinny African boys across the bay at Nyali Beach scamper up palm trees to gather coconuts. To my surprise, and slight embarrassment, an Arab boy a bit older than me was given the job of fanning me with a small palm frond to keep me cool in the heat of the day. For the next few hours he sprinkled rose water on my face and arms and laid offerings of Turkish Delight dusted in a powder of fine sugar beside me. Sitting on my magic carpet, the wafting scents of rose water and sugary sweets lulled me into a dream world. It was as if I had effortlessly stepped back into the myths and legends of Arabia when the stories of *One Thousand and One Nights* first fired the world's imagination. My impressionable young mind conjured up all that was exciting about distant lands and their peoples and instilled in me a lifelong thirst for travel and adventure.

SAFARIS AND ZEBRAS

Apart from being at the coast, the buzz of going on safari two or three times a year never wore off. On the day of departure we all piled into the Land Rover at dawn and headed south on bone-rattling dirt roads for the five hour journey to Amboseli National Park. In the early days, Ndebu, Dad's driver, followed in a lorry with all the necessary gear—our tents and bedding, canvas chairs, food and water, pots and pans, gin for my mother and whiskey for Pa. I spent most of the time gazing out of the window watching small game, conjuring up faces and animals out of the fleecy white clouds, or playing an addictive Solitaire card game invented by Dad. Sometimes we sang 'One Man Went to Mow' in Swahili—anything to hurry the hours along. After stopping off at Namanga, a border town with Tanganyika, for a quick spartan lunch, we continued until we neared the foothills of Mount Kilimanjaro. Between us and our campsite lay the vast dried up bed of Amboseli Lake which we needed to cross. In the heat haze mirages of giant beasts and towering figures danced and shimmered as they floated dreamily above the horizon towards us. Once when my maternal Grandfather was on safari with us we came across six hundred Cape buffalo—huge herds were common in those days—standing silently, solidly, on the lake bed. They completely blocked the area and refused to let us pass for well over an hour, something which made him extremely cross. Dad tried to calm him down,

"Pop, don't be fooled into thinking these buffalo are placid. They play a dangerous game and give no indication they are going to charge. Then suddenly they come for you, their heavy boss and wide horns head-on. They charge at fifty kilometres an hour, trampling everything in their path. So there's nothing we can do but sit it out until they move away. You'll just have to be patient."

As soon as we arrived at a chosen spot the tents were put up by the Africans and nestled unobtrusively under the giant yellow-fever trees. Far off the forest echoed with the crash of elephants and as the light faded different animal noises, sounding like the sections of a symphony in rehearsal, drifted on the wind to camp—the low growl of a lion, zebra barking and the ghostly sound of hyenas—all gearing up for the night's performance.

We rose before dawn, cold and shivering, for our first game drive, the perfect time when the big cats were hungry and out stalking their prey. I could hear the cheerful early morning voices of the Africans starting their day, one of them going to my parents' tent to wake them up with a quiet, *chai tayari*—'tea is ready' and placing the tray on a table outside. Pa soon came out dressed in his starched, knee-length khaki shorts and cotton bush jacket, knee socks and desert boots. He was very particular about his clothes and was always immaculately dressed, whether for safaris or dinner. Ma was quite casual on safari—slim-cut trousers, white Airtex shirt and cardigan slung over her shoulders. After hot cups of cocoa for the children, we jumped into the lorry and set off. In those far off days Amboseli was heaving with large numbers of elephant, buffalo, rhino, lion, cheetah and smaller game and although the elephant constantly stripped and tore down branches, much of the park was still laced with the flat filigree tops of acacia trees.

If we had driven round for an hour without finding a lion my father would shoot a zebra in order to leave a trail scent. This was in the early 1950s when white men were still allowed to kill game. A couple of Africans jumped out and put a long rope round the lifeless creature's neck to drag behind our lorry. Sooner or later the smell of fresh blood lured out a lion or two from the thicket where we had a front row view of them tearing at the flesh. Watching the once unlimited freedom of the big cats was to see nature at its best and most raw. It was while driving that same lorry on safari that Pa had gone down wind too near a long horned white rhino, an animal with weak eye-sight, when it suddenly turned. I was standing up in the back of the lorry with one of the African men, adrenaline pumping, when the huge charging animal caught us and tore three planks of thick wood off the tail-end of the lorry with its horn, barely five feet from where we were standing. That was pretty heady stuff for a child. Dad shouted out of his window,

"Sorry about that, Tupps. Are you still in one piece?"

"Yup, I'm fine," I squeaked, holding tightly onto the African's arm.

If we were unsuccessful in attracting any big cat on the game drive we dragged the dead zebra back to camp with us where the early morning fire was blazing—a cooked breakfast of bacon, eggs, baked beans and fried bread awaited us, expertly done by the *pishi*, the cook.

The Africans gathered round and pulled the heavy animal over to an area behind the tents where they had built their own fire. Using the sharpest of knives they carefully cut the skin away from the muscle as I stood there watching. This would be sold in the market at Arusha to make the men a bit of extra money on the side. When I got slightly older they gave me a small knife to help them peel back the skin. I was excited and nervous at the same time, but quickly got the hang of it. For some reason my sisters and brothers-in-law still tease me when it comes to my tales of skinning zebra. They laugh and say,

"Dal, come on. Aren't you just exaggerating all this?" (When little, my sisters couldn't say Caroline, so called me Daline, then shortened it). However many times I reply, "Absolutely not," they remain sceptical. But it was exactly how events appeared to me, no more and no less. Besides, my siblings were younger and unlikely to have been involved in the gory process.

Once the zebra had been gutted I remember the mass of grey foul-smelling intestines spilling wet and warm onto the blood-soaked ground of the camp. The men worked without pausing until the lacerated carcass lay discarded, like a forgotten relic. Vultures, swirled patiently in the sky before taking their chance to devour the remains. It's strange to think of now, but I remember those skinning sessions with a certain nostalgia.

Some years later Amboseli became the proud owner of a basic *banda*, a small thatched house with two rooms, where we could sleep. A hut next to it, lit by a hurricane lamp, served as a bathroom. It possessed a tin bath which if we were lucky would quarter-fill with brown water spitting out of a temperamental tap, along with the occasional snake. Taking turns to lie in it at the end of the dusty day we were conscious of bats in their hundreds hanging upside down from the rafters. Human and winged mammal watched each other carefully, especially human when it was Mum's turn. Not long before she had been sitting on the *choo*, which was just a simple long drop, when a bat flew up from the depths and thwacked her hard on the bottom. She shrieked and ran out at top speed, knickers down, not caring whether a lion or hyena had its hungry chops waiting for her and she remained frightened of bats for the rest of her life.

TRIBAL WAYS

While the small privileged minority of whites were the administrators, along with farmers and white hunters, of areas of Kenya bigger than Ireland, Africans had little say in the land that had once belonged to them and their forefathers. To them all white people were *mzungus* and when we were young they sometimes called us *memsahib kidogo*—little mistress. With their good humour and their natural ability to be so emotionally and physically alive, so open and caring of children, it was easy to become fond of the Africans who worked for us. They had a particular gift for communicating and listening, and we would hear them singing Kikuyu and Luo songs as they went about their work. Machakos, our main house-man in Kajiado had teeth sharpened to a point, as was his tribe, the Kamba's, custom. This came in useful when Susie put her finger into a hole of a large stone and was stung by a scorpion. Machakos heard her cries, ran to find her and bit straight into her finger with his pointed teeth to suck out the poison.

One of the strengths shared by all the tribes, traditionally animists, was the belief that everyone and everything on earth had a spirit—people and animals; trees, rivers and stars. When faced with a particular problem or situation, *Shauri ya Mungu*—'the will of God'—was another certainty rooted deep in their psyche.

The Maasai was the tribe I knew best while I was growing up, though their time-honoured intimate rituals were naturally unknown to me.

"Why do the young *moran*—warriors—suddenly have their hair shaved off?" I asked my father one day.

He was always patient in his answers,

"After their *Eunoto* ceremony which celebrates their transition to becoming senior warriors, they are encouraged to marry. The life of being a single *moran* is over and so their hair is shaved off by their mothers," he explained.

I watched them bleeding their cow's jugular into a gourd as part of their diet; jumping and chanting a low, almost animal sound, from deep inside their bellies, which I found hypnotic. Many times I have sat in their dark dung and mud *manyattas*—homesteads—where smoke from a fire in the middle filled the small space and burned my eyes.

The men possessed great physical beauty about which they were known be as vain as peacocks. The decoration of their lean, muscular bodies was important to them in peace as well as war and anxious to attract the girls, the *moran* decorated themselves with red ochre mixed with fat and braided their ochred hair into long plaits, symbolising the African lion's strength.

When I was young the traditonal killing of an adult lion with a spear was still considered a rite of passage for a *moran*. A boy could not be a man until he had undertaken his first kill. Only then was he allowed to wear a tall helmet of lion mane as a prized trophy, proving his great strength and courage. I never witnessed a lion hunt although my father did. If the hunt had been successful the celebrations lasted for a week. There was a magic about the warriors' dances, as if the song of Africa stretched, quivering, out of the depths of the land and offered itself to pagan gods through the chants and primeval ecstasy of its people. Long before the new moon sliced the sky, the moving bodies snaked their way one by one into a semi-circle and started swaying to the rhythms of their tribe. Rows of colourful beads rose and fell on the necks and wrists of both women and men as they undulated towards each other. The *moran* held their handsome heads high, the sweat of their gleaming brown torsos caught in the early evening light. As the chanting grew louder, the men jumped higher and the swirl of feet sent dust billowing into the air. Tension and excitement. Laughter and sexuality. Teeth whiter than the moon. The jaunty breasts and agile arms of the ululating girls provoked their partners into a frenzy of showmanship and for many hours, the chorus of voices and the stomping of feet challenged the distant noises of the wild.

My parents were considerate and fair to the Africans who worked for us and listened carefully to their problems. We were well aware that Mum frequently topped up their monthly rations of tea, sugar and maize meal for their culinary mainstay, *posho*. Our staff seemed to like both my parents who, unlike others, never shouted at them. Around this time in Nairobi we had a Seychelloise nanny, instead of our normal ayahs, who was firmly wedded to favouritism. Whichever child happened to be her beloved that week would be the dubious recipient of a raw egg cracked over her head, the whites nimbly chucked away and the smelly yolk squelched firmly into the hair. There it was left for ten minutes, egg dripping silently down our face before being washed out. This was supposed to make our hair blonder and shinier. We were confirmed tomboys but secretly, when I wasn't mucking around with horses, I quite enjoyed my hair being shiny on trips to see the ballet or *The Boyfriend* and *Salad Days*, then all the rage, or even Gilbert and Sullivan's *The Pirates of Penzance*. But at twelve I was seldom her favourite. My new little sister Rachel, whom we nicknamed Digs, had just been born and nanny was much keener on babies.

MAU MAU

Although the following story combines the memories of 'young white colonial teenagers', I hope it will be understood in the light of considerable turmoil at that time. It involves the only really unsettling period of my adolescence when I became conscious at thirteen that Kenya was embroiled in the Mau Mau uprising, a frightening time that few young people today have ever heard about. In 1952 the Kikuyu, the largest tribe, feeling robbed of their country's best land, initiated a ferocious guerilla war which lasted for over five years. It was brutal. My parents rarely discussed the 'Emergency', as it was referred to, in front of my sisters and myself but occasionally I overheard them whispering, and snippets of the latest atrocity stayed with me when I went to bed. I was aware that like most other grown-ups both of them concealed guns beneath their shirts and jackets, though my dear Mama actually hitting her target was doubtful. Dad always kept a gun under his pillow at night.

Our days at school were too busy for us to give the Mau Mau much thought, but the undercurrents of fear still made a deep impression on me; twice we saw escaped prisoners with their Rasta dreadlocks blowing out behind them as they ran through our garden and into the nearby belt of forest. It was the nights in particular which made me nervous, especially when we drove to friends' farms at weekends. Rumours of Mau Mau gangs rolling large boulders off the Escarpment in an attempt to flatten a passing car at dusk became seared into my mind. I felt sure that would happen to us. My father often attributed his children's apprehension once night fell to growing up in those uncertain years. But my story was nothing compared to others.

Aware of simmering discontent and tension among the Africans, the Governor, Sir Evelyn Baring, declared a State of Emergency in October 1952 and arrested Jomo Kenyatta, then reputed to be leader of the rebels. He spent seven years in a detention camp as an early advocate of land reform and independence, and became a symbol of Kikuyu resistance. However, it was fanatics like Dedan Kimathi, the high priest of the Mau Mau forest armies and feared by many, who made the secret society such a symbol of barbarism, bestiality and black magic. The Aberdares, where much of the fighting took place, lay in the heart of the Highlands. Mist hung heavy in the early morning and the pungent smell of cedar enfolded the dark sweeping forest. Wisps of woodsmoke from huts circled upwards, seeking a path through the dense foliage. The nights were cold and people warmed themselves around fires of pine and cedar. Scattered on the slopes of the mountains stood the mugumo trees, the huge wild fig sacred to the Kikuyu god and revered by his people. To the west, the escarpment fell away to the pastures and billowing brooks of Wanjohi, once the infamous 'Happy Valley.'

Although the Mau Mau was in theory anti-white the terrorists killed nearly one hundred times as many fellow Kikuyu as Europeans and the Government did little to placate the aggrieved tribe. By the time the British Army and the King's African Rifles became involved, thousands of Mau Mau sympathisers had fled to the forest. Long haired and unwashed they lived high up in the Aberdare range and on Mount Kenya. At night they swept through the reserves and settled areas stealing food and money and murdering nearly two thousand Africans loyal to the Crown, as well as thirty two whites and twenty-six Asians. Towards the latter part of the emergency their rituals were increasingly bestial. They would cut off breasts, bury people alive and kill children or parents piece by piece in front of each other. A few members of less fortunate families in the European-own farms were hacked to death. Farm houses were destroyed, crops set on fire, horses and livestock killed.

Understandably the settler community were horrified by the sudden rebellion which threatened their very existence. In order to infiltrate the terrorists and sympathisers living in the forests, small 'pseudo gangs' of loyal Kikuyu disguised as Mau Mau, headed by a white man, were formed. In 1956 two who went on these dangerous missions were Captain Francis Erskine of the Kings African Rifles and Ian Henderson, a local Special Branch member and guerilla hunter extraordinaire—later the author of the acclaimed book, *The Hunt for Kimathi*. They matted their hair, blackened their faces, hands and feet with burned cork and stove polish. Filthy cloth caps or wide-brimmed felt army hats were pulled down well to hide blue eyes and straight hair. They crouched in old army greatcoats, which were favoured by the Kikuyu, in thickets on the edges of gatherings of Mau Mau rebels. There in the dense night mist, when it was often cold and raining, they listened to planned attacks as the Kikuyu guerillas, in reeking animal skins that had not been removed for several years, hunched round their fire. It was a dirty war in which atrocities and torture were committed by both sides. The security forces killed around twenty thousand rebels.

My close friend, Jacinthe Delap, whose grandmother once had a passionate affair with Ewart Grogan, famous for being the first man to walk from the Cape to Cairo, has been affected to this day by the events in her childhood on the highest farm in the Kinankop, within the Aberdare Range. As a small child, she or her brothers and sisters would find Ju Ju headless chickens and parts of a goat or bones in their beds at night. Animals were killed and strung up on the farm gate. Unbeknownst to them at one point the malcontent Dedan Kimathi worked as a cattleman and milk recorder on their farm. Bill Delap, increasingly perturbed, built a huge three story stone fort with no ground floor windows, for his family to sleep in at night. The five-inch thick door into the fort from the house was made of solid oak and iron and on the top was a powerful search light to flash neighbours should the need arise. For years they continued their nightly ritual as they went through the long, many-roomed house.

"Being the youngest I carried the paraffin lamp. With the darkness closing in behind me we walked silently into the fort each night and I found that very frightening," Jacinthe recalls.

The Mau Mau continued to kill their farm animals and poach their cattle, driving them vertically up the mountain while constantly whipping them so that their tendons broke and crippled them. On one occasion the kitchen *toto*—child—warned the family that there were ten Mau Mau crouching up in the roof who planned to kill the whole family at six o'clock that evening. They were quickly caught by the police.

On the other hand my great pal Appley had an entirely more enjoyable experience at her primary boarding school. The Beehive, a school of forty pupils, was situated near Nanyuki on the lower slopes of Mount Kenya and run by the avuncular Colonel Delaforce and his headmistress wife. Appley had been a boarder there since she was six and by the time she was nine, Dedan Kimathi was reputed to be hiding out deep in the forest only a few miles away from the school. Gangs frequently came down to Nanyuki at night to try and recruit new members and forage for food, often entering the terrified staffs' quarters at the school. A battalion of Black Watch soldiers had recently been stationed outside the town to keep law and order in the area.

Near the school lived a tribe of bow-men who specialised in homemade bows and arrows and were expert at fashioning small metal arrowheads. These short friendly men had been employed by The Beehive to prowl round the grounds each night and protect the children. In the day they taught them how to correctly pull the bows and make the simple arrowheads. Appley recalls, "Twice a week after bedtime, emergency drills were conducted in our dormitories and we were told to turn our old iron beds on their sides and kneel behind them. Our bows and arrows were quickly brought out and pointed towards the dormitory door in preparation for a possible attack."

Eventually the parents of the young children became so worried about the encroaching Mau Mau they threatened to take away their offspring.

The Delaforces came up instead with the bright idea of taking the whole school to Watatu on the idyllic south coast of Kenya for a year. There the children lived in separated dormitories—primitive round bandas with roofs made out of coconut palms. Appley remembers that time fondly, "We hardly had any lessons. If the tide was right, a couple of friends and I went off in the canoe, without a teacher in sight. We were free as birds, swimming naked in the sea with plenty of places to explore." They quickly became wild children, their hair growing long and bleached by the sun, their skin a golden brown, straight out of *The Lord of the Flies*. They got used to snakes, went to the loo outside, lined up each morning for their anti-malarial pills, and sat on the floor of the main *banda* to listen to Queen Elizabeth's Coronation in 1953 on the radio without really understanding a thing. In the afternoons some of the children wandered off through the bush to the *duka* run by Indians a mile away from the school, to buy tins of condensed milk. A fire was lit on the beach each night, and the children sat round watching the moon create a dazzling path on the waves down to them.

Four years later in 1957 the ten foot high fences of barbed wire and tall look out towers, each manned by an African guard with an antiquated rifle, which surrounded the grounds of mine and Appley's boarding school at Limuru, eventually came down. The Kikuyu rebellion was defeated that year, soon after Dedan Kimathi was captured deep in the Aberdares after being shot in the leg by one of Henderson's men. Although he was hanged at the age of thirty-six, the struggle for freedom and independence continued and the old regime gave way within a few years. Independence came in 1963 making Kenya the first British colony to achieve African rule.

HOLLYWOOD COMES TO TOWN

Films and the theatre have always been a passion and every Saturday morning I went to the cinema in Nairobi when films suitable for children were shown—Burt Lancaster in *Trapeze*; *East of Eden* and *Gone with the Wind*. Luckily for me in the 1950s film companies had become fascinated by Africa for its raw beauty and majestic mountains, exotic tribes and raffish colonial characters. MGM Studios caused great excitement when they came to Kenya to film part of *Mogambo*, directed by John Ford. Nearly forty years later when I was researching material for my biography of Joy Adamson, I spent a day with Terence Gavaghan, who had known both Joy and my father when he was the District Commissioner at Maralal at the time of filming *Mogambo*.

"I was absolutely firm, if they wanted to film on land full of Samburu tribesmen, then the Africans must benefit," he told me.

Over a dinner with the stars of the film—Clark Gable, Ava Gardner, Grace Kelly and Donald Sinden—Gavaghan struck a hard bargain with the producer. In exchange for one thousand tribesmen to be used as extras in the film he insisted that one thousand spears were to be specially fashioned by the tribal spear-maker, plus three hundred head of cattle to feed the men.

"I also insisted on three yards of the best quality red silk cloth per man and would also retain the animal skins on the tribesmen's behalf." Much to Gavaghan's amazement, the producer agreed. To prevent an attack by terrorists it was rumoured that MGM made a secret payment of £50,000 to the Mau Mau's reputed leader Jomo Kenyatta.

By all accounts *Mogambo* was not a happy set. It became the talk of the town and I remember grown-ups' chat—"Ten white hunters for the actors' protection is quite absurd" kind of remark. My young parents, who were considered quite glamorous and fun, met the stars one evening at the infamous nightclub, the Equator Club, in Nairobi and everyone partied long into the night.

Terence recalled the first day of shooting: "It was disrupted by a large baboon that kept getting into camera range to watch Clark Gable and Ava Gardner film a love scene which we all found most amusing!" Grace Kelly became infatuated with Gable and began a steamy affair on set that continued after filming ended. But the actor, still a romantic lead in his fifties, had no wish to become seriously involved with a girl thirty years younger. While in London, the distraught actress sought Ava Gardner's advice and her co-star counselled, "He likes to conquer and when he's done, he's through with them and leaves."

Terence continued, "It was common knowledge that Clark Gable's chest was completely hairless so he insisted that no other actor should expose a hairy torso on film, considering it an affront to his 'manliness'". Each day make-up men armed with electric clippers prowled around ready to pounce on any actor sprouting a suspect chest hair.

Frank Sinatra came out to keep an eye on Ava Gardner, his beautiful wife. Theirs was a famously tempestuous marriage and Sinatra was increasingly edgy as he waited to hear if he had got the plum supporting role of Private Angelo Maggio in the film *From Here to Eternity*. He was wildly jealous of Clark Gable as he was of all Ava's leading men and in a short time became a 'royal pain in the neck' according to the other actors. As soon as his longed for role was confirmed, he left for Hollywood and everyone, including his wife, was more than happy to see the back of him.

"While Ava Gardner was shooting a scene with a baby elephant, the creature pushed her into a mud pool," Terence chuckled. "She screamed for help but John Ford motioned the crew to keep on filming." The scene proved to be one of the best in the film. After each day, Ava bathed in a canvas tub set up and filled by a local African boy assigned to her. When the Colonial Government complained about her appearing unclothed infront of the Africans, she laughed, threw all modesty to the winds and ran naked as a jaybird through the camp.

The previous year a British company came out to film *Where No Vultures Fly* on location in Amboseli, part of my father's remit in Kajiado. Set against the backdrop of Mountain Kilimanjaro and its large herds of elephants it was the perfect setting for a film on ivory poaching. It became the big family film of 1951. The romantic leads were the handsome British actor Anthony Steele, (who a few years later married the Swedish bombshell Anita Ekberg), with Dinah Sheridan. My parents became good friends with the actor and we would travel to Amboseli, which was like a second home to us anyway, to watch the filming. Having been slightly in awe of 'the famous filmstar', I still have a photo of the actor standing by a papyrus swamp which he gave to my mother. On the back, he wrote,

"Dear Dinah, keep this away from Leslie. Otherwise a Maasai spear will be missing, to my detriment."

His was one of the first films I enjoyed, but *Mogambo* remains my favourite childhood film—I have always thought Ava Gardener was the most beautiful star of them all.

There was no television in Kenya but we were more than content with the radio, our gramaphone and books. The McMillan Library, an imposing building with towering columns and huge stone lions, was built by Lady McMillan in 1931 in memory of her husband, the American philanthropist Sir William Northrup McMillan. Lady Mac, as we called her, also formed an important stud, producing the largest string of racehorses in the county. At its zenith, the library contained two hundred thousand books and it became an essential part of my growing up. In the holidays, if we weren't on safari or at the coast, I would go there with my mother and choose two or three books. At twelve I yearned to be the heroine in *National Velvet*, dressing up as a boy so I could ride in the Grand National. That was soon followed by the historical novel *The Scarlet Pimpernel*, about a handsome English hero in the French Revolution. Much later, like other love-struck girls leaving their teens, I became smitten with classic stories of tragic women obsessed with romance. Those few who were brave, or foolhardy enough, to pursue their passions, tormenting themselves mercilessly in the process until alas, their pursuit becomes fatal. The ruined and beautiful Emma Bovary swallows arsenic. And the captivating, tragic Anna Karenina throws herself under the carriage of a passing steam train. My dying heroines. Oh, the tears, the sadness of it all! But then, young girls are creatures of extremes.

MOMBASA TRAIN

Strong memories of adolescence come flooding back and mine usually wind around travel. There were few things more exciting than taking the old fashioned steam train from Nairobi to Mombasa. At the time of its building, the railway was known as the 'Lunatic Express'—in 1895 cheap labour had been imported from India to help construct the tracks from the coast to Uganda. As soon as they reached Tsavo, famous for its man-eating lions, all hell broke loose once lions became adept at dragging Indian workers off into the bushes and eating them. Before the Second World War trains were stopped at the slightest pretext, to let passengers shoot or photograph animals. One well-known story concerned Lord Delamere, who arrived at a station with his bull terrier bitch and a litter of four puppies, which he was taking to Nairobi. In getting them comfortably settled he forgot to purchase tickets for either himself or the dogs. When the train had left, the station master telegraphed a warning to Nairobi: "The Lord is on the train with one bitch and four sons of bitches. No tickets. Please collect."

Leaving in the late afternoon we followed our parents closely as they wove their way through the chaotic and crowded platform at Nairobi station. Africans, burdened with their over-loaded *kikapus*, baskets, tied up with rope, struggled towards carriages at the back of the train. We were ushered into comfortable compartments where at night we could look forward to sleeping between crisp white sheets and bedding which had been carefully prepared on our bunks. As the train pulled out of the station the clickety-clack of the wheels were soon reverberating along the track. Rattling across the silent land we were glued to the windows to see the game. It was like turning the pages of an animal book. Giraffe on dancer's legs stretched their graceful necks to graze on the thorny branches of the tallest acacia tree; wildebeest, the ugly clowns of Africa, took fright at some imagined threat and careered over the undulating landscape. At seven o'clock sharp came the sound of a gong announcing it was time for dinner. It's bearer was a beaming African steward, immaculately dressed in a white kanzu, a red cummerbund and fez, lurching unsteadily through the corridor. A dinner of solid English fare always began with soup ladled out of a huge silver tureen, all of us waiting with bated breath for the swaying waiter's ladle to spill the hot liquid all over our laps as the train joggled along.

Sensing the proximity of the sea early the next morning we played exactly the same games as always. Who would be the first to see a tall coconut palm or a young local boy running with his small basket, holding up his skinny little arms and begging us with a winning smile to buy his peanuts? The most exotic prize of all was the first one to see a bare-breasted woman from the coastal Giriama tribe in her short tutu-skirt made of sisal or strips of cloth, standing outside her small hut while her children played in the sandy earth. Then we really knew we were nearing our destination. Huts and clumps of mango trees gave way to spreading mangroves and the coral buildings of the tropical lowlands. Once we arrived in Mombasa and the train screeched to a halt, we gladly surrendered to the heat, humidity and the salty sea air.

During the rainy seasons the monsoons swept up the East African beaches, silver sheets of rain falling in short bursts. After the storm clouds passed fat drops of rain continued to drip from banana leaves and small beads of moisture glistened in the throats of the moonflowers. The smell of the earth hung low, clean and fresh as a child's breath. At night we lay beneath our mosquito nets, listening to the chirring of the night jars in the trees and the pounding of the Indian Ocean. If our holiday wasn't at Malindi, Nyali or Tiwi we stayed at Government House, high on the cliffs in Mombasa. It was large and white with green shutters, airy and open so that it seemed at one with the sky and the sea below. On the ground floor, tall rounded white pillars were built around three sides of a verandah which enclosed the open courtyard facing the sea—the first thing one saw through an archway when driving up to the house. I am sure that beautiful building started my interest in architecture.

When travelling to Malindi on the north coast, we needed to cross the Kilifi creek by ferry. Moving slowly over the deep waters, a line of Africans pulled on chains to ferry our Land Rover to the other side. The wet slap of the chains rose and plunged in rhythm as the men sang, *Memsahib na Bwana na kwenda safari*, ('Memsahib and Bwana are going on safari.') In Malindi our simple whitewashed house, constructed of mud and wattle, was built on a long stretch of beach. Thick walls held up the *makuti* roof made of palm fronds. Early each morning after a breakfast of sweet mangoes and pawpaws, we could barely wait to step out from the shadows of the coconut and frangipanis and run down the hot path which burnt the soles of our feet, to the beach. Casuarina trees were feathered against the sky where the whitest of sands began and the round, grass-green leaves of the Ipomoea creeper snaked their way along the ground. In front of us lay the vast coral gardens of the Indian Ocean. Rippled sand ridges, covered with layers of soft brown seaweed, led us down to the water's turquoise edge and further out the Africans' dugout fishing canoes bobbed up and down in the strong breeze.

I was allowed to wander off down the often deserted beach on my own and would say a cheerful *jambo* to the fishermen as they came up to the house to show my mother their fresh fish and lobsters each morning. The coastal tribes were friendly and easy-going. The main religion was Islam and the Swahili fishermen, a mixture of Arab and Bantu, were soft-spoken. It was also then that I began my love of shell-collecting and would spend hours alone weaving along the edge of the tide and picking up small abandoned butterfly shells. But one day when I was seven I became lost. I was alone somewhere on the the endless beach and couldn't find our house. There are few things more frightening to a child than becoming lost, as if you have been swallowed up in a terrifying dream and absolutely know you will never see your family again. I began crying and called out for my mother but no one could hear me over the roar of the waves. When I eventually found my way back with the help of a kind fisherman, sunburnt and still tearful, my mother immediately swept me up in her arms and covered my salty cheeks with her kisses, telling me that everything would be alright. She was my rock and my world.

One of my favourite pastimes was wading into the water before lowtide with my goggles and finding myself in a silent world of moving colour. Swimming along the reef I uncovered the secrets hidden among the waving sea fronds and bright corals; dark brown spotted leopard cowrie shells and large red helmet shells, their slit gaping like orange wounds. Innocent looking red and white striped lion fish, whose feathery quills gave a powerful sting, gliding past waving sea anemones. A line of yellow and black angel fish, rather like nervous sea-horses, followed each other. As my flippers stroked the water the scales of the blue and green parrot fish sparkled iridescent in the shafts of sunlight and shoals of tiny fish, the lapis lazuli colour of a butterfly's wing, shimmered past. Those days were a fairytale existence.

SIR EVELYN BARING, GOVERNOR

The Barings lived in Government House, a stately building overlooking a beautifully kept, English-style garden in Nairobi. Sir Evelyn, the Governor from 1952-59, had a booming laugh, once heard never forgotten, especially by us children who developed a deep affection for him and his wife, Lady Mary. When my father was his Private Secretary the two men became close, sharing the same sense of humour and remaining friends all their lives. Sir Evelyn took over as the Mau Mau terror was rising and he had the unenviable task, through controversial and often harsh methods, of restoring law and order after detaining Jomo Kenyatta. Although fate cast him in the role of "colonial oppressor" he was the least racially minded of men at heart and he conceived an abiding love for Kenya and its people. He mastered Kiswahili, combined firmness as a tough governor with a liberal, encouraging attitude towards African aspirations and managed to push through land consolidation along with newly sited villages that welcomed many Africans into the modern benefits of schooling, medical welfare and water.

Sir Evelyn cared little for the pomp and circumstance of high office. He had extremely long legs and his white ceremonial trousers were always too tight. The only way for him to get them on was by soaking them with water, lying on the bed and frantically pulling and stretching them up over his limbs. This caused much merriment to those around him trying to help. His charming wife, Lady Mary, good friends with my mother, was the daughter of the fifth Earl Grey, after whom the tea was named. I once came across the extraordinary sight of the ageing Earl at the poolside in his heavy Edwardian woollen bathing suit sagging to his ancient knees; long thin straps over his bony shoulders. I thought he looked so old and frail he might be blown into the water and dragged swiftly to the bottom by the weight of his soaking wet costume.

The younger Barings who came out to Kenya seemed impossibly sophisticated to my fertile mind, having been brought up and educated in England and Europe where culture seemed to saturate the very air. I was at an impressionable age and they were a seminal influence during the early days of my adolescence. Clever and artistic, witty and goodlooking, they were unfailingly kind to me and my sisters. They sang amusing Noel Coward songs round the piano; played Charades after dinner and made up *risqué* songs on a bongo drum in the evenings at our house. Katherine, the eldest daughter, drew like a dream and didn't seem to mind me hanging around watching her sketch. The adults took me to the Nairobi Races where I won my first ever bit of money, the huge amount of seventy Kenya shillings. The film star Danny Kaye signed my first autograph book in their house and of course I can't forget Princess Margaret-who-never-came-to-tea. The Princess was staying with the Barings after her breakup with her lover Peter Townsend and was pretty miserable but not quite enough to stop her taking a fancy to my father at a Government House ball where she insisted on monopolising the dancing with him all evening, much to my mother's displeasure. After dancing the Princess smiled up at him coquettishly with her big liquid blue eyes and purred, "See you later, alligator," to which he was meant to reply, "In a while, crocodile," after the snappy popsong of the day. The following afternoon she was due to have tea with Susie, Pods and myself and we were sitting down in our best frocks, thrilled to be meeting a real princess. At the last minute she changed her mind and refused to come down which was hugely disappointing. It's funny how we recall so many small incidents from our childhood.

As our house was in the grounds, Susie, Pods and I were always running in and out of the main house and swimming in the pool. Many childhood accidents happened there but we were fearless. I once jack-knived off the ten foot high diving board, trying to be very Esther Williams—the Hollywood star—just as Pods was coming up from the depths, but instead of breaking both our necks I chipped my front tooth on her head. Then there was the time Susie was skimming a stone through the water and it hit Pods standing on the opposite side, badly cutting he above her mouth. Parents were called, doctors arrived. Stitches were needed and she still has a scar.

My first girl-crush was on the beautiful eighteen year old Baring cousin, Clare, whom I stuck to like a second shadow. Most of the Governor's ADCs (*aides-de-camp*) were in love with either her or another pretty cousin, Mary Dawnay. I often listened to the young adults discussing whose heart was currently broken and who was mad about whom, so for a delicious moment I lived in the grown-ups' world of love and romance. Whenever Clare was off to play tennis with the ADCs she wore a teeny-tiny pair of white shorts. Twirling round in the long mirror before leaving her bedroom, she would ask me,

"Do my legs look too fat in these?" Her legs were complete perfection and I blabbered,

"Oh no, Clare, your legs look wonderful. Can I carry your racket for you?" I couldn't do enough for her.

✳

At that time we had a little black and white mongrel called Binker who was curious and energetic. He and I enjoyed exploring the land down in the valley by the river in front of our house. Small animals crossed this land looking for food and pilfering vegetables and roots from the Africans' *shambas*— meager plots of land which augmented much of their daily nutritional needs. Sometimes we came across porcupines or jackals, small buck and the odd snake.

One afternoon Binker bounded ahead down the slope and when I caught up with him I found him barking and sniffing at the base of a thick hedge where he was frantically trying to dig a hole. As he disappeared through, I heard a sharp yelp. Thinking an animal had attacked him, I broke through the hedge, and looking down, found Binker had fallen onto a long sharp stake in the middle of a deep hole in the ground built by the Africans to catch trespassing animals. An ointment or scent was put down to attract small creatures to their dismal fate. Binker was pinned on the stake which had gone right through the fur and flesh on his right side and he was just hanging there whimpering in pain. There was no way I could climb down and prise him off so I ran home to get Thomas, our *Pishi*, our cook, and we rushed back together to rescue poor Binker. Wonderful Thomas jumped into the hole and lifted the dog gently off the stake. We took him home, bloodied, in a blanket and nursed him back to health.

LOITOKITOK

I have always thought of Mount Kilimanjaro as my magical mountain. Whenever we approached it, the ethereal grandeur of the mountain, shaped like the curved back of some vast whale, filled the sky in front of us. Thin wisps of clouds drifted and coiled like the seven veils below the deep snowline, as if teasing the plum-pudding crown into covering its secrets. Listening to rain thrumming on the corrugated iron roof of our small house in Loitokitok was music to me and as I lay in bed at night, cradled in the folds of the mountain, it gave me a safe, secure feeling. And when the sun came out the next morning, there was a lightness in the air and the sky danced with myriad colours.

The ground was covered with smooth red seeds from the 'Lucky Bean' trees. How I loved to collect them straight after the rains had fallen. Africans would patiently carve sets of three tiny elephants out of the cream-coloured pulp before putting them back into the empty seed pod, closing the lid and selling them for a few cents. We had a meandering brook in the wild garden, with clumps of white arum lilies lining the sides. My sisters and I would have races in the stream with our Lucky Beans and see which won before they slipped over the small waterfall. Birds darted everywhere and the snap of a branch, caused by some prowling animal deep in the mountain forest occasionally broke the silence. One day we were out walking when my father, looking rather pleased with himself, suddenly stopped, placed his legs far apart and exclaimed,

"I am now straddling two countries. I have one leg in Kenya and one in Tanganyika!"

Rumour had it that when the German Kaiser, Queen Victoria's grandson, complained that it was unfair she had two mountains in Kenya, she gave him Mount Kilimanjaro for his birthday present.

LIMURU GIRLS

Limuru Girls' School was in the Highlands, rich agricultural land on the eastern edge of the Rift Valley and forty five minutes from Nairobi. It was lush with tea plantations; rolling hills and perfect countryside for hunting. The Limuru Hunt, which I joined, was well known. Off a small road beside plump tea bushes and wattle trees lay what was considered the best private girls' school in Kenya, run along strict English boarding school lines, where one hundred and fifty privileged white girls received a good education. But that journey back to school sitting silently between my parents in the front of the car with a sense of impending doom the nearer we got, can never be fully buried.

Brief reunions with our families only happened on two Sunday exeats either side of a halfterm weekend. However, the force of youthful friendships was intense and I made rock-solid pals for life at Limuru. Our gang of eight are still alive and in touch, Appley and I see each other nearly every day as she lives round the corner from me in London. Gentle Stork, another member, also lives a mile away. We worked pretty hard at school, played hockey, tennis and netball like it was going out of style; mooned over James Dean or the latest soppy popsong; managed to get hold of a copy of *Forever Amber* to read the naughty bits, and cleared away our desks after class to dance crazily, endlessly, to Elvis. I was also an enthusiastic member of the chapel choir, singing at our daily morning service in a rather fetching purple surplice with a white frilly collar and tried to ignore my friends who did their best to make me laugh when the choir walked two by two down the aisle. If you are fortunate enough to be taught by just one great teacher, you reap the benefits for the rest of your life. My heroine was Miss Hayes, a wise woman who was our science and biology teacher. Haysie as we called her, was Russian-born, middle-aged to us and had lead an extraordinary life, once giving birth on a trans-Siberian train on her own, with no doctors or nurses onboard. We were lucky enough to learn many of the most important things in life from her. Her lessons enthralled us but whenever we had a fit of giggles when dissecting a frog's private parts or something equally amusing, Haysie had just three words for it—"Ah, adolescent hysteria"—and just shrugged her shoulders as she went on teaching.

Being in the larva stage of life, we were always hungry. After the rains, to fill ourselves up if the school food had been particulary grim that day, we would run outside to catch handfuls of flying ants as they came out of their holes in the earth and rose up into the air in their hundreds. We gleefully pulled off their wings and stuffed them between the two slices of bread filched at teatime. Any teacher we unfortunately bumped into on our starving way out never failed to bark, "No running or talking in the corridors girls, only walking one behind the other. Please behave more like ladies." (Something my mother eventually gave up as a hopeless task.)

Most of us underwent various acts of mild brutality at school. Corporal punishment was considered pretty normal though I was beaten only once at my primary boarding school—for tucking into a forbidden midnight feast. Six of us, all roughly nine years old, were hit hard on our bare bottoms with a *tackie*, an Africaans word for a gym shoe. "Ow, ow" slipped unforced from our lips. That heavy thwack hurt a good deal and afterwards I could hear another girl sitting on the lavatory next door to mine, balling her little eyes out. No doubt she could hear me too, but once we reached puberty teachers never beat us again. However, at Limuru our perpetually grubby geography teacher, Miss Robinson, was a crack shot with a piece of chalk whenever we weren't concentrating. Quivering in anticipation and rocking on her great gnarly feet, she would ping us in the forehead as accurately as a dedicated darts player. Bullseye, she never missed. Another particular favourite of hers was coming up behind us and cracking us hard over the back of the head with the edge of a wooden ruler when we were least expecting it. Somehow, we all took it in our stride. The combination of boarding school and early childhood separation from family instilled in us an inner resilience and lack of self-pity. These days parents would have had Robbie, as we called her, up for child abuse. But Kenya girls, having the ingrained ability to just get on with things, grew up feeling anything was possible.

A few weeks before our mammoth 'O'-level exams, my two best friends, Appley and Hut, and I made the monumentally foolish decision to nip out of school and see the bright lights of Nairobi during the Royal Agricultural Show, a yearly event. We had already joined the Young Farmers' Association and quickly entered forms to compete in the Show.

We were given the disastrous task of choosing the best chicken in some obsure category we'd never heard of. Alas, my own knowledge on the subject of our feathered friends was severely limited.

How on earth do I tell a 'Cape Coop' from a 'White Leghorn'?" I muttered.

Appley, looking equally bewildered, announced:

"And afterwards, apparently we are going to be shown the quickest way to behead one of them!"

This seemed a bit drastic considering a few minutes before we would be extolling the poor creature's considerable virtues.

The three of us had been invited by our fledgling boyfriends to a dance at the Duke of York Boys' School in Nairobi on the night of the Show and told our parents we had been given permission to attend by Miss Cable, our hirsute headmistress. We would be spending the night at Appley's parents' house. Needless to say the 'permission' was a bit of a fib but it was all strictly highjinks at the time.

So there we were out of school, failing miserably at the chicken business and merrily jiving and square-dancing with the boys under the beady eyes of two teachers, when the headmaster suddenly whipped us into his office. In all the years we had been at Limuru, no headmistress had ever taken a roll call but when Cable called out our names at supper, a deathly silence had filled the hall. She guessed where we were and was coming down to Nairobi to collect her wayward girls. No doubt she imagined us being ravaged on some damp rugby field instead of innocently doing a bit of American 'do-si-doing.'

But within minutes our bravado had melted and we began to panic. Two of the boys 'borrowed' a school lorry, shoved us in the open back with a couple of blankets and off we shot to Limuru. After a freezing drive, we ran as fast as we could across the hockey pitch in the dark, scarpered up the fire escape and jumped into bed, falling asleep instantly. Cable was understandably furious when she returned and panted up the stairs to the top floor to find us sleeping like exhausted angels.

First thing in the morning we found ourselves being frogmarched to the sanatorium and firmly locked in with no food or water, while Cable discussed our fate with the governors. The head of them was the Archbishop of Canterbury, Reverend Dr. Geoffrey Fisher, who had crowned Queen Elizabeth at her coronation and christened my sister Digs in Government House a few years previously. His neice Miss Fisher had until recently been our scary headmistress and had she still been so, we would never had gone 'awol.' She was a formidable woman who went on to become headmistress at Arundel Girl's School in Salisbury, Rhodesia, where Susie and Pods went, before becoming head of the prestigious Wycombe Abbey Girl's School in England. Later, aged nineteen, I had accompanied my mother to an Arundel Open Day, dressed up quite decently I thought in a slim fitting dress, high heels and a glam hat. When it was my turn to shake hands with Miss Fisher, she looked me up and down before saying loudly,

"Caroline, what do you think you look like?"

'Actually Miss Fisher, I now feel like a crushed macaroon thanks', I longed to say. Instead I blushed furiously and wished the ground would swallow me up before recalling only too well what a cow she could be, one that excelled at the ultimate putdown.

The upshot was we all left school rather earlier than anticipated but not before our diminutive Latin teacher whom we were fond of, and named *Twiga*, Swahili for giraffe, spoke to us sternly in the quadrangle.

"Your behaviour is very disappointing, girls. Going to a boys' school dance without permission leads me to believe you are girls of loose morals."

She might also have thrown in the word 'tart' somewhere, a favourite insult spat at one in those days. We were obviously on the road to Sodom and

Gomorah and divine retribution was unlikely to come our way. This all rather stunned us. We'd only gone to a square dance for heaven's sake which was hardly a Federal crime. Besides, we had only had one or two bumbling kisses up until then and were still, unquestionably, 'virgo intacta'. Crying parents came to collect us which we found rather sobering and brought us swiftly down to earth. My father was most upset, especially as I had been doing so well at school, and suddenly our escapade didn't seem quite as amusing.

The one thing I did find funny was a stern letter from the head of the Girl Guides' Association who had never laid eyes on me—I was an enthusiastic Sea Ranger three hundred miles from the sea and making do with sailing and piping my bosun onto a rickety boat on a nearby lake.

"Dear Caroline, your behaviour is more like that of a Brownie than a Girl Guide." Oh, such damnation!

I was obviously a lost cause. For a while we were considered scarlet women by narrow-minded matrons in Nairobi. One or two of them would cross the road, pernickety noses pointing to their own particular heaven, rather than speak to our mothers. These sanctimonius biddies with their permed hair and large trousered bottoms were most probably the prudish offspring of parents who had been part of the 'Happy Valley' crowd. Famous for excelling at louche behaviour they were more than acquainted with the three elements that made the country so notorious: altitude, alcohol and adultery. Meanwhile the three of us had to go to a crammer for a while where we were taught by a very clever teacher, an old Oxford don. He wore the same old cardigan every day and would sit in his worn leather chair with his feet sticking out of the window in the sunshine.

Allowed back to school for our exams, we were firmly locked up in Cable's house after being driven up each day by Appley's family driver; pupils were forbidden to speak to us. But on the final day of the exams as we drove down the long jacaranda drive, the entire school rushed out, lined the driveway and waved us goodbye. Soon afterwards, Apples and Hut went off to a finishing school in Switzerland to learn perfect French and flirt with dishy ski instructors while I followed my family to Northern Ireland.

KWA ZULU AFRIKANERS

When I occasionally think back to Mr. Jacobs the Kajiado farmer, I realise that Afrikaners have loomed large in my life on only one other occasion, a memorable encounter nearly forty years later in Kwa Zulu Natal, South Africa. I was travelling with my Kenyan friend Jacinthe and her South African musician husband, Bry, on a long, hair-raising drive over a dirt road late in the evening across the Drakensburg Mountains on the border with Lesotho—down a steep valley into Rhodes, a small town—known as a *dorp* in Afrikaans. More than anything we looked forward to the luxury of a hot bath and a strong drink.

As Jas and I sank into our tubs, her husband came back from the restaurant of the charming bougainvillea covered hotel we were staying in to tell us there was no way he was going to allow us into the bar as it was spilling over with drunken Afrikaners. Naturally we took absolutely no notice but once we got there, we felt we had stepped back a century—rather like stumbling on an old settlement of Pennsylvanian Amish who had unwittingly taken to drink. Huge young men with beer guts and builders' bums sat on flimsy looking bar stools, firmly clasping their Castle beers and looking at us defensively. They had never liked the British—the Boer War and all that. It didn't matter that we were white Africans ourselves, to them we were one step away from being *Rooineks*, the English soldiers in pith helmets who were greatly mocked by the Boers for burning bright red in the sun.

Behind the bar stood a diminutive but fiery blonde with short peroxide hair and small bra-less breasts sticking up perkily beneath a thin white t-shirt. Whenever the men thought she was looking the other way, one of them would nip behind the bar and try and grab a beer or a swig of whiskey. Quick as a ferret she would turn and zap them in the chest with an enormous electric cattle prod which she hid on a shelf underneath the bar top. The men would yelp as they were knocked backwards, retreating like beaten whippets until their befuddled brains forced one or another of them to try their luck again. Amazed, I nudged Jas and said,

"Try doing that in 'The Slug and Lettuce' in Chelsea!"

She laughed. Then one of two of the beer-swillers started to speak to us.

"Ach, we are the lost tribe, we are the lost tribe, hey," they wailed in thick Afrikaans accents as we sat on our stools nervously knocking back our vodka and tonics. Zap, Zap.

"No one understands us. Where would we go if we were booted out, hey?" Zap, Zap.

The men were being slowly stunned into herd-like submission and it soon became blindingly obvious that more than a few brain cells had, over the years, been left on the bar top. To ease the tension Bry brought out his guitar and began to play *Sarie Marais*, the traditional folk song beloved by all Afrikaners. His was a melodic voice and one young suddenly friendly woman started to cry with emotion,

"Ach, that was really *lekker*."

The atmosphere instantly changed and the evening soon became rather jolly. We all became the best of friends until, accompanied the by now thoroughly ill-tempered blonde zapper, the inebriated herd stumbled out into the night to go to a party and we three went to our beds.

A Colonial Family

MY FAMILY COMES, on both sides, from six generations of colonials. Brave and educated, curious and creative, since the 1750s they
were drawn to the furthest corners of the British Empire and tales
of their pioneering spirit have long captivated me. Some were adventurers;
many were soldiers in the Indian and British Armies and fought in the two
World Wars; others served as administrators in the Colonial and Political
Service. Although I cannot defend the British Raj in India, I am certain that
as far as my intrepid maternal great-grandfather in Malaya, paternal grandfather in India and my own father in Kenya were concerned, their motivation
was as genuinely philanthropic as human intentions can be. They had followed their parents and grandparents in abandoning a safe and predictable
life in England, Scotland and Ireland to enjoy the challenges of new hori-
zons. An ardent belief in doing good for the people of the country in which
they were to live decided their chosen path.

Two of my forebears stand out for their particularly striking and eccentric lives, and indeed fates.

THE CHINESE GOLDSMITH'S BATH-HOUSE

I like to imagine my forebears having either the swashbuckling derring-do of
Horatio Hornblower, or sound political nous and a flexible way of governing.
Alas, this was not always the case with my maternal great-great grandfather,

but you can't win them all. Teetering on the brink of what should have been a successful new posting, he found himself instead plunging headlong into a fiery abyss.

In 1874 James Wheeler Woodford Birch was appointed as the 1st British Resident to Perak, one of the oldest hereditary seats among the Malay States. He found it a tussle from the start and for a year he struggled to impose his authority on the young state ruler Sultan Abdullah, whose use of opium and refusal to give up slavery was abhorrent to him. Now middle-aged, he was considered an expert in colonial administration after twenty-seven years, having mostly gained his experience in Ceylon. He arrived in Malaya from the post of Colonial Secretary of the Straits Settlements in Singapore as a senior officer who believed in a policy of 'firmness with the natives'. Although his personal qualities were mostly admirable—preaching against debt-slavery and protecting runaway slaves, being kind to the poor, the sick and oppressed—at forty-eight, he was probably too intractable to learn the hundred ways in which Malay etiquette may be infringed through a stranger's ignorance. Birch's reforms and his methods of urging them eventually created a fierce opposition which extended, almost without exception, to all the Perak chiefs. Birch quarrelled openly with both the Sultan and the chiefs until they unanimously plotted to kill him.

Many of his trips in the more remote parts of Perak were done on the back of elephants. On the last occasion, during *Ramadan*, the month of fasting, he travelled up the Perak river with an English officer and his interpreter in his own 'Dragon' houseboat which mounted a three-pounder gun. They were accompanied by a *sampan panjang* for his twelve Sikh *sepoys,* carrying a small mortar, and another for a dozen Malay boatmen which was also used by the servants as a floating kitchen. Of Birch's physical courage there can be no doubt. He had heard the rumours of death threats against him, but in a further attempt to ensure British control of Perak, he had come to the village of Passir Salak to talk over the situation with its angry and resentful ruler, Maharajah Lela, the most senior of the eight major Perak chiefs.

Birch's boat arrived late at night and was moored close to the bank near a Chinese goldsmith's shop. At dawn the sepoys and boatmen went ashore to cook their rice and clean their unloaded guns. When Maharajah Lela refused to come down to meet the Resident, a large crowd of armed Malays began to assemble near the Chinese shop. Ignoring the abuse of the restless crowd, Birch entered the Chinaman's adjacent small riverside bath-house with only a single Sikh sentry armed with a revolver standing outside to guard him. Eventually there was a signal for a rush on the bath-house and Birch was speared through the thin palm-leaf walls. Taken by surprise, naked and vulnerable, he was hacked to death with a sword and his body fell into the river, floating past the Malays on the bank. Birch's bloodied and mutilated corpse was recovered a few days later and he was buried with full military honours. His murder, instigated by Maharajah Lela, was followed by two days of feasting in the area. Ten years later when his son Ernest visited Pasir Salak, a local man handed over the murdered Resident's gold watch and gun.

Though Birch left no will which might have established another family, the facts remain that on numerous occasions 'Sultan Abdullah's girls,' many of whom had been reduced to prostitution, deserted the Sultan or other chiefs for the Residency knowing that Birch would either give them refuge or help them escape disguised as boatmen. When the cases of the runaway slaves he harboured were examined, the slaves are found to be girls only. An angry chief once called on the Resident to give up a girl who gone there and was invited on a fruitless search of the house. Birch had told the woman to hide in the adjoining jungle. The next day he took her and another girl, disguised in Chinese dress, in his own boat, to Pangkor. Some historians felt certain that Birch had sexual relations with the Malay girls, and a local historian pointed out that a Malay manuscript had described Birch as 'an over-sexed man.' Others refused to believe the rumour, convinced that he would have been above it.

Throughout the years there has been much talk within the family as to our possible Malay-Chinese heritage, in particular the pattern of distinctly Chinese shaped eyes in some—alas my generation missed it. My grandmother flatly refused to discuss it during her lifetime. A totally forbidden subject. But two of her own sisters had a definite Oriental look as did my mother and her first cousin, the humorous stage and television actor Patrick Cargill. Even my children and Cal, my eldest grandchild, have this attractive feature. Despite any concrete evidence my sisters and I would still like to believe that an illicit affair could somehow explain 'the look'.

ZARH IN TAHITI

One relation whose dreams were realised on the opposite side of the world one hundred and twenty year ago, in particular fascinates me. I like to muse that my paternal grandfather Colonel Hugh Pritchard's brother Zarh, my eccentric and talented great-uncle, is responsible for a smattering of my passion for the sea. Always a romantic figure in our eyes, Zarh was an unusual character with a wacky streak, whose fame came from being the world's first acknowledged underwater painter of oils on canvas. One of nineteen children from two mothers, he was born in 1866 in Madras in India, as was my grandfather and most of their seventeen siblings, a number of whom were killed in the First World War. Packed off at the age of ten to boarding school in Scotland, Zarh took art classes in Edinburgh and spent his summers free diving in the bays. At fourteen he discovered the picturesque fishing village of Portobello where a party of boys frequently gathered on a raft. He watched them dive deep by casting loose the cork-headed ropes of sacks of sand which they used to pull them under water. With ears and noses stuffed with cotton wool and holding their breath they played tag for up to a minute. Zarh soon joined them but with each dive he found himself increasingly entranced by the mysterious watery world. To see better he fashioned a set of goggles out of cow horn after a pair he saw in a travel book and within a few years had begun to create his first serious undersea views. He frequently dived thirty to forty times to observe a scene, rose to the surface, swam hurriedly ashore and attempted to draw it from memory. Many years later Zarh told a *New York Times* reporter,

"I rebelled against my parents' wishes to join the army and fled to London to become a struggling artist, having to make do at times with a crust of bread and a cup of hot chocolate a day." However, he was determined to follow his two passions, art and the sea. Luck would be a lady one night in 1890 when, at the age of twenty four, Zarh attended a stage performance of *Cleopatra*, starring the eccentric French actress Sarah Bernhardt, who was noted for her elaborate costumes and her interest in their authenticity. In one scene her robe represented a sea-sorceress and when they met Zarh, who spoke fluent French, explained to the actress her robe was quite simply all wrong. Instantly liking and trusting him, she ordered her jewelled sea-gown to be remade from the designs that he drew on scraps of paper and to celebrate the occasion she bought two of his paintings. The Divine Sarah, as she was called, was known for charming the most handsome men of her time but she also set Zarh on his life's work. For the next fourteen years, their friendship provided him an easy *entrée* into London's world of decorative arts, which resulted in numerous commissions for costumes, stage accessories and murals.

After recovering from a dangerous bout of pneumonia which permanently damaged his lungs, he took off for the dry, warm climate of California and on to Tahiti in 1904, regarded at the time as an earthly paradise by so many artists, pre-eminently Paul Gaugin. Unlike them Zarh continued his interest in the life below sea level and soon found himself befriending fishermen and local Tahitians. First he had to rebuild his weakened body. Donning his precious cow horn goggles, he waded out into the lagoon and gazed with amazement on mountains of red coral, gardens of delicate sponge and bright tropical fish. Once his breathing improved, his ability to descend deeper increased. To protect his white skin from sunburn he developed a curious outfit vaguely reminiscent of his Indian background: cut-off trousers under a knee-length skirt, a long-sleeved work shirt, cloth shoes and several bandanas wound around his neck. Some considered him rather peculiar.

Within weeks Zarh met Narii Salmon, the brother of beautiful Marau, the last Queen of Tahiti, born to an English Jewish merchant and a Tahitian princess. Both children were privately educated in Sydney until Marau came home to Papeete at fifteen to marry Crown Prince Ariiaue, the future King Pomare. Popular and friendly, she counted Robert Louis Stevenson, Gauguin, Pierre Loti and Somerset Maugham among her friends. Her brother Narii happened to own the only diving outfit in Tahiti. It turned out to be a helmet attached to a simple old sou'wester, its seams waterproofed with the sap of a breadfruit tree. Over dinner one evening the gentle, handsome Narii bet Zarh that he could not produce an oil painting on canvas under water. The two friends agreed on a bet of $500.

Sitting at his iron easel Zarh produced the first real paintings of marine life and scenes ever painted under the sea—he later became known as 'The Merman', a moniker given to him by the *Los Angeles Times* art critic. Attached to a coral or stone weight, Zarh would sink to the seafloor, preferring the depth of around thirty feet where he found the light clearer. He used lambskin and brushes soaked in oil and kept his tubes of paint in a special belt similar to those used to hold cartridges. The helmet was serviced with air through a tube, made of the skin of a llama, from a tank on a boat above. Once he selected the view, his canvas and materials were lowered to him from the boat and he painted for roughly half an hour. Whenever his Tahitian boatmen became careless when pumping his air supply, allowing water to seep into the exhaust line, Zarh had to furiously signal them. Occasionally while he was painting, Narii, with a mischievous grin and wearing a loin-cloth, would appear unexpectedly at his side, to watch his friend at work.

In the calm waters off Tahiti Zarh could leave his easel on the seafloor and go back the next day to finish his picture. Most of his underwater work was used as sketches for later completed pictures. Focusing on the sensual colours of the exquisite flora and fauna, his interpretations were mystical and dreamy and many people responded to the spiritual side of Zarh's haunting compositions. The artist wrote about the world where he most loved to work: "On reaching the bottom, it is as if one were temporarily resting on a dissolving fragment of some far planet."

There was always an element of danger, including an octopus with eight-foot tentacles which almost seized him before his safety diver managed to spear the creature. As he explained to a *New York Times* reporter: "There is the tiger shark, who likes the warm, bright, clear, lime-bearing water... Also the giant ray, fifteen feet across, which crushes his victim by descending. You must move quickly when a shadow covers you. Sometimes fish eight or ten feet long have come close. A tiny mistake there because one has come too near, and the whole sketch is spoiled. A submarine painter can make no alterations."

Zarh eventually returned to California with hundreds of sketches and paintings. Many were shown at his first American exhibition at the Paul Elder Galley in San Francisco in the month of the massive earthquake in 1906 in which fifty of his most important works were destroyed by fire. After recovering from their loss and basing himself in Pasadena, he continued to travel and exhibit throughout the world. In his prime Zarh was an international figure whose collectors included Queen Victoria, Prince Fushimi of Japan, Prince Albert of Monaco and numerous museums, including nine paintings in the American Museum of Natural History where they can still be seen. His first appearance in his full diving regalia was recorded in the *Illustrated London News* in January, 1922, along with five of his paintings. The artist died in 1956, aged ninety and was buried in Austin, Texas.

SIR ERNEST BIRCH, MY GREAT-GRANDFATHER

My mother' side of the family has already been introduced with the assassination of J.W.W. Birch. This naturally left his son, my great-grandfather Ernest, bereft, but by all accounts he turned out to be a remarkable man. Born in Trincomalee, Ceylon in 1857, he was sent to Harrow, went up to Oxford for a year and at 19 entered the Colonial Office.

Two years later Ernest was sent to the Secretariat in Singapore, where in 1882 he met and married Margaret Niven, eldest daughter of the Director of the beautiful Singapore Botanical Gardens, Lawrence Niven. (The actor David Niven was another of my mother's cousins.) One of their six children was my grandmother, Margaret Idris, named after her father's great friend, Sultan Idris of Perak. Ernest was a man with a great personality, an all-round sportsman who introduced western sport to the people of Perak—he loved the Malays who in return gave him ample proof of their affection. In recognition of his valued services he was knighted by Queen Victoria and received the KCMG. After being Governor of North Borneo he followed in his late father's footsteps by serving as the 8th British Resident of Perak from 1904 until his retirement in 1910. In 1975 my parents travelled up a river deep into the heart of Perak to find the memorials to Mum's grandfather—a marble fountain and clock tower. When they arrived a small festival was held in their honour by the friendly people.

GRANNY, LADY WHELER AND GRANDPA,
SIR TREVOR WHELER (13TH BARONET)

Ernest's daughter—Granny—was called Idris all her life. She was the second of four girls and two boys, one of whom drowned in Malacca at the age of seven. At the same age she was sent back to school in England with her three sisters Omme, to whom she was very close, Winnie and Hilly, later known as Hitler for her dictatorial character. Winnie was so tiny she once got carried away by an open umbrella in a gust of wind. Like other colonial children at the time, the girls spent most of their holidays at school and didn't see their parents for seven years. My mother explained, "Although that seems too terrible for words, they had each other and didn't seem hurt by it all."

Once she was a bit older Granny lived a rather ritzy life with her own maid and under-maid in a big house belonging to her parents in South Kensington. On the day she was presented at Court her father had fresh red roses sent over from Paris to pin on her long stylish silk designer dress—which she kept all her life. At twenty-one she married my grandfather Sir Trevor Wheler at the Holy Trinity Church Brompton in London in 1915 and they remained married for over 70 years until their deaths. My grandfather was fond of saying, "And to think you only get 25 years for life!"

My memory of Granny in Kenya, where they lived near us in Nairobi, was that of a very amusing, elegantly dressed woman never seen without her pearls or one of her diamond brooches. She always seemed to be wearing stockings and high heels—she had marvellous legs—and holding a long cigarette holder on which she drew furiously until she was 93. Granny was quite eccentric, very social, rather selfish and as much as she loved her gin and tonic her real passion in life was bridge, at which she excelled, becoming All Sussex Bridge Champion on her eventual return to England. What I admired most about her was her independent spirit and ability to set up bridge clubs wherever she lived, her last one being in Bexhill, to which she would bicycle in her high heels well into her eighties. I remember Grandpa in Nairobi looking after us when my parents went out to a dinner party, but what I cannot recall is Granny ever doing anything with me at all. I realise that was a different time as far as grand-children went and I never really expected anything from her; as my mother loved me so entirely it didn't matter. It is only in my later years, when I am so involved with my own four grandsons that I have wondered about it.

Grandpa was a kind-hearted, funny man and I was very fond of him. Unfortunately he had a propensity to chippiness, mainly because he had suffered greatly from being bullied at Radley, his public school, due to his lack of height—five foot seven inches—and the fact that he had inherited his baronetcy (granted by Charles II in 1660) at the difficult age of fourteen when his adored father, the 12th Baronet, died. To make matters worse his mother, in trying to protect her only son, kitted him out in all the wrong clothes for boarding school; combinations—an all-in-one pants and vest affair—which no other boy had. Carrying a parrot's head umbrella with his brand new uniform proved the final straw. In defiance of the bullying, he proved himself by being excellent at games—cricket, football, golf, squash and tennis, at which he became a first class doubles partner. According to my mother his arrival at Radley coloured his whole life.

INDIAN SUMMERS

Christened Diana but always call Dinah, my mother was extremely pretty, vivacious and full of laughter. Kind and loving, above all else she adored her husband and four girls. Apart from being gutsy and brave, not much in the wild phased her other than bats. Thick wavy brown hair was brushed away from her face, small blue eyes sparkled, and she kept her enviably slim figure for many years. She was one of those people who, throughout her life, drew people of all ages to her with her positive spirit and great sense of humour which she had inherited from both her parents. But it was her father, Sir Trevor, to whom she was particularly close.

Mum was born in 1918 in Dalhousie, a hill station in Himachal Pradesh in India, established, along with Simla, in 1854 by the British as a summer retreat for its Raj bureaucrats and troops. By all accounts in its heyday Simla was a mass of parties and balls, tennis foursomes and croquet, and the British, waited on hand and foot, had a rollicking good time.

After the First World War Mum's family returned to England where Grandpa ran a game farm for a close friend, Henry Horne. Horne was not only very rich, he was a full-blown *bon vivant*. Racing car drivers, actresses and maharajahs roared down in droves at weekend for shoots. Henry was always in between marriages when Granny acted as his hostess. My mother explained, "I loathed the shooting parties but both my parents shot. Actually I think Henry was absolutely mad about Mummy but she only enjoyed the admiration, like we all do."

When Mum was eight Henry Horne gave her some large fitted boxes with gold tops from Asprey's plus exquisite gold and enamel cigarette cases; a couple of fox furs as well, all of which delighted my mother who thought 'everything was so pretty'. They were obviously all for my grandmother but she let her daughter have them as she had absolutely no interest in accepting gifts from her admirer. Granny's best friend was the Countess of Durham, and her children Tony Lambton and his brother often stayed the night. Mum smiled, as if it was yesterday: "Each night Tony and I were shoved, giggling, in the bath together and thoroughly scrubbed by nanny."

Three years later the Countess was killed in a hunting accident and Granny was utterly heartbroken.

MY FATHER'S SIDE

My paternal great-grandfather was Thomas Pritchard, a British Captain in the Madras Fusiliers, who came from a long line of soldiers; he was the father of Zarh, the underwater artist, and my grandfather Hugh, called 'Do' in the family. Like Zarh, Do was born in Madras and went to school in Scotland. After attending Bonne University Do joined the Indian Army. He married my grandmother, Mot, a kind, gentle woman with long wavy light brown hair and soft blue eyes, also born in India.

Do was handsome and tremendously capable but grew into a stern patrician, a stickler for manners, abiding by strict protocol at all times. He became the Resident in Mewar, Political Agent to the Governor General of Central India, followed by Political Agent to the Governor General of the Madras States, then India's two main states.

At 46 and flying increasingly high in India, Grandpa then did something rather bizarre: he refused a knighthood—"Because I couldn't stand the Viceroy and thought the whole thing was a load of bollocks"—convinced himself he had angina and returned to England to retire. Perhaps, after his refusal, it was the only way to prevent the impossible situation of being given any higher posting without an accolade.

MY FATHER

My father Leslie had also been born in India, in the same year as my mother, but unlike hers his was not such an unblemished upbringing. He was born in Loralei in the North West Province near Lahore, where his father was stationed as a young man.

Dad was a reserved, thoughtful man who possessed a talent for succeeding in anything he undertook. Tall and good looking with fair golden-brown hair and large blue eyes, gentle by nature and modest in demeanour, he was an honourable man who effortlessly commanded respect. He tended to draw a veil over his emotions and more often than not gave the impression that his life was as calm and smooth as an alpine lake. But those who really knew him understood that his ideals and feelings ran deep.

Pa's early childhood was a happy one riding ponies and living in grand

Indian palaces which had been turned into residencies for the British rulers. But the inevitable day came for him, as it did for so many other children of the British Empire, to be sent back home to prep school at the age of seven and enter into the bewildering fray that was the English public school. From that day on he only saw his beloved mother, Mot, every four years when his parents came back on home leave by sea. Her absence in his life caused him great unhappiness.

Grandpa Do was tough on Dad who, at the age of twelve had the misfortune to stay for the holidays with a Vicar he disliked intensely, and his wife, at the Rectory in Lamberhurst in Sussex. Taking any opportunity to escape, he spent as many hours as possible in the indoor riding stables at Dewhurst, where he was taught by Old Mrs Selby. She told my mother fifty years later, "I still remember him as a shy, well-mannered child with a good seat."

When life grew too difficult Dad twice ran away—jumping on his bike and peddling for miles across the countryside to find his older sister Jotto and her husband Ralph who were often forced to send him back. At the height of his anguish, in one of his Prep school reports, the headmaster wrote "The flame of ambition that flickered last term has died down again but I do not think it has gone out." All this changed when Pa went to Blundells, his public school in Devon. He thrived there at the subjects he enjoyed, including rugby and running; he was popular, ending up as Head of House. Dad also made a life-long friend of Philip Nind, who later went up to Balliol College, Oxford and became my much loved godfather. In the winter holidays the two of them went skiing together; in the season they queued up for tickets to see opera and ballet at the Royal Albert Hall in London. Philip was passionate about ballet, my father was an opera buff, in particular anything by Wagner. Many years later he took me to my very first opera, an unforgettable production of Verdi's *Aida* at the Royal Opera House in Covent Garden. That special evening spent together is one of my cherished memories.

At times Dad had been forced to deal with a less than robust constitution at school and in a letter he wrote, aged seventeen, to his parents from Blundell's he confirmed his life-long need to help others: "...I am increasingly interested in the medical profession. French [his house master] is all in favour of it and seems to think it would suit me. Also the thought that I would be doing some real good in the world is an added satisfaction..." He was in the midst of his studies at Guy's Medical School, in London when the Second World War broke out. Together with Philip Nind my father immediately joined up as an Officer in the British Army in the 12th Battalion, Royal Fusiliers and attended Staff College Camberley.

By then Henry Horne had gone bust, leaving a trail of bad debts, and my maternal grandfather Sir Trevor Wheler had his own pheasant farm near Amersham. "That is how my father lost nearly all his money," Mum told me indignantly. "Yet Henry became a millionaire twice again in his life. It was such a terrible thing to do to anybody, especially my father who was such a generous man."

My mother never forgave her father's nemesis. "Years later when I was at Quaglinos one night, Henry was there, this utter cad who had wrecked my father's life to a great extent. He recognized me after all those years and I was so angry I just wanted to kick him. Instead I remained extremely cool and unforthcoming, and turned away to carry on dancing". At eighteen Mum started a job at Molyneux Fashion House in Mount Street for three years and was greatly enjoying life.

"My fabulous Aunt Murie had a flat in Berkley Street in Mayfair where I was able to stay. I used to go roaring up from Amersham to dances; then we'd all go to Lyon's Corner House for breakfast at about seven in the morning, having danced literally all night at the Embassy or the 400. Then I rushed back to the flat, changed quickly and be back at my job at Molyneux in time."

I can just imagine my mother getting ready to go out to a dinner party, sitting at her dressing table and dabbing herself behind the ears with her favourite Worth's *Je Reviens* scent which she wore all her life. Or putting on her bright red lipstick, having formed her mouth into a large 'O' for the purpose. Mum yearned to be an actress but Grandpa put his foot down at the very thought. God forbid! It was far too racy and usually the first step to becoming a '*grande horizontale*'.

"Then the war came and I couldn't stay in London any longer as Pa was too worried about me," she continued. Her parents had planned to have a dance and a large party for her 21st birthday. "Of course Hitler decided to declare war the day before, so many people couldn't come. Just a couple of dozen came for drinks and we went up to London. When we came back the sirens were going off so we spent that night sitting in the car. On the night of my 21st!"

That was also the year my parents met, on a Saturday night at The Mill House in old Amersham which had supper and dancing at the weekends. Granny had taken Mum and friends of hers were going to join them with someone she had never met. Mum recalls, "When they came upstairs with their friend Leslie, he looked too wonderful for words in his dark blue regimental evening dress. I thought 'Oh my God! How glorious'. Dad introduced himself and of course he was absolutely delicious." A few minutes later he asked my mother to dance and they went downstairs but as she already had her head in the clouds, she tripped on the last two steps and ended up sprawled on the floor. Mum pulled herself up, dusted herself down and, both laughing, they began to dance.

"Daddy instantly said, 'There is a hunt ball next weekend. Will you come with me?' I told him I couldn't as I was busy. He was frightfully disappointed, saying, 'But you must. I want you to.'" My pretty mother was much sought after but remembers every minute of the night she met my father. "I went upstairs after the dance and Mummy, who knew about the hunt ball said, 'You are silly not to go, darling, because that's the man you are going to marry!'" Two months later my parents got engaged on the 9th May, a day before my father's twenty-second birthday and the day Hitler invaded Belgium and Holland. "All leave was cancelled and we were not able to see each other which we were heartbroken about", sighed my mother.

My father was on field exercises in the New Forest and wrote letters to his new fiancée every day. This is part of a letter written to her in 1940 during their engagement:

"... I went to bed last night with your voice still in my ears and I lay on my old camp bed with a perfect moon shining into my tent—just dreaming. All my life I've managed to live way up in the stars, often for days on end miles away from the earth and surrounded by ideals. I loved to be alone and get away from everything sometimes. People have often laughed at me for this until eventually after the war had started I gave it up as a bad job. I had no ideals any more. But now it's all come back again and when you live your whole day and night always in the open, all thought somehow becomes quite clear and vivid, my imagination is even more active and my longing for you is a hundred times more acute. I've new ideals now, full of sincerity and faith founded on our unshakeable love and I thank God for this chance of solitude which brings me such tremendous peace of mind..."

MARRIAGE, CEYLON AND SINGAPORE

My parents were married a year after they met, in Weymouth near my father's regiment. Mum told me, "I couldn't have been happier because my mother-in-law Mot, whom I adored, was there but luckily without my father-in-law whom I found to be a harsh and fearsome man."

After finishing Staff College Camberley, my father embarked for service overseas and was appointed GSOII 11th Army Group in the Royal Fusiliers. He arrived in Delhi in 1944, eighteen months before the end of the war, eager to be a fighting soldier. Instead, he joined Earl Mountbatten's staff as a Major at Joint Planning Staff, Rear Headquarters, Supreme Allied Commander, South East Asia (S.A.C.S.E.A) in Kandy, Ceylon, where he proved to have a great flair for administration. He stayed with Mountbatten, known as the 'Supremo', for the rest of the war and by the time they sailed to Singapore when the Japanese surrendered he was on his way to becoming a Lieutenant-Colonel at the age of twenty-six, one of the youngest in the army in the Second World War. In Singapore on 6th September 1945 my father was appointed Overseeing Commander, No. 7 War Crimes Investigation Team. While my mother was driving ambulances and lorries to Tilbury docks as part of the London war effort, my father, busy on the other side of the world, wrote numerous letters to her. The following is part of one of them.

> ...My little LCQ was the first British ship to enter Keppel Harbour for three and a half years and we sailed in with our battle ensign flying, covered by the guns of the Fleet. There was, however, absolutely no resistance and not a shot was fired. We were met on the wharf by a party of senior Japanese officers who had come to "welcome" us!
>
> Our first job was to get out to the prisoners and so we turned a Jap officer out of his large car and set off for the main camp which was at the other end of the island. We were the first British troops to drive through the town and the welcome we got from the local population, mostly Chinese, was quite overwhelming. They have suffered horribly. There were Japanese sentries and picquets everywhere and they all came to attention and bowed as we went by. It was almost unbelievable and you can imagine what a tremendous kick I got out of it!
>
> Our reception at the camp was equally moving even though some of our boys

had parachuted in several days before. We were literally besieged and at times it was more difficult to move than it ever was coming away from rugger matches at Twickenham! They all shouted questions at the same time and seemed literally intoxicated with joy. From the walls of their prison they had watched our mass of ships sail into the bay and I think that must have been the greatest moment of their lives.

We spent the rest of the day with the camp staff and listened to their story of the last three and a half years. They have suffered great hardships but their morale is higher than ever. I can't tell you what a tremendous impression these chaps have made on me. The organisation of the camps has been wonderful and they have banded together making the finest team in the world to counter these bloody Japanese. Their spirit has never been broken and they have stood up mentally to the treatment they have received far better than I ever thought possible. I expected to find a collection of mental and physical wrecks but this is NOT so although there are of course a lot of sick.

Today I have been to the civilian internees' camp with which I was almost equally impressed. The women were especially remarkable. I suppose each of them had tried to keep one dress for this great day and they certainly made the best of it! Some of them would have done justice to Bond Street and to me they looked quite incongruous with their pitiful surroundings but ye Gods I admired their pluck. When the huge gates were opened Lady Shenton Thomas, who had refused to bow to the Japanese, walked tall out of Changi wearing a ragged old blouse, a sacking skirt and no shoes—the wife of the Governor!

My jeep has been the most terrific sensation and I spent an hour today giving the children a ride. I took six at a time and they simply adored it. One little nipper had never seen a car before and asked his father if it was a house on wheels! Actually our transport situation is super for although the Japanese had precious little military transport there are still plenty of luxury limousines in Singapore. I have nabbed myself a big Packard Straight 8 and several other roadsters for the chaps.

The Japanese are behaving well and there have been absolutely no incidents here. I've interviewed the Japanese General in charge of prisoners and he seems only anxious to try and save his skin by doing all we require. They seem completely demoralised and a little shouting reduces them to pulp very quickly. One sword has been surrendered to me by the Japanese General and I am allowed to keep it! I have unearthed so many pretty awful things and have got to address the press so that all the world can know what has been going on in this part of the world these last three and a half years. It won't make pleasant reading but I will say that it's not a patch on the horrors of the German concentration camps, thank God.

We are working flat out but have ourselves a lovely E Group bungalow which is beautifully furnished which makes all the difference. I have actually got a spring bed and a bathroom of my own! We have gone onto half rations in order to give the prisoners more to eat—it leaves us a bit hungry but who cares. I have now been put in charge of the distribution of supplies by air to prisoners and civilians in Borneo, Celebes, Bali, Java and Sumatra. It's the hell of a job and after a day of solid thinking I'm only just beginning to see daylight as to how I'm going to organise the show. I am sending all my E Group boys out to these places with our doctors and I have a squadron of Dakotas to fly in the medical supplies, food and clothing. They will also bring out casualties, the desperate, starving and broken POWs. We've got the Japanese working in the city cleaning the streets and generally doing the worst jobs possible."

After nearly two eventful years abroad, the time came for my father to return home to England.

Distance Yearning

I WAS SEVENTEEN when my father left the Colonial Administration and joined the tobacco giant, Gallagher. He was forty years old, had never set eyes on a tobacco leaf, and was to spend the next year learning the ropes at the headquarters in Belfast, Northern Ireland before returning to Africa to become Managing Director in Rhodesia, one of the world's main tobacco growing countries.

Belfast, of all places! What could possibly be more dreary after the sun and beauty of Africa? I was by nature an adventurer but this place had me stumped. I found it a bleak, unfriendly place with rain permanently skidding off the roofs; drab parks and grey pebble-dash houses clamped together in terraced rows. A town where the first two young girls I met enquired, "Hey, youse, what's your religion?" I had never been asked that before and like a typical teenager, I replied with a shrug, "Heathen, actually."

They left, looking slightly peeved, without asking my name. Outside the center of the city, soggy green fields surrounded by thick hedges dotted the Irish landscape. I felt utterly bereft, torn away from everything I knew and loved.

I soon began suffering from *mal d'Afrique*, the deep-seated homesickness of those who have to leave their own particular patch of Africa. Only in my dreams was I back where I should be, among the eucalyptus and the casuarina trees, smelling dust and frangipani. The salty taste of tears was never far away. I was lonely, with no friends in this wet, frayed country and spent hours in my bedroom, listening on my record player to Ella Fitzgerald's soulful rendition of Cole Porter's "Give me land, lots of land, with starry skies above, don't fence me in..."

My younger sisters seemed reasonably happy in their new schools, but my mother, father and I disliked the place equally. Eventually, after a brief spell at an art school attached to Queen's University where nobody could be bothered to talk to me, I was packed off to Cheltenham to a secretarial college for the remaining seven months of our exile. Secretarial! God help me.

"Do I really have to, Mum?" Before she could utter a word, Dad said firmly, as so many flummoxed fathers have done before him, "Yes, so you will have something to fall back on."

Although my father was aware that he could be a target for the IRA there was little indication of the turmoil that would engulf Northern Ireland a few years later. Simmering social and political issues gradually surfaced after civil rights activists began protesting government discrimination against Catholics and Irish nationalists. Eventually tensions were ratcheted up until wholescale violence broke out in Belfast and other parts of the country. The thirty years of civil strife that followed became known as 'The Troubles'.

I have no happy memories of that short time in Northern Ireland but there was one summer day that I remember well mainly because I managed to survive it. It was a breezy morning when, still trying to deal with my new life, I went for a walk to try and chase away the shadows. I wore a plain white t-shirt and my mother's rather tight, snazzy red trousers for which I had developed a bit of a penchant. They suited me, she didn't mind lending them and I felt rather more jaunty as I set off alone. After a long, meandering walk I lay down in the middle of a big grassy field and closed my eyes. The sounds of the birds and the infrequent sunbeams on my face felt soothing. Perhaps I drifted off for a few minutes but I was suddenly startled by a gravelly male voice. I sat bolt upright to find a large burly man standing there blotting out the weak sun as he looked down at me. "Aren't you afraid, being out here all by yourself, missy?", he asked.

"Not really. I'm from Kenya and like exploring," I replied with a certain tomboyish bravado. I was an innocent abroad but after five minutes I began to feel uncomfortable with his questions. I politely said goodbye, carried on walking and eventually sat down in another field half a mile away to continue my pondering.

It was barely fifteen minutes before I heard someone whistling loudly as they walked up and down the other side of the hedge at the bottom of the field. I instinctively knew it was the burly man and that, like a predator in the wild, he was out to get me. What if his terrifying face suddenly appeared over the top of the hedge? I sprang up and ran as fast as I could up the hill on my side of the hedge. My pursuer ran up panting on his side, though slightly behind me, as I was younger, a quicker sprinter and was the first to reach the woods at the top. Crouching in the darkness, I tried to muffle my breathing as he thrashed around in the dense, rustling rhododendron bushes trying to find me. I could hear the crunching of broken twigs as he tore at murky shapes in the underbrush. Mustering the small amount of imagined bush craft from my younger days I began crawling on my belly through the undergrowth to his original side of the hedge, then ran like the wind down to the bottom of the hill. I could still hear his noisy grunts far above me as he continued searching. Jumping over an old wooden farm gate with my feet barely touching the muddy lane, I rushed back to our house. With the terror slowly dissipating, I lunged for the garden door and found Mum writing a letter in the sitting room. Gasping, I blurted out the story of my narrow escape.

"Oh really, darling?" she replied, not taking my plight in the least bit seriously. "Are you absolutely sure? Aren't you exaggerating it all just the tiniest bit?" before telling me to get ready for lunch. Bloody hell, I thought, I could have been raped, or even murdered! Sighing, I climbed the stairs and put Ella back on the record player.

Thank heavens I did go to Cheltenham for within two weeks I met my first love at a swimming pool one sunny weekend. He was nineteen and his name was Rullygullian which I thought was wildly romantic. Everyone called him Rullie. He was tall and well-built with a shock of blonde hair and green eyes, rugby-mad and had taken a job as a lifeguard at the pool for the summer months to make some money. I thought he was the most beautiful man I had ever seen. His warm and welcoming family lived in an old, sprawling cottage in Coombe Hill, just outside town. I became close to his parents and two sisters and spent most weekends with them, tucking into his mother's delicious lamb stews and homemade apple pies. They were like a second family to me and Rullie and I were blissfully happy for the eight months I was in Cheltenham.

The college's only real treat was taking my class to see the Royal Shakespeare Company's production of *The Taming of The Shrew* at Stratford-on-Avon. The young, unbelievably handsome actor, Peter O'Toole, played a rollicking, larger-than-life Petruchio opposite an older Peggy Ashcroft as Kate. He was magnetic, a sensation, and his acting in my first Shakespeare play was something I will always keep close to my heart.

Rullie also took me up to London to see my very first West End musical, *West Side Story*, which to my mind is still the best of them all. He had arranged for us to spend the night with his best friend, a charming, well-educated son of an Indian maharajah. Shivay had rented a convenient flat in Hornton Street in Kensington and was due to leave in six months to return to India where his father had finalised an arranged marriage for him to a suitable and very beautiful Indian girl. They were to be married in the centuries-old Moghul Palace belonging to Shivay's family. After our scintillating night at the theatre we went back to the flat and slept soundly. The three of us were abruptly awoken in the early morning by Shivay's acid-tongued landlady, accompanied by an uncomfortable looking policeman.

"Right. Out. I'll give you two hours to pack up," she said. Shivay was evicted on the flimsy grounds that he let an unmarried couple stay the night. But the real reason was because he was Indian. Those were the days of the reptilian London landlord Rachman, who spent years turfing out black tenants who could no longer pay his increasingly unfair rents. I always felt guilty about Shivay's eviction because we had been the immediate cause, or excuse. It must have been so humiliating for him but he behaved with great dignity through-out the whole unpleasant ordeal. He finished his studies in London and left immediately for India. It made me furious that the draconian practice of turning decent renters' lives upside down on a whim was still tolerated.

At the end of our idyllic, carefree time together, Rullie accepted a job working on a rubber plantation in Malaya while my family and I were soon to depart for Southern Rhodesia, now Zimbabwe. We took a long, sad fare-well at the London train station on his way to catch the ship. I returned to Belfast having cried the whole night on the boat-crossing, my heart twisted in a tight knot. Unbeknownst to me my aunt Jotto had guessed I had begun a love-affair with Rullie, which, at seventeen, was just not on in those days. Very odd, when she got married in India at either the same age, or just a few months older. My father called me into the sitting room, sat me down beside him and asked, " Is it true?"

"Yes, Dad, and I am in love for the first time." He put his arm round me and said with a sigh,

"Oh Tupps, we must pull our socks up, mustn't we?" Our uncharacteristic moment of intimacy surprised and moved me. But I wasn't quite sure what was exactly required of me since I could hardly return to being a virgin, so I nodded in agreement, gave him a big hug and went back to being in love.

But I never saw Rullie again. We wrote impassioned letters of love to each other over the next two years in which we planned that I would travel out to Malaya from Rhodesia to be together again before deciding our future. Then one day I received two letters, one from his family and the other from Klaus, a Dutch friend who was with him at the time, to tell me Rullie had been killed in a car accident on a muddy road in the monsoon rains. He was only twenty-one, a kind and good man. It was a harrowing, heart-breaking time for me, one from which I thought I might never completely recover.

SOUTHERN RHODESIA

The family arrived in Salisbury, the capital, in 1961 and I knelt down and kissed the tarmac when we got off the plane. Africa at last. But how different this landlocked country, bordered by Bechuanaland, Mozambique, Northern Rhodesia and South Africa, turned out to be compared to the one I had grown up in. There were immaculately-kept tobacco estates and rich farmlands in this breadbasket of Africa, but no coastline, no snow-capped mountain; the indigenous tribes were not as exotic; even the white people appeared not as varied. Although I found the massive Victoria Falls and trout-filled rivers of Nyanga spectacular, I found the topography with its endless miles of scrub bush and rocks monotonous. I never felt in the six years we lived there that the country really touched my soul. Still, Salisbury was an attractive town with a mass of jacarandas lining the streets from east to west and the large ruby red blossoms of flame trees filling the sky from north to south. We lived in the pretty suburb of Borrowdale near the racecourse in a long white house—rather 'Equatorial Ealing' in Evelyn's Waugh's immortal putdown on Kenya's colonial dwellings—surrounded by a partly wild eight acre garden. A few houses were dotted sporadically on either side of the long dirt driveway leading to our property. We soon learnt that our nearest neighbour in Grasmere Lane had only one arm—the other had been bitten off by a shark whilst swimming in Durban. Another neighbour had been walking with his two girls on a nearby hill when a flash of lightening killed him and badly burned the hands of his children. Rhodesia is one of most lightning-prone countries in the world, killing a number of people every year, most of them Africans.

Our garden was carefully tended by my mother who was a keen gardener, together with Teasy and Ninepence, and in time, Johnny. They also kept the swimming pool clean and swept the eucalyptus leaves off the tennis court. Older African parents, like Ninepence's, sometimes gave their children English names in the belief that it would attract the white man's power. The gardeners spent their days trimming the lawns, weeding and looking after the large rose garden, the pale blue agapanthus, sweet-smelling gardenias and cannas and all the myriad smaller flowers that make gardens in Africa so alive with colour. The view from the house and pool was down a long peaceful valley edged in pine trees and thick with a carpet of pink and white cosmos flowers.

The gardeners also looked after the fruit trees and the vegetable garden which grew all that we needed. Teasy was careful to oust any cobras or mambas living in the dense clump of bamboo trees near the pool which drew us like a magnet in the heat of the day at weekends. Whenever a snake appeared, Mum would pelt off and fetch my father's old ceremonial sword which he had taken off the surrendering Japanese General in Singapore, and whack off its head. That reminded me of an incredibly stupid thing I once did at Malindi when I was fifteen when the whole family had gone off to the beach. I was alone in my bedroom and suddenly saw a good sized, sleek brown snake gracefully oiling its way along the edges of the room. From its colour I have always been convinced it was a young black mamba. Without a moment's thought I picked up a shoe, went over to the snake, bent down closely and bashed it on the head, killing it instantly. Mambas can be deadly and it could have bitten my hand or arm in a flash. Naturally I wouldn't dream of unnecessarily killing one now.

Domboshawa Rocks was not far from where we lived. With its ancient rock art, panoramic views and unparalled sunsets it was a special place for us. The country had many intriguing landmarks called kopjes—huge boulders which sat, often at odd angles, on top of much smaller boulders, like a child's lopsided building blocks. Although they looked precariously unstable, they had balanced like this since prehistoric times. Dombashawa consisted of an immense granite hill with an overhanging rock filled with cave paintings, some dating back almost six thousand years. Red and brown earth pigments produced fine depictions of humans and animals striding across the sides of the cave, which was sacred to the Shona tribe. In times of drought the people came to this hallowed place bearing small offerings to the Rain Spirit.

Pods and I often visited Dombashowa with our friends. Walking up on a clear evening with a picnic and bottle of wine and sitting on the smooth bald dome under the stars was exhilarating. We always looked forward to listening to a large Shona tribe in their village far below in the valley, beating their drums, made out of hollowed-out logs and cowhide, and singing late into the night. Although the indigenous party-goers were too far away for us to see in the dark, the music and voices echoed round the surrounding hills and floated clearly up to us. We imagined them performing an ancient ritual, stamping down on the rich earth and dancing trance-like around a huge fire. One night on top of our rock Pod's boyfriend Don began dancing in his own idiosyncratic way to the rythym of the drums, with a bottle of Castle lager in one hand—beer being the favourite tipple of most white Rhodesian men. After a particularly spectacular leap in the air, he landed hard on his left leg which went straight down a narrow crevice in the rock and disappeared up to his groin as if cleaved cleanly in half by a butcher. However painful, he somehow managed to hold his arm aloft, thus keeping his precious beer intact. The hills around us echoed with loud peals of laughter from the rest of us.

During the year that Susie was away in Europe and America, I became very close to Pods. In those days, Rachel, being twelve years younger was still a gentle little girl in blonde pigtails coming home every afternoon in her yellow and white gingham school uniform, playing in the garden with Prince, our part Alastian, part Rhodesian Ridgeback, or watching the only television shows available, Dr. Kildare and hospital dramas. But of course we had fun together.

"Come on Digs," I'd say, "Let's take you to the drive-in tonight and see a totally unsuitable film!" She was nine years old, under-aged and thrilled.

"Sit down and Pods will give you your beehive hairdo. I'll put put on tons of bright pink lipstick, mascara and eyeshadow on until you look like a mini Dusty Springfield!"

And to make Digs taller we plonked her on three cushions in the back of Mum's car 'Lucy', all of which she thought of as a great adventure.

My parents had insisted that all the staff and their families live with us on the property, each in one half of a *kaya*—house. Few people in Salisbury offered this accommodation at the time and instead the wives and children lived in their real home, their *musha*, in distant tribal homelands called 'reserves', where their husbands could only visit infrequently. Some of the Africans were Shona, others came from the Matabele tribe or were Mozambican, and all our house staff wore long khaki shorts and a pair of Bata tackies. Their wives could often be seen walking round the vegetable garden with their babies tied to their backs in vividly printed African shawls. In those days, in both Kenya and Rhodesia, we did not know the surnames of any of our staff, only their christian names. All Africans also had to carry identity cards, a *situpa*, with a number on them. Ours were loyal and with us for many years and I have endless memories of their friendly faces. But I never understood how African cooks, often taught by Mum, could make western dishes with such aplomb when they had little idea of what it should taste like—*sadza*, maize meal porridge being their main food. Axon, who somehow managed to pull off my favourite hot chocolate pudding every time, was dignified, imposing and well-educated. His eyes missed nothing and he wrote letters in a fine cultured hand, having been taught in a country that had produced Africa's most literate population. The day my family eventually left Rhodesia, Axon was so upset he was unable to come outside to say goodbye, instead staying in the kitchen. But he and my mother kept up a correspondence for many years.

Quiet and gentle Douglas, the main house man, was kind and conscientious to a fault. I remember well the time that he proudly brought the Christmas pudding into the diningroom, already lit with the flame burning high from too much brandy. He ran round the table and in his distress managed to catch the curtains on fire before rushing outside and throwing the whole blazing dish on the grass. A few weeks later, when my parents were giving a dinner-party, my mother asked Douglas to decorate the chocolate pudding. He did so by covering the top with Mum's pink contraception pills which he found nestling handily in the fridge.

Next to the main house was a white-painted thatched square *rondavel*, hut, where I lived when I got older. Once after a robbery or whenever there was rumoured to be a prowler around, a night guard with a knobkerrie, a club, was employed to hide in a msasa tree in our driveway nearest the *rondavel*. Every night, within an hour he could be seen fast asleep with his legs dangling down, clearly visible on either side of the branch he was sitting on. How he didn't fall off was a mystery to us all but his skinny legs, rather like some strange nocturnal animal hanging there in the dark, were slightly disconcerting when we returned from an evening out. Needless to say he never caught an intruder.

Whenever I came back from work, longing for a swim, there would be a freshly made cake from Axon. Ma was always around, often busy on her Singer sewing machine. She was an excellent dress maker and had made most of our frocks, many of them smocked, in the 1950s, as so many other mothers did in those days. I remember Butterick and Vogue patterns strewn all over the table as she started on a new little number.

Both my parents were passionate about fly-fishing and whenever they could get away they went up to Nyanga where there was superb trout to be caught in the icy rivers. One morning, knee deep in cold water next to Rachel, Mum, with the grand flourish of an opera conductor, cast her rod wide as usual. Alas, she managed with some innate talent to catch herself—hook, line and sinker. It had gone in deep into her cheek, over the barb and was impossible to pull out. After quickly cutting the fishing line and shaking like a freshly caught trout, Mum returned with the others to find a doctor at the rambling Troutbeck Hotel where they were staying. Looking at the little feathers sticking out of her face, the doctor briskly told Mum,

"All I can do is push the hook through your cheek and cut it off." He continued cheerfully, "I'll just get some whiskey."

"How kind of you," whispered my mother. He walked over to his medical case and pulled out a flask of whiskey. Instead of giving it to Ma to calm her down, much to her amazement he took a large slug to steady his own nerves before putting it away again.

Back home, one afternoon while he was gardening, Teasy and his wife asked Ninepence to look after their toddler while they were busy working near their *kaya*. Ninepence had made a large bonfire that day to burn all the swept-up leaves. At some stage the little boy fell into the fire and was badly burned before the gardener could catch him. He shouted for Teasy who rushed down with his wife, picked up his burning child in his arms and ran up to my parents' house. They immediately bundled the family into the car and tore off to the African Hospital in Salisbury. The toddler's devastated parents quite understandably blamed Ninepence for the accident.

Each day they would wrap up a small sandwich and a piece of fruit prepared by Axon for their injured child and sit silently by his hospital bed. As it was difficult for the traumatised couple to get a bus directly to the hospital, and I had a Mini Minor, I dropped them off there on the third day on my way to work as a minion in the office of Sir Roy Welensky, at the time the prime minister of Rhodesia and Nyasaland. They made a sad picture walking off with their little parcel of food and their heads bent in sorrow. The following day my mother and father took them to the hospital and when the four of them arrived at the ward they found his bed empty. The child had died and his body been taken away. No one at the hospital had bothered to let either the desolate parents or mine know and Teasy and his wife never saw their little boy again. The couple's dreadful grief was raw, overwhelming, and the sound of wailing and keening could be heard coming from their *kaya* for many days. For a long time afterwards the bad feelings between the two gardeners and their families was intense and only partially solved through time.

Looking back, without rose-tinted glasses, I think my father, with only male dogs for companionship, was tremendously patient with his four daughters. He never lost his temper or shouted at any of us; he was kind but firm, thoughtful and often silent. Digs and he, however, had a special bond and the two remained very close for the rest of his life. I'm sure Mum and Dad discussed their children's problems *ad nauseam*, but he was the one who had to be the tough guy, to bring up the subject, or deliver the occasional *coup de grâce*. Mum was there to soften the blow, even though throughout her life she was fond of saying with a gentle sigh, "Jacks, (her nickname for me) you really have been a bloody nuisance since you were six, darling," referring to my numerous accidents and illnesses. At six I had undergone a radical mastoid-ectomy, a major procedure on my right ear, caused by Mica minerals from the sandy beach getting into the inner ear. The Nairobi surgeon explained to my parents that my chances were 50/50 but if they didn't operate I would most certainly die once the Mica hit the brain. I still remember the pulsing agony in my ear and the pain from seventy-five shots of penicillin over the following three days which helped save my life and left me with wonky hearing and a terror of needles.

Although I loved Dad very much there were times when I was scared of him, as were my closest girlfriends, particularly in our frivolous teenage years. We weren't wild, just full of bounce and curiosity, but I always felt more relaxed around my mother, our vigilant keeper of the domestic flame. Even so, whenever she was also cross with me over some misdemeanor, I found it difficult being the eldest; the experimental one on whom parents try out their stricter-rules and tighter-boundaries regime, subliminally fearful their adventurous daughter might get into all sorts of trouble, which of course I did. All it took was for Dad to beckon me aside and utter the killer line, "Tupps, I think it's time we had a little chat", for a fistful of butterflies to disco round my tummy as I followed him into his study. Once there he never raised his voice but, with a certain inaccessible look in his steady blue eyes, he quietly and methodically demolished any flubbery explanation or excuse I gave. These encounters often reduced me to a gibbering wreck, frustrated by my total inablility to find the punchy words and perfect phrases I needed to defend my youthful actions.

ZAMBEZI CROCODILES

When I look back at the dumbest thing I have ever done—many jostling for pole position, which I never told my parents about—my mind zooms back to crocodiles floating lazily down the Zambezi River. Although the memory and love of Rullie still echoed strongly in my heart, I had started going out with a clever young Welshman named Dai. He had emigrated to Rhodesia, loved all things Welsh and taught me to understand Dylan Thomas's work, starting with *Under Milk Wood*, which I learned to love. At weekends we itched to get out of town and explore, often pitching our tent on the banks of the Zambezi River. After the long drive, we collected piles of dry wood and built a crackling fire for the nights were cold. Under the beginnings of a starry sky we listened to the night noises of the animals—the splash and crashing of crocodiles and hippos, the master dwellers of the river. We were particularly wary of the latter which wallow, often barely seen except a flicker of a pink ear, in the deeper pools by day and come out to forage along the banks when night falls. They can plunge through the water and onto land at astonishing speed and in the process kill more people in Africa than any other wild animal.

After an uncomfortably cold night in our flimsy camp beds, we went down to the sandy bank. Knowing I was a strong swimmer Dai bet me five pounds I couldn't swim across the river and back without getting caught by a croc. I was always ready to accept a sporting bet and as it was only forty yards across it seemed rather thrilling to see if I could outwit them. Driving along the bumpy, rutted road the day before we had seen plenty of the reptiles basking in the sun a few hundred yards upstream but naturally in unfettered minds youth equals immortality. I changed into my bikini and stepped gingerly into the cold water. After a furtive glance upstream where the sun hit the water in shafts of silver spears, I took off like a sea snake in a Speedo. Battling a reasonably strong current I reached the other side in a few minutes and threw myself, panting, onto the warm sand. Once I caught my breath I suddenly began shaking with nerves at the thought of having to complete my return swim. The only thing to do was leap back into the fray, put my head down and swim like a creature possessed. Midway I checked upstream again and to my horror saw the head of a large crocodile cutting silently through the surface. It was coming straight towards me, its amber eyes already viewing which juicy body part it was going to crunch into first. I began swimming quite frantically, at a pace I had never thought possible and noisier than a snorting hippo. But I already knew it was a losing battle—there was no way I could escape an attack. Its powerful jaws would be clamped onto me in less than thirty seconds. But, like a true blue desperado I refused to give up until the bitter end and continued my by now flailing, panicky strokes. The monster floated nearer and nearer until, oh my God, it finally hit me. Bang! I closed my eyes and was ready for the big chomp when I realised that my 'crocodile' was, in fact, a long floating log with two large knots on either side exactly where the reptile's eyes would have been.

I limped back like a deflated balloon to the bank and collapsed in a heap of tears. I turned to Dai who had of course watched the whole, presumably highly entertaining, scene. Although he was slightly apologetic for encouraging me, I told him huffily,

"I will never, ever again take on one of your stupid bets," and flounced off dripping wet into the tent to change. This time I had been lucky but I wouldn't be chancing it a second time.

Most young white Rhodesian men never did much for me; besides, country-cowboys entertained some rather dodgy ideas of having a good time. Pods and I were travelling up to Lake Kariba and stopped off at a farm belonging to friends of the man with us. They turned out to be strong testosterone-fuelled farm guys with little to do in the evenings. With more than a few Lion beers under their belts, they found nothing more amusing than the 'steak game.' Each would grab a large raw steak from the kitchen and sit down cross-legged on the floor facing a blank wall. When a whistle was blown they flung their dripping steaks high up onto the wall where they stuck for a few seconds, blood dripping down in bright red rivulets. Soon the meat started to slide to the floor and the young farmers hooted with laughter, as if they were at the races in reverse, urging on other's steaks to fall faster while begging their own to remain longer on the wall. The last one to fall won this imbecilic game.

LONDON SWINGS

After two years of Rhodesian life I began to feel the tug of travel again. Needing to stretch my wings and broaden my mind after a sad but necessary departure from Dai, I flew to London, where I wanted to explore museums and galleries, soak up art and theatre. They still remain two of my great interests. A few years ago I was lucky enough to see the mesmerizing play *Jerusalem* by Jez Butterworth, with one of the finest performances I have ever seen, by the great English actor Mark Rylance. And if there was an exhibition of my favourite artist, the Spanish painter Joaquin Sorolla, one of the best of the natural painters, I would put on my running blades to get there. Some years ago my close friend Jean Harvey, a talented American artist living in London, had seen Francis Bacon's retrospective at the Royal Academy the day before she bumped into the famous man at the local newsagent.

"I have to tell you," she said, "that you are the greatest artist of the 20th century."

"Oh, that's terribly sweet of you," Bacon replied. "Most people hate my work!"

When I arrived in September 1963, I lived with my aunt, Jotto, my father's sister, and her husband Ralph in their charming house in Holland Park. Over time I became very close to Jotto, bonding as we sat round their diningroom table and listened to the reports on the wireless of President Kennedy's assassination. It was almost impossibly sad, as if we all knew him personally. Everyone remembers where they were on that fatal day.

My aunt and I were both passionate about ballet and were lucky enough to see Margot Fonteyn and Rudolf Nureyev dance *La Bayadere*. These days to watch the remarkable Cuban, Carlos Acosta, dancing with the exquisite Spanish dancer, Tamara Rojo, is a particular pleasure.

Jotto had been born in India in 1908 and spent her childhood there with her parents and later her brother, my father, ten years her junior. In the evening I listened, riveted, to her stories of her life there and we spent hours poring over the hundreds of photographs of Moghul palaces and tiger shoots, of bejewelled maharajahs and balls. Under the watchful eye of her nanny, Jotto played in the garden of one of their large Residencies which employed the busy hands of one hundred Indian gardeners. She showed me a photo of the men all lined up in rows which I found quite astonishing. Jotto was tall and lovely, had a beautiful voice and always wanted to be an opera singer. When she was seventeen she was sent to Vienna to be trained but dropped the whole idea after a trip back to India where she fell in love and married Ralph, a gentle, good-looking officer in the Indian Army. The Mararajah of Udaipur, a friend of my grandfather's, lent his glorious Lake Palace, in the middle of a glassy lake, to the couple for their honeymoon.

But I also remember the pure agony when the four of us children were on home leave from Kenya and staying with Jotto. Before kissing us goodnight she would stand at the end of our beds to sing us a song in her pure but by then slightly tremulous soprano voice. She only need get to the end of the first line of 'When Nanny Puts the Lightie Out' before we began squirming, trying desperately not to let her see us heaving with giggles under our eiderdowns.

On their marriage when Jotto was eighteen my uncle inherited a considerable fortune but within ten years a fraudulent business brother managed to financially ruin him and also swindled him out of a thriving orange farm in Uganda, where the young couple lived and which Jotto loathed. They were eventually forced to return to England to live in a cottage in the Sussex countryside with their two small childen, their new straightened circumstances being the reason they were seldom able to keep my father, her schoolboy brother, in the holidays. When she grew older, Jotto would sit in her dark green velvet chair in the sitting room sipping a sherry by the fireplace, and say to me with a hint of nostalgia,

"Darling, you think you had a good life growing up in Africa but it simply didn't hold a candle to how we lived in India". Probably not, but she was wonderful to me and our evenings were full of easy, leisurely conversation.

For many of us the 1960s was the flowering of youth and London was the most fashionable place on the planet. It was perfect timing to be there. The Beatles' first album *Please Please Me* had come out as the Swinging Sixties were beginning to blossom—bursting with colour, innovation and youthful energy. Young people of all classes were moving to the foreground of the cultural and creative scene, in a state of rebellion against the previous generation. London life seemed exciting and sexy to us. The explosion of the youth culture in fashion, art and music could be seen everywhere and creative juices were flowing in the art colleges.

For the following seven months after leaving Jotto's house my friend Appley and I lived in one big dingy pink room at the very top of an old Victorian house on Bayswater Road, overlooking Hyde Park. Like a once-beautiful old woman sighing for her glory days but now on her last, unsteady legs, it's faded grandeur resembled the sort of gloomy, neglected house that Mortitia Adams would have killed for. Large original stained glass windows captured the beams of sunlight and spread them in waves up the grand ornate staircase. The rooms on all the floors except ours were tall and elegant with intricately carved cornices and ceiling roses and in them you could dream of being in Paris until a chunk of peeling plaster fell on your head. We didn't care; we were young and full of life. Along with a Nigerian and his white lover, Appley and I shared a grotty little kitchen, and a bath covered in earwigs that must have been in use ever since the Plantagenets were around. The couple's relationship was still quite unusual in 1964. Being pretty liberal and from Africa, we thought it excitingly *risqué*. Their contented life together threw me back to that unpleasant time in London four years previously when the unfortunate Shivay found his landlady hadn't been quite as accommodating. Alas, our rickety old house was demolished many years ago but whenever I drive past the spot on Bayswater Road where it once proudly stood I look in despair at the hideous modern block of flats in its place and feel a perverse pang of nostalgia.

Appley and I worked at various mundane temporary jobs in advertising, where we had our fair share of bosses making flirtatious comments about our bosoms or pinching our bottoms. These we managed to brush off knowing that we wouldn't be there long. Our weekly take home pay was £8 but we somehow saved enough each month after paying the rent for a pretty £2 dress from Biba or an occasional Mary Quant frilly collared shirt. I suppose, like most young girls, Appley and I were reasonably conscious of how we looked. I usually wore my hair long or in a fashionable pony tail from the top of my head, or made it 'big' by backcombing. I have always been partial to a slick of make-up and really have no eyes unless framed by lashings of mascara. So I outlined my eyes heavily in black pencil and put on a pouty pale pink lipstick, all of which was copied from Paris and *de rigeur* in the '60s. If only we could look like Julie Christie or Jean Shrimpton in her Liberty prints—perfection, trendy and hip. Carnaby Street was buzzy, Vidal Sassoon was the hair stylist of the moment. The whole scene just blew our minds, even though neither of us had, up to that point, drunk alcohol nor taken drugs. If we had a few shillings to spare, we'd shoot off to Paris or Florence and marvel at the art and architecture. We skied in Austria when the winter Olympics were on and fell in love with Amsterdam where we ran out of money and lived on raw herrings and chocolate.

In London we hung out with others from Kenya, South Africa and Australia in Earl's Court, known as Kangaroo Alley, where my newly acquired Kenya beau shared a dowdy basement flat with two other boys from home. We had all enjoyed such a different upbringing from the young here and had little in common with the London debutantes and upper class young men, known as Debs Delights, we either met or knew through our families. 'Wah-Wahs' we called them. And so our tribe stayed together. The thing that really saved me on Sundays, a day I would be at my most homesick for Africa and the family, was having a delicious Sunday lunch cooked by Jotto, an excellent Cordon Bleu cook. The rest of the weekend would find us with our friends dancing wildly anywhere we could to the Beatles' music. Paul was my total crush. Little did I dream that many years later one of my daughters would work as his personal assistant for a number of years and I would get to meet him. Sigh!

SPANISH EYES

It was Spain that really grabbed my heart and African sensibilities. The hot sienna and red colours of the earth, and the parched rolling landscape reminded me of home. Appley's father Jamie lived in the south near the then unspoiled little fishing village of Marbella, with his third wife Gillie. He owned a 60 foot yacht which he invited us on to crew for three months. We would be sailing over to Morocco quite often, he explained. Morocco! The Mecca of exotic hippiedom and louche behaviour. Naturally we leapt at the idea. My generous parents had given me some money for my 21st birthday in London so once Appley and I had saved a bit, we chucked in our jobs in June and headed off for Spain. Like many other matador-swooning girls of my age I had devoured Hemingway's novel *The Sun also Rises* and longed to see the country, particularly Pamplona in the Basque country. Each year the 'Running of the Bulls' was the highlight of a traditional local festival in honour of San Fermin, Pamplona's patron saint. The perilous chase down cobblestoned streets finished in the bullring where the animals would meet their end that afternoon.

We stayed in a small hotel overlooking the narrow street down which the bulls would be running, craning our necks over the balcony to see the race start. Young men, dressed in their whites with a red sash and *pañuelo* necker-chief, tried to control their jittery nerves as they waited anxiously for the six bulls, each weighing half a ton, together with six steers, to be let out of their corral. A roar immediately drowned out our voices as the boys tore down the street, attempting to dodge the angry bulls. The strongest, or drunkest, jumped amongst the massive animals to show off their bravado, knowing full well that a sharp nick from one of the horns would open them up like a razor-blade. Those that got caught were tossed in the air or trampled upon, but it was thrilling to us, like some crazily dangerous street party, even though we would say, laughingly, to each other, "I wish we were running with the boys!"

Once they had passed, the laughing crowd, drinking wine in a graceful arc into their mouths from a goatskin *bota* bag, surged into the bullring to be greeted by four loud Spanish bands in separate areas of the ring, each playing different music. Bands were big in Pamplona. Later, we sat in the bright sunshine waiting for the bullfights to start, listening to the cacophony of competing music all round us, which seemed to fit in with the extraordinary energy of the day.

Appley and I then hitch-hiked to Barcelona and hopped on a ferry to Majorca to stay with her former stepmother, Anne who had built a palatial stone house onto the walls of an old Moorish castle in Capdepera. She was a strange, lonely old bird, only about forty-eight though she seemed ancient to us, but she was kind and seemed fond of Appley. She was also very rich. Each night we dined on gold plates, which might have been a bit excessive, and ate copious bowls of borscht soup which in her opinion was the very finest of all vegetable soups and to my young untrained palate, utterly revolting. Occasionally, if Appley and I weren't cavorting round with our friends at beach parties in Cala Ratjada we sat in the vast drawing room after dinner with Anne, watching her imbibe flagons of wine as she got out her needles and wool and started knitting. Dozens of booties and bonnets, endless little jumpers and soft shawls by the yard. Like a worker bee busy building its hive, her nesting work hardly ever stopped. Plain stitch, pearl stitch, in, out, in, out. And each day as she knitted her tummy got larger and larger. She had never had children but to our eyes was quite obviously pregnant. Whom on earth by, we wondered?

During dinner one night Appley plucked up the courage to ask her who the lucky fella was and Anne said, "Well, your father James, of course".

We nearly choked on our borsht. She had continued to pine for him after their separation but as far as we knew, he was madly in love and very happy with Gillie and hadn't been anywhere near Anne for well over a year. But Anne stuck to her guns, continued to knit and drink and swell to the size of a small *finca* until one day a few months later it all went 'poof' and her phantom pregnancy was over. It had been the drink all along and two years later her liver gave up and she died of cancer. Instead of giving her stunning house to either Appley or her brother as everyone thought she would, she left it to charity. Ah, well.

We hitched a ride to Madrid, taking the charitable driver one hundred miles out of his way. Ah, the power of youth and the kindness of men who think they might get lucky. A third class ticket for Malaga found us sitting amongst poor Spanish peasants travelling with their goats and chickens. Small groups of men dressed in the Spanish Army uniform kindly offered to share their food with us, while a few listless Moroccan soldiers sprawled in the corridor, sweating from the heat. It was practically impossible to step over the dozens of legs in a swaying carriage to get to the loo. At one point I got so irritated with one particular Moroccan who refused to let me pass that I used the only French swearword I knew, 'Merde'. He immediately narrowed his eyes, sprang up and pulled out his knife ready to stab me until two of his fellow soldiers pulled him back and calmed him down. We travelled on to the south of Spain without any more mishaps to be met by Jamie at the railway station.

Appley's father was a tall, avuncular man with a touch of Churchill about him. He was retired, and had been Air Vice Marshall in the Royal Air Force during the Second World War, after which he worked at Whitehall. Highly intelligent, he smoked cigars by the dozen, had a booming, friendly laugh, and was supremely knowledgeable about boats.

During our first week his pretty third wife Gillie invited a female couple to stay. They were much older than us and one of them weighed in at least two hundred and fifty pounds with enormous thighs and an unflattering, short cropped masculine haircut. Her favourite outfits were cream coloured waistcoats with wide white linen trousers, very Cecil Beaton strolling along the Corniche. Her girlfriend was more feminine in appearance, neat and slim with long manicured fingernails painted bright scarlet. The couple had been given separate bedrooms on the first floor at the back of the house next to where Appley and I were staying.

Jamie nicknamed us Apples and Pears due to our nubile, though fully-fledged, embonpoints. The two of us spent most of our time swimming in the sea in our Bridget Bardot look-alike bikinis—mine was pale blue and white checks—which we thought were rather cute. In our second week as we were looking for shells, two members of the Guardia Civil strolled up and without any warning, promptly arrested us. We knew little about draconian Spanish politics and were oblivious to the fact that in dictator Franco's Spain bikinis were strictly forbidden. Despite our pleas of *"No, No, señor, per favor! Per favor!"* they marched us off to the local Police Station, put us in a cell where we waited, half-naked and hapless for a couple of hours until Appley's father came and bailed us out. He, of course, thought the whole thing 'bloody *estupido*.'

That afternoon, following a long, boozy lunch I decided to go up to my room to read. I was nearly at the top of the stairs when I came across a startling sight. The larger guest's room was directly opposite the staircase. Her door was wide open and she was sitting stark naked on the end of the bed like a snorting Spanish bull, staring straight at me. Over two hundred pounds of willing, jubbly flesh, legs akimbo, and sporting a huge black dildo-thing strapped onto a thick leather contraption around her formidable waist. She was one of the most fearsome sights I had ever encountered. It was obviously difficult for her in her indelicate position to exude a suitably seductive 'come hither' look and she spoke not a word of enticement or encouragement. But there was little doubt that she was waiting for either Appley or myself to come upstairs so she could tempt us into the exacting arts of Sappho. I nearly fainted with shock. To a twenty-one year old, or any age actually, she was monumentally unappealing. Averting my eyes best as I could as I slid quickly past her door and ran to my room, shut the door firmly and lay panting with nerves, waiting for Appley to come up and rescue me.

Once I had poured out the story of the would-be Mounting Cavalier,

"Good God, Apples, I thought she might come in and land on top of me like a large cupboard," we collapsed in a heap on my bed.

Back then Appley and I were innocents when it came to lesbians. That evening we explained our small, or rather large in this case, predicament to Jamie and after a heated discussion with Gillie he gave the women their marching orders. They left with their Louis Vuitton suitcases in a flurry of indignation the next morning and we sailed off to Tangier.

Why is it that most skippers, the minute they set sail, become mini tyrants with the crew? Jamie was no exception. Plus, I struggled to help Appley cook for six guests and crew. After ten minutes below deck I'd say to her for the fifth time that day,

"I feel as seasick as a drowning mullet. Again."

She'd reply evenly,

"Just keep de-boning the sardines and look at the horizon."

Oh, that fish and diesel smell! I spent regular intervals lying prone on deck wanting to die, which probably didn't thrill Jamie. The thing is, I love everything about the sea, the waves, the freedom, sailing into the big blue and the thought of adventure; but wretched seasickness lets me down every time. So annoying. One thing that did amuse us on these trips was an unfortunate trait of one of the crew, a small Moroccan. It was his job once we reached Tangier, to jump from the boat and tie the rope round the bollard. Perhaps he was as near-sighted as a tree shrew but every time he jumped he misjudged the distance, hit the wall, cracked his elbow on the stone quay and fell head first into the water twelve feet below. Some of us would be unusually busy swabbing the deck, whispering to each other, "He's about to start, look, he's going to jump!" while waiting for the inevitable mishap which would have us in fits and which we tried to hide behind our mop heads. In the end the poor man broke his arm and that was the end of him.

Jamie took us to some extraordinary bullfights and we watched two of the major bullfighters of the time—the great, flamboyant El Cordobes and the wildly handsome Miguel Mateo 'Miguelin'. After one of the latter's fights Jamie took us back to his dressing room and when Miguelin took off his magnificent 'suit of lights' jacket, richly beaded and embroidered in gold, our eyes widened in amazement when we saw that his muscled torso was crisscrossed with a mass of jagged scars from his years of bullfighting. He later came to Appley's twenty-first birthday party which caused quite a flutter amongst the girls.

There was another man in Guadaranque whom we had a soft spot for, a Spaniard named Geronimo who worked for Jamie. On a certain night each month Appley and I made sure we were crouching in the shadows of a twisted cork tree near Geronimo's little *finca* behind the main house. There we would find him sitting on his outside step, happily frothing at the mouth as he gazed up at the full moon.

Coming home to Africa on a Union Castle ship was fun. In Kenya civil servants, including the family, had travelled to England for a month of long leave every four years. Three weeks on the high seas was a boon to us, except for Mum who was permanently seasick, off colour to the point of appearing spectral, and spent much of the time suffering alone in her cabin. Somehow, on one herculean occasion she managed to make our fancy-dress hula-hula outfits which won first prize.

This time Appley was with me and we were sailing from Gibraltar to Beira in Mozambique where my parents would meet us and drive us up to Salisbury. Little did we know that within a few years, Appley would marry a charming, piano-playing Austrialian advertising man, and become the country's best known French country antique furniture dealer for the following thirty years, before moving back to London where she continues to thrive.

The cold clear air of the African dawn always caught my breath. The senses became alert to each new sensation as random washes of purple and red streaked the sky, as if an artist's palette had been left out in the rain. Out of the mirage, date palms waved their ghostly fronds. Shallow saltpans, carved out of the sandy landscape, fringed the entrance to the deserts of Egypt, land of Pharaohs and fakirs, pyramids and friezes as the liner slowly sailed, like a venerable dowager, into Port Said. The haunting sound of the muezzin calling the faithful to prayer was drowned by the cry of eager young boys scrambling up ropes lashed to the side of the ship and forcing their pistachio nuts and dates into the hands of the travellers. The harbour was a noisy, ramshackle place and the air was filled with the pungent aroma of spices and burnt coffee beans. From there we travelled down the Suez Canal towards the Red Sea, through the Gulf of Aden and out into the indigo waters of the Indian Ocean. Our path would follow the concave curve of Africa down to our destination.

I had been away a year but from the day I arrived phone calls and flowers began to flood in from Dai. We had gone through so much together in the past, good and bad, that little by little we started to see each other again, eventually becoming engaged. All the important men in my life have made me laugh (much to my friends and family's amazement) and Dai was no exception. But I had to admit that I remained confused. As the day of our wedding came closer I woke up each morning feeling I was one step nearer the guillotine. I tried to appear cheerful but the final straw was flying up to Kitwe, a small, depressing copper belt mining town; a pimple on the backside of the universe in Northern Rhodesia, now Zambia, where Dai had been posted. As soon as he flew me up there I immediately thought, "This, I no can do." I felt living in the Gobi desert with two yaks and a goat would have been preferable One evening my parents, both having noticed my increasing lack of enthusiasm for the upcoming nuptials, decided to confront the situation. My father said,

"Tupps, you seem unhappy. You don't really want to get married, do you?" I admitted tearfully that I didn't. "Don't worry, your mother and I will sort it out".

What a relief. I think I would have gone through with it if we hadn't had that talk. The marquee came down, my bridal dress and the bridesmaids' outfits were given away, the presents were sent back. It was all rather traumatic. I felt incredibly guilty and sad about Dai, plus I had put my parents to so much expense and heartache over the last few years, particularly as they had never really taken to him. Both of them were so understanding when it mattered.

A circus came to Salisbury soon afterwards and Pa and Ma took the four of us as a treat. We were ushered to the best ringside seats in the tent—a hard wooden bench in the front row. The first act was a macho lion tamer with a large whip which he cracked with relentless enthusiasm as his snarling lions prowled restlessly round the wooden barriers of the circus ring. One enormous, full maned male seemed particularly bored with the proceedings and decided to take time out to relieve himself. Males urinate backwards and upwards very fast and since the spray can reach up to four metres, he managed to hit my smartly dressed mother and father squarely in the solar plexus. Their clothes were soaked, much to their astonishment and our amusement. To give her her due, my mother, who found humour in most things, managed to laugh.

Later it was the turn of a compact little man to be shot out of his cannon into a safety net on the far side of the ring. All eyes turned upwards as the drums rolled dramatically. The daredevil human cannon ball shot out in a perfect arc like a midget Superman, sailed high into the air, completely missed the intended net and with a loud thud, slammed his head slap into the wooden barriers circling the circus ring. Nervous titters as the confused audience started clapping, convinced this must be part of the act. But within minutes families saw the acrobat unconscious, slumped on his side as the circus master rushed over, crowded round his limp body with other officials and carried him out on a canvas stretcher. It was difficult to see this circus making it to the big time.

UNILATERAL DECLARATION OF INDEPENDENCE

In November 1965, Ian Smith, the leader of the mostly white minority government, announced that Rhodesia, a British territory that had governed itself for forty-two years since 1923, unilaterally declared independence (UDI) from the United Kingdom. This was done without devising a set timetable for the introduction of black majority rule which was bound to be of huge concern to the Africans. Rhodesia had modelled its tobacco industry on the United States, adopting American production to grow Virginia tobacco and was one of the largest producers in the world. With UDI, international sanctions hit the country hard, eliminating many export markets and as a result the Rhodesian tobacco crop declined dramatically.

Besides being a politician, Ian Smith was a farmer and had been a fighter pilot with the Royal Air Force during the Second World War. He was shot down over Italy, suffered permanent debilitating facial and bodily wounds and escaped by hiking over the freezing Alps in only his shirt, trousers and socks. His supporters lionised him as a man of integrity and vision while critics, including my parents, described him as an unrepentant racist. The determined Prime Minister of the new rebel colony would eventually lead his country into seven years of civil war.

AMORE

With the news of UDI, the world's press descended on Salisbury. Being the head of a major tobacco firm and in Ian Smith's Little Black Book, my father found himself becoming a useful source for foreign correspondents. At weekends they were invited round to our house in Borrowdale for lunch followed by a game of tennis and a swim. If not involved in our various sporting activities—usually tournament tennis, riding or hockey—we girls would usually be around to help entertain them. Among them, in May 1966, was the *Time* magazine bureau chief in Nairobi, Dean Fischer, an American. He was six foot three, fair-haired and broad-shouldered with blue eyes, serious but with a wry sense of humour. It wasn't long before I realised that Dean was there rather more frequently than the others and was becoming a firm favourite with my parents. I found him interesting, warm and refreshingly different from Rhodesian men but it was only a year since I had broken off my engagement and was understandably nervous about launching into another relationship so soon. Nevertheless he was keen and persuasive and so we started dating.

Dean had just returned from interviewing Emperor Haile Selassie of Ethiopia, a sparrow of a man, five feet four inches tall. An orthodox Christian, the Emperor granted interviews while sitting on his throne in his palace in Addis Ababa, guarded by two large lions, one on either side. Once an interview was over it was customary for the visitor to walk backwards, still facing the Emperor until he reached the far end of the room. Just as Dean was about to congratulate himself on having completed the walk without wobbling, instead of passing effortlessly through the opened door, he hit the back wall with a loud smack. He told me he felt his cheeks flush as he edged himself sideways, like the Pink Panther to the elusive exit.

The Emperor's name at birth was Ras Tafari and many in the Rastafari movement in Jamaica who looked at Africa as the Promised Land, revered the Emperor as a messianic figure who would lead them into a future golden age, but he came to grief following a coup d'etat. After being imprisoned by Marxist revolutionaries, the frail eighty-three year old was strangled in his bed.

It seemed to me that being a foreign correspondent was a pretty glamorous life, always hopping on a plane and rushing off to a faraway place to write some interesting story; I enjoyed listening to Dean's descriptions and anecdotes of his trips. It soon became apparent he was easy to be with, had a similar sense of fun and a strong set of values. I admired his obvious intelligence, and the hesitant, protective manner that I found endearing—he was seven years older. We soon found ourselves falling for each other. Three months later, after a morning of marlin fishing at Malindi, Kenya, Dean proposed very romantically by writing the words in large letters in the sand. And so began what became a supremely happy time for us.

Rhodesia was going through a strange period and items were becoming scarce. Economic sanctions meant one could not buy books or records and there were endless blank pages in the 'Rhodesia Herald', the country's main newspaper which was heavily censored. I will always have a soft spot for the late Henry Grunwald, then the foreign editor of *Time* magazine, who was visiting Rhodesia. He had been a refugee from Nazi-dominated Austria who rose to become the magazine's top editor and did an exceptionally thoughtful thing for me. At the time I badly wanted the Andy William's album, *Moon River*. When he got back to New York he arranged for it to be sent to me. A small but much appreciated kindness in those blinkered days.

I was working for the Japanese Ambassador in Salisbury at the time. His name was Mr. Fukai and his number two was Mr. Oda. Mr Fukai, who was plump and full of himself, and the silent, insipid Mr. Oda quite simply loathed each other. They were constantly spying on one another and I found both of them equally unfathomable. One day my father came to see the Ambassador on business. Mr. Fukai had a strongly developed sense of superiority towards white people and knowing full well who it was, kept my father waiting for nearly an hour, which always infuriated him. The family knew when Pa was about to lose the plot—a small piece of bone in his jaw would start twitching. It was definitely twitching. Throughout that hour the Ambassador kept calling me into his office on some pretext or other so I could see him with his fat little feet up on his desk, sipping a glass of whisky. My father, to put it mildly, had not been overly fond of the Japanese since his war experiences in the Far East. One of the things that continued to offend him in the 1960s was that Meikles Hotel, the best hotel in Salisbury, allowed in Japanese who were firm trading partners with Rhodesia and thus considered white while the Chinese, some of whom were friends of my father's, were considered coloured and therefore not allowed to cross the sacred threshold.

To make up for all this Ambassordial sniping and petty behaviour, I enjoyed working with Mr. Fukai's personal secretary, a lusciously beautiful and very sexy, very married, thirty year old Rhodesian girl with shiny flowing black hair and long legs—needlessly long from my point of view—which she showed off to great effect in her miniskirts. Her office was between the boss's and mine and was filled with shelves of empty different sized scent bottles with fancy tops which she told me she used as sex toys. Once or twice a week when Mr. Fukai had gone out for a lengthy lunch she would have one of her lovers into her office for a hidden hour of passion; thank God the walls of the building were thick and and doors well built. Actually we got on very well and I liked her husband but however cool I acted at the time, I was continually amazed that she got away with it.

In September news broke that the Prime Minister of South Africa, Hendrik Verwoerd, known as the 'Architect of Apartheid', had been assassinated. He had been stabbed in the House of Assembly in Cape Town by a mixed-race Parliamentary clerk who later escaped the death penalty on the grounds of insanity, saying a large worm in his stomach told him to kill Verwoerd. Dean had to leave immediately for Johannesburg to cover the breaking story and asked me to accompany him. Also coming with us was a close friend of his, the great *Time-Life* magazine photographer Priya Ramraka, a young, extremely good-looking Kenyan of Indian descent from Nairobi with whom many girls there were hopelessly in love. Priya liked to be where the action was and it was clear from his pictures of war, of conflict and civil unrest around the world—in the Congo, Prague or Nigeria—that he was a brave man. *Time*, then the most powerful magazine in the world, was regarded by the paranoid South African government as a 'pinko' magazine, a pejorative term for any publication deemed to have Communist leanings, which was patently absurd. However, when we arrived in South Africa with numerous other foreign correspondents, we never got any further than Johannesburg airport. Told we were not allowed into the country, we were immediately escorted to a holding cell for whites to await the next plane out. With a feeling of anger and embarrassment we watched Priya being marched off to a similar cell in the 'coloured' section. A few hours later we were reunited when we were all shoved on a British Airways flight to Nairobi. But in 1968, while Priya was photographing the Biafran war, he was shot and killed. In his last roll of film he captured many spectacular images of the frightened soldiers and the utter confusion of battle. His untimely death left a big hole in the world of photography and in the lives of his many friends.

Five months after our whirlwind courtship Dean and I were married in Christchurch, a simple, white church in Borrowdale filled with white flowers. My parents organised the wedding with great precision and care. It had rained incessantly for two weeks before the day, stormy and thunderous, threatening to wipe out all Ma's beautiful flowers so carefully tended by Teasy and Johnny. But when we woke up on the big day the skies were blue and the sunbirds and paradise fly catchers were flitting all over our sunny garden. Ours was a very sixties wedding; I wore a flowing full length veil over a long simple embroidery-anglaise dress which clung to my twenty-three inch waist—oh how I long for those taken-for-granted days. My three extremely pretty sisters were my bridesmaids in empire pink and white gingham dresses with small white flowers in their piled up hair, which Pods told me later she loathed. When Priya took our superb wedding photographs in the garden we didn't know that it was the last time we would see him. At the end of the afternoon with a huge lump in my throat and eyes brimming I said goodbye to my beloved family, my friends and our dear staff whose small children had all been dressed up in their best clothes for the day. Dad's driver, Ben, took us to the airport and off we went to start a new life in America, a country I had never been to. Looking back it was the best decision I ever made although I had no idea how much I was going to miss my parents, how I would ache for the laughter I shared with my sisters, how I would feel a piece of me would be forever left in Africa.

From Sea to Shining Sea

D URING OUR LONG, meandering honeymoon Dean and I stayed in London at the Dorchester Hotel, where Appley got kicked out for wearing a trouser suit. Women weren't allowed to flaunt such frippery in hotels and formal restaurants in those days. We travelled to Paris, New York and Washington, finally arriving in Chicago in late December, 1966, where Dean was to join the *Time* magazine bureau. Whilst in New York he interviewed King Hussein of Jordan in his opulent suite at the Waldorf-Astoria and had asked me to take down the King's words of wisdom. I told him my shorthand was as rusty as an old oil tanker but agreed, thinking it would be easy as an Arab was bound to speak English hesitantly. Once inside, there standing by the mantlepiece was the twinkling, very good looking though rather short, King Hussein who, with perfect manners, welcomed us in.

Within five minutes of having notepad in hand and pencil pertly poised, my shorthand totally disintegrated. I had no idea the King had been educated at Harrow before going on to Sandhurst and had never heard anyone speak English so fast in my life. My dismal attempt was later confessed to my rather surprised husband, but being a seasoned journalist he had luckily jotted down the salient points. When later relating the story to a Kenyan friend of mine, Jock Leslie-Melville, who had been at Sandhurst with the monarch, he recalled the day something went wrong during his drill. The flustered sergeant-major wasn't certain how to address him so he shouted at the top of his voice, "Mr King Hussein, Sir, what the bloody hell are you doing?"

Time magazine put us up in a big old downtown hotel in Chicago and it was there that I met a beautiful American girl who was to become my life-long friend, the poet Wendy Larsen. Her journalist husband John Larsen had also been posted to the Chicago bureau. Being trapped in our hotel with the city waist deep in thick drifts of snow, forcing many people to ski to work down Michigan Avenue, it was easy for the four of us to fall into an instant friendship.

Time magazine was first published in 1923, the weekly publication being the brainchild of patricians Henry R. Luce and Briton Hadden, whose friendship was forged at their prep school and cemented at Yale. But it was after his visionary co-founding editor and friend died aged thirty that Henry Luce went on to become the most influential publisher in modern journalism. John's father Roy E. Larsen was also involved from the beginning, later becoming President of Time Inc.

Being suddenly thrown into the storm of American politics, about which I knew nothing, affected me deeply. The Vietnam War had barely impinged on the minds of Kenyan and Rhodesian youth and I wouldn't have recognised Richard Daley, the ultra-tough Mayor of Chicago, if he fell on me. It's an unsettling feeling living in a strange new country where you know absolutely no one except your husband, who one day goes back to work. Added to that I found myself in an extremely well educated, well informed, sophisticated and often rich journalist crowd. Thank God for Wendy who came to my rescue. I was forced to learn quickly which, bolstered by Dean's unending patience and help I did, and in the process my love for him continued to grow.

I had not met my parents-in-law before we married and soon after our arrival we drove out to see them. Three hours west of Chicago lies Alpha, a small hamlet, a charming word which conjures up Mrs Tiggy-Winkle cottages, but alas not immediately obvious in Alpha's case. Although much of America had exquisite scenery, I found the mid-west and in particular the country-side around Chicago, decidedly uninspiring. The land is flat and the trees are few, occasionally seen on the horizon next to a solitary farmhouse and silo. Driving past cornfields of such banal repetition, I half-expected to see Howard Keel and the entire cast of *Oklahoma* thrashing their way through rows of tender green stalks.

Many people living in Illinois had never heard of Alpha which was quite understandable as one could pass through it in seconds with a twitch of a big toe on the accelerator. On either side of the main road stood small bungalows with open, carefully mown lawns, next to a few attractive Victorian style clapboard houses with porches and rocking chairs, similar to Bate's creepy mother's in *Psycho*. Most of the inhabitants in the area were of German and Swedish stock, good, solid, God-fearing folk to whom alcohol was anathema. Since many of them were Baptists, the local church did a roaring trade. The preacher must have rubbed his hands with glee when Dean's parents gave us a second wedding reception in his dark pipe-filled church basement. It was sans alcohol naturally, forcing me to sip a mouth-twistingly sour cranberry concoction while I was being introduced to many of the town worthies. Blimey, life in Alpha was simple. By comparison our African towns seemed mired in decadence straight out of 1920s Paris.

Elmer, Dean's father was a quiet, hardworking man and respected Head of Schools. He came from a German background, his grandparents coming to The Land of the Free as immigrants shortly before the First World War. I regarded him as a bit of a saint on the domestic front. Frances, my mother-in-law was a well-meaning piano and French teacher at primary school. But my goodness, she could talk—not only the hind leg off a donkey, but each limb off an entire herd. Her long-suffering husband turned his hearing aid off at regular intervals whenever he could bear her incessant jibber-jabbering no longer.

My parents-in-law were rightly very proud of their son and daughter Alice. Dean was clever and hardworking and after being educated in Kewanee, Illinois, he had a hankering to try his luck abroad and went off to the University of Calcutta in India as a Rotary scholar. For some reason I remember him telling me that each evening as he walked home through the park, Indian prostitutes, crouching behind the bushes in the dark, would jump up like beguiling and bejewelled jack-in-the-boxes to offer their rough and ready services. Back in the States, having narrowly missed being a Rhodes Scholar at Oxford, he took a post-graduate degree at the University of Chicago where he also excelled in the Little All-American Football team. After graduation and bent on being a journalist, Dean began his career by joining the *Des Moines Register* in Iowa, a daily newspaper, as a novice reporter.

Each day the family sat down to dinner at 5pm, to my mind practically indecent. But dear old Fran did her best. Her *pièce de resistance* was making crêpes, describing it as 'flipping the crap' which of course tickled me. Both my in-laws were considerate of my 'newness-to-America' and I became fond of them, especially Elmer; I tried hard to fit in and it wasn't as if I had to live up to a firm set of expectations. On their fortieth wedding anniversary they threw a lunch party for their friends. Looking at the huge glass punchbowl of colourful fruit juices prepared that morning, I thought it lacked a certain *elán*. So before the guests arrived I laced the concoction with two bottles of vodka and everyone had a whale of a time. Some said they hadn't been to such a good party in years.

THOUGHTS OF CAPOTE

In 1966, the year we arrived in America, Truman Capote wrote the book *In Cold Blood*, a detailed account of the brutal murders of a prosperous farmer in Kansas, his wife and two of their four children. Before the killers were captured Capote travelled with his friend and fellow writer Harper Lee to Kansas to write about the crime. His book gripped the imagination of the American public and was universally acknowledged as one the greatest crime sellers ever written. I had recently read it and, like many others, found the harrowing descriptions difficult to forget.

The following summer Dean decided to introduce me to his homeland. There are few things more invigorating and stimulating than a driving jaunt across America. Forever associated with that country, it's the ultimate trip. One white Mustang convertible, hood down, hair blowing in the wind and sun on our faces, Coke bottles to hand, music blaring. We were young, in love and everything was an adventure. Over the three years we lived in the midwest we took many trips in this sleek, cool car, travelling out west two years in a row. I was bowled over by the beauty of the country, especially when camping in the national parks in the northwest. On our first trip we ran out of money for a campsite on our way home through Ohio and decided to sleep in a small country churchyard off a dirt road where no one would see us.

We pitched our small pup-tent near the church and laid out our sleeping bags. After a light supper of beans on toast we were soon tucked into our sleeping bags and fell fast asleep. In the dead of night we were woken up by the sound of a car, the tyres crunching on the gravel as the driver took the track towards the graveyard before turning off his engine. He was obviously alone as we heard no talking or laughter and his car radio was silent. For the next couple of hours we lay there listening to the sound of the car boot being opened and closed and the distinctive sound of digging. What on earth was he up to? Capote's grisly book still fresh in our minds, we could only imagine the very worst—the gruesome disposal, bit by bit, of a body into one of the graves. We decided our best plan was to pretend to be sound asleep. Dean had his trusty knife in his right hand and I always kept my whistle and a large stick beside me, both of which had reassured me in Mt. Rainier National Park, in Washington state, where there had been a spate of bear attacks that summer.

Eventually the sounds stopped. As the man was turning his car round, his headlights suddenly picked out our tent which he had obviously missed on the way in. His brought the car up to the very front of the zipped-up tent and pressed his bumper against the canvas with his headlights full on. We were sitting ducks. Terrified of what he might do, neither of us dared move a muscle, convinced that had the man seen any movement he would have either just run us over or got out of his car and shot us. And so we pretended to be asleep for nearly half an hour which seemed an eternity. Once he had presumably convinced himself that we had neither seen nor heard any-thing, he backed up his car and left. Dean told me later that he had been ready to tell the man that he was a friend of Bobby Kennedy's and should anything happen to us, our killer would never get away with it. I remained unconvinced. We couldn't sleep after that and early in the morning we went to inspect the graveyard. There seemed to be so many newly dug graves that we had no clue where his dubious handiwork might have begun. We couldn't tell the police as camping there was probably illegal, but that was certainly one of the most terrifying nights of my life.

ANTI-VIETNAM WAR PROTESTS—1968

I was just getting to understand the rhythms of the country when the Rev. Martin Luther King was murdered in Memphis, Tennessee in April, 1968, shocking the entire world. Two months later we watched the news in

disbelief as Robert Kennedy was fatally shot. America was reeling and people's increasing discontent sparked the most intense period of protests and
marches against the hugely unpopular Vietnam War. President Lyndon B.
Johnson was mired in crisis and loathed by many. In August the National
Democractic Convention to nominate a presidential candidate was held in
downtown Chicago when the Vietnam War was in its thirteenth year. The
city tensed as word got out that the city's water was going to be poisoned by
members of the Chicago Seven, the Youth International Party (Yippies)—
which included Jerry Rubin, Abbie Hoffman and Tom Hayden, later to
become the actress Jane Fonda's second husband. In 1972, Fonda herself
caused huge controversy when she was photographed sitting on an anti-air-
craft gun on her visit to North Vietnam, which earned her the derisory nickname 'Hanoi Jane.'

Dean and John Larsen suggested we all go down to Grant Park to gauge
the war protesters and see how Mayor Daley's cops were dealing with the
situtation. Both our husbands had their Press badges fixed onto their jacket
lapels and handed Wendy and me two to wear 'for safety' as we parked our car
on the road leading through the Park. Within five minutes two hardnosed
Chicago cops, who had immediately spotted the Press badges, came up and
pushed Dean and John roughly up against another car, twisting John's arm
behind his back and manhandling them both. The police had long regarded
the media with suspicion, bordering on disgust. All four of us were then
deliberately shoved by the police into the main road and into danger as cars
sped past, narrowly missing us. In the ten years I lived in America, I have
always thought of Chicago police as the most aggressive I have ever come
across. The chaotic streets of the city were soon spilling over with riots and
bloodshed involving police, anti-war protesters, activists. The police seemed
to have lost control and were letting off tear gas in every direction. We later
heard that inside the International Amphitheatre where the Convention
was being held, the highly respected TV journalists Mike Wallace and Dan
Rather were roughed up by Security; both these events were broadcast live
on television.

The next day we went down to Grant Park again to check out the scene.
Vice-President Humphrey was giving a speech inside the Amphitheatre
and we were amongst the ten thousand protesters milling around the Park.
Those inside were oblivious to what was happening on the outside. We saw
armed soldiers lining up on top of the Chicago Museum as Mayor Daley was

worried these 'unwashed, unimpressed' young protesters would ruin his show and there was no way he was going to put up with that. As we stood watching a stand-off between a row of cops, rifles and bayonets at the ready, a mass of young protesters were giving the Peace sign in front of the Hilton Hotel, and shouting "Hey, hey, LBJ, how many kids did you kill today." Police were hitting women with billy clubs. Young people passed by, blood streaming from head wounds caused by the truncheons. Many of those beaten and arrested were shoved into police vans. People handed out soaked hankies to help those affected by the searing tear gas in their eyes as Wendy and I ran down into the subway to get away from the fumes but got gassed again anyway. The chaos lasted eight days and turned out to be the most tumultous political convention in American history, radically changing the country's political and social landscape. The Chicago 7 were arrested, tried and then released, while a major report later condemned the night of August 28th as a 'Police Riot'.

THE REVEREND JESSE JACKSON

Four months previously, in April, riots had occurred in the ghetto on the South Side of Chicago. For the majority of black people the outbreak was a spontaneous overflow of pentup aggression following Martin Luther King's murder. It was one of a hundred riots in the country. Dean was asked to write a story on the Reverend Jesse Jackson, the charismatic American Civil Rights activist, Baptist minister and politician who had inherited the mantle of future leader after Dr.King's death. We nervously travelled in our white Mustang through the streets on the South Side full of burnt out houses and shops, looking like a ghost town. People shouted, "Go home Honky" at us as we passed through a hopeless looking landscape of burning rubble with wind howling through abandoned alleyways.

Jesse Jackson lived in a dark double story house covered inside with brown panelling and when we arrived we found him lying ill in bed but willing to talk. Our host invited me to sit on the end of his bed while Dean sat in a chair beside him taking notes. Even though Jackson was under the weather it was difficult not to be mesmerised by this articulate, attractive man who I already knew was a brilliant orator with a rich, powerful voice and exciting ideas for the future. He talked for an hour and a half about his great passion, 'Operation Breadbasket', an organisation dedicated to improving the economic conditions of black communities across the country. I would have been happy to listen to this dynamic speaker for hours and when the time came, we said goodbye reluctantly.

It was easy to appreciate this exhilarating capsule in America's history—the era of 'peace, man', 'free love' and 'flower power'—with an outsider's eyes. Dean spent an exhilarating day interviewing the great singer Aretha Franklin; we experienced our first disappointing marijuana joint with Wendy and John; frequented many of the jazz clubs for which Chicago was famous and saw the sensual Miriam Makeba sing at 'Second City', having been exiled from South Africa for protesting against Apartheid.

While we lived there, my sister Pods and her childhood friend, Diana, came from London to stay. They were eighteen years old, very pretty, adventurous and fun. Pods had long blonde hair, bright blue eyes and an easy charm, and I was so happy to have her around again. Keen to show them the real America, one day we locked up the apartment in Old Town and took off in our Mustang, a car perfect for two but not four. The girls might not have possessed the long, celebrated legs of Elle MacPherson but they were wildly uncomfortable being scrunched up like two munchkins in the back, made even more cramped by Dean's insistence on taking an ice box, nicknamed the Pleasure Chest, on the floor behind his seat. This was continually topped up with cold drinks which he was convinced would save our lives if the car broke down in Death Valley in the Mojave Desert, but mainly because he wanted his ice-cold beers on tap. Needless to say this was in the days before drink-driving ever saw the light. We three women pioneers got to hate the wretched Pleasure Chest which was severely hampering our lower limbs. And even if we had been struggling on burning foot across Death Valley, we wouldn't have had enough strength to carry the stupid thing.

Somehow we managed to reach the Rockies in Colorado alive but barely kicking. After a good night's rest on the rim of the mind-blowing Grand Canyon, we awoke to find several mules eyeing Dean with disbelief when they saw he was six foot three and a mite over 200lbs. Their relief was palpable on realising he was not allowed to ride them, instead having to walk the

Right: my maternal great-great-grandfather, James Wheeler Woodford Birch,1st British Resident to Perak.

Below: Great uncle Zarh Pritchard, artist in Tahiti, 1905.

Below right: Zarh Pritchard, Illustrated London News, January 1922.

Above left: Sir Ernest Birch, ICS, CMG, KCMG: maternal great-grandfather (Indian Civil Service, Companion and Knight Commander). 8th Resident of Perak, Malaya, 1904-1910.

And above: Sir Ernest in his favourite Malay outfit.

Left: Sultan Idris of Perak, great friend of my great-grandfather.

My paternal grandfather Colonel Hugh (Do) Pritchard as a young officer and his wife Letitia (Mot).

My maternal grandfather Sir Trevor Wheler Bt, and his wife Lady Wheler, née Idris Birch.

Great-aunt Winnie's wedding at her father Sir Ernest Birch's Residence in Perak.

Aunt Jotto (my father's sister and my favourite aunt) being carried by her Indian bearers, with her nanny beside her; and right, Jotto as a young woman.

My father in his prep school uniform with two Scottish fishermen and right, saying goodbye to me before going off to WII.

My father and mother and my godfather Philip Nind and his wife Faye, sitting on the back of the car, with army friends; and right: my mother with a bald me. Below: our first house in Kwale, Kenya.

Our house at Kajiado.

Left: *Pods, me and Susie on boardship a Union-Castle liner to England.*

Below: *Pods and me on the Kilifi ferry.*

With my Cousin Christopher in Tiwi, Kenya.

English actor Anthony Steele on location in Amboseli filming "Where No Vultures Fly".

Maasai warriors chanting as they perform a dance.

A Kikuyu police post pulling up the drawbridge at dusk to keep out Mau Mau from their village.

Picture of lions taken by my mother, for which she won a photography competition.

whole way down then up again which is no mean feat, although he beat us both ways. The whole idea held zero appeal for Diana who stayed up at the top reading either Proust or movie mags, I cant remember which. Pods and I mounted our indifferent mules with their fly-blown saddles and rumbling bellies as we stumbled off for the Canyon's bottom. That particular bottom was not our chief concern. The endless foul-smelling plop, plop coming from the mules' rear ends, into which each animal behind neatly stepped, over-whelmed the fresh pine-scented air. But I was happy to be riding along, at one with my mule. Just as I was taking in the jaw-dropping splendour of the red ochre mountains opposite, the mule on the winding path above did its best to send me hurtling down the cliff to my certain death by kicking over a loose boulder which just clipped the right hind leg of my own sturdy pack animal. It was a close call, my mule fortunately held steady despite nervous 'whoops' and 'whoas' from Pods, who was right behind me and has never had a natural affinity to anything that looks or sounds like a horse. After five hot hours of twisting our way down the five thousand foot canyon we reached the bottom, dismounting as bow-legged as two old cowpokes. Dean was there to greet us with a smile and a beer. After munching through our shoe-sized steaks, swigging a couple of bottles of wine and singing along with the guitar-playing ranch hands, we fell onto our beds in a freezing log cabin beside the Colorado river, a river on which I would one day run the rapids. Early next morning, as stiff as two dug up mummies, Pods and I started the mighty climb upwards while my stalwart husband strode forth like Beowulf and vanished into the pine trees.

In California we stayed at a ranch in Santa Ines belonging to the large eccentric family of my friend Wendy. It was there that I met my first real cowboy, Virgil, who worked with the cattle and horses. He was lean and wiry and had the lined leathery skin of a man who has little acquaintance with the indoors. One morning a few of us were sitting on the split log railings around a dusty corral watching Virgil and his men lasso the young bulls to pull them in and castrate them. Each experienced throw hit its moving target with perfect precision. As soon as the bull hit the earth, two or three men grabbed its twisting horns and the testicles were swiftly cut off. It was the job of those on the fencing rails to rush in to the middle of the arena after each chop and hand Virgil the required bottle of medicine to prevent any infection in the wound. When it was my turn I jumped off the rails and like a pro, grabbed what I thought was the right brown bottle, ran like Mo

Farah up to the men, and with a breathless, "Here you are, Virgil," promptly handed him a bottle of beer. His look of contempt for this clueless foreign woman sent me scurrying back red-faced while a more experienced ranch-hand completed the simple task. The others sitting there sniggered with amusement at my blunder.

The next morning at breakfast we were all introduced to the delicacy of 'mountain oysters'. Having no idea what they were, we later discovered they were the intimate parts of the bull we had so blithely watched being taken off.

TARA AND THE MOON

1969 in Chicago started out as a strange year. I had miscarried the previous year amidst great sadness and pain (partly due to the idiotic doctor forgetting to give me any aneasthetic for the D&C he performed) and being placed in a ward where happy young mothers were holding their warmly-wrapped newborns.

When your own baby has gone, it is hard to adjust to the emptiness, the loss. Apart fom Dean and my mother no one wanted to talk about it. Miscarriages were mostly dismissed in those days. You were expected to smile, keep silent about it and carry on. So the thrill of becoming pregnant again was slightly dampened by having to stay in bed for four months to prevent another loss. Mum came over to look after me, while my craving for tinned chicken livers rose to new feathered heights. Dean, my father and Elmer, with sighs of relief, went off to Colorado to fish and do some male bonding as the doctors had forbidden me to fly. During the day Mum would sit in a comfortable arm chair by my bed and we either read or recalled stories from the old days. One day as she was knitting a small shawl for the baby, she said rather wistfully,

"Jacks, I think you girls probably had an even better childhood than I did. Being brought up in Africa took a great deal of beating because of the lovely freedom of it all. It was Kenya which we all loved so much."

Apart from having my adored children I think the most extraordinary event in my life was seeing the two American astronauts landing on the moon in June 1969. Half a billion people were watching television as the Apollo

Lunar Module Eagle landed in the Sea of Tranquility. As my tummy was fast resembling a moon-let, we had a party in the garden of our apartment on Astor Street, off Lake Shore Drive and everyone, including both sets of parents, was there to watch the historic occasion unfold on television. It was practically impossible to take in the fact that we were seeing the first human foot being planted on another world. Copious amounts of wine and whiskey enhanced the mounting excitement and tension on that summer night and when the American flag was placed on the moon, we all erupted into wild cheers for this huge ambition, so faultlessly accomplished.

TASMIN AND WASHINGTON D.C.

After three tumultuous years in Chicago, Dean was posted to Washington where, in my semi-delicate state, *Time* magazine put us up in the grand Hay Adams Hotel opposite the White House until we could find a house. Soon after, John Larsen was posted to Saigon where his wife Wendy spent a year teaching English Literature at the University. I missed her a great deal. She later wrote *Shallow Graves*, her extraordinary verse novel about her time there.

When I think back to our time in Washington in the 1970s, apart from a few health dramas, I consider them halcyon days in many ways. Dean became *Time's* White House correspondent when Richard Nixon was President. But everything I had experienced until that moment paled in comparison with the birth of our much longed-for daughter, Tara. I was a mother possessed, and revelled in the first-baby, unpredictable rhythm of our lives. Since I was clueless about babies, my mother and sweet fifteen year old sister Digs, came to the rescue for a month and gradually organised the domestic front. From the start we were infatuated by our totally delicious blue-eyed, strawberry-colour haired baby who, with her distinctly Chinese-shaped eyes, looked like a little smiling Buddha. It was a time full of joy.

Outside our cosy nest, the war seemed to be winding down. Then Nixon, heavily supported by Henry Kissinger, suddenly announced the invasion of Cambodia on April 30th, 1970, triggering protests across college campuses. A peaceful anti-war rally held on the commons at Kent State University in the rolling green hills of a small town in Ohio, ended with twenty-eight guardsmen from the Ohio National Guard opening fire on the crowd. They killed four students and wounded nine. The horrific massacre, which cut our hearts to the quick, was regarded as an historic moment of public unrest during the Vietnam War. Turbulence across the country escalated even further and thousands of people in the United States, including my friends and I, were by now actively protesting the Vietnam War by going on marches.

The following year our beautiful second daughter Tasmin was born, with blue eyes and a mass of dark hair. She fell ill within a week of arriving home and with the help of Pods, who had come from England to help, we rushed her to hospital where she was kept for a month suffering from spinal meningitis. Gut-wrenching days followed, convinced my tiny baby was going to die. I wandered around in a fog of bewilderment and unhappiness. To this day I feel incredibly lucky that she pulled through and that Pods was such a stalwart helper, cheering up Dean and myself with her eternal streak of optimism. She also introduced us to Todd Civardi, her tall, very good-looking future American husband. Supremely sportif, he was an ardent collector of pre-Columbian artifacts and fossils, loving nature and all things outdoors. They had met skiing in Verbier, Switzerland, where she and Susie were 'chalet girls' for two seasons and Todd was a barman.

My tiny Tasmin turned into an adorable, gutsy child and fearless tomboy who bore her health issues for the next three years with great courage. It was a time of zero sleep for her parents and I cannot imagine how Dean was able to function at work. Early one morning, when I looked particularly unattractive, ashen-faced from weariness with Worzel Gummidge hair, crucial mascara absent and droopy eye-bags offered up instead, the door bell rang. Aargh! I staggered to the door to see a very young, very tall Englishman, Henry Wyndham, Dig's future husband, whom I had never met and was coming to stay—but rather too early. As he handed me Elton John's latest album *Don't Shoot the Piano Player* as a present, he spluttered with what I took to be an expression of horror, "But you don't look anything like I was told you did!"

When something from long ago stirs in my memory, I try to catch it like a firefly before its light dims in my mind. When she was three Tasmin was holding my hand as we walked down "O" Street in Georgetown where we lived. It was a breezy spring morning and all the pink cherry blossoms were scattering their petals in the wind. Looking up to me she said, "Mummy, soon it will be summer and then we can do sommersaults!" That made such perfect sense.

All through my life memories of my children have brought me solace and happiness and they are the achievement I will always be the most proud of. I know how fortunate I am to be so incredibly close to them. Another memory floats back when we were trying to get Tara into Sheridan School, one of Washington's best, when she was five. As the Headmaster was rubbing a sheet of paper with Tara's pretty basic drawing of a house and placed it on the glass window, he asked, "Tara, what makes this paper stick to the window?"

"Static elecricity," she shot back—never heard before nor since. The total surprise of her answer nearly made me fall off my chair. It must have been learnt from the brilliant children's television show, Sesame Street.

NIXON'S PRAYER BREAKFAST

As a White House correspondent Dean attended President Nixon's Prayer Breakfasts at the White House, events that bring together people from different religions and walks of life for an hour devoted to faith. I went along with my husband one cold winter's morning and as we arrived Henry Kissinger, who was soon to become the U.S. Secretary of State, was the first person Dean introduced me to. I distinctly remember two things about him. His intense, twinkly blue eyes and the aura of power that exuded from his short, rotund figure. He spoke in a deep German accent, was charming and worldly compared to others around him. But of course one couldn't forget his damning involvement in Cambodia.

Power was not something I was naturally drawn to although I had by then met a number of influential Americans and Washington high-flyers. On our honeymoon Bobby Kennedy, then the charismatic Senator from New York, had invited Dean and myself to tea so he could meet his friend's new bride. I found him fun and easy; he smiled a lot but had a way of gazing at me like a prize heifer which slightly unnerved me. Dean also introduced me to former President Johnson around that time—another man who exuded power. My husband told me a rather unfresh, oft-repeated story about Johnson. He had a habit of calling in a journalist while he was sitting on the lavatory doing his business, and insisted on the door being left open. The mortified member of the press would then stand beside it and interview the President, a degrading position for both. Dean was once one of those unfortunates and never forgot it.

I was now twenty-seven, but still relatively new to the corridors of powers. The first of my invitations to the White House filled me with excitement; I imagined it to be similar to stepping into Buckingham Palace and having a quick chat with the Queen. It is a lovely building though much smaller inside than I expected. We were all ushered into the stunning East Room where ten rows of chairs filled the space between the front of the room and the area where a choir was to stand. As we sat down, what appeared to be the entire membership of the Mormon Tabernacle Choir walked in one by one, women in blue, men in black. Row upon row of them and only six feet from where we were sitting. Finally President Nixon and his wife Pat walked in, nodded to everyone and sat down.

The Evangelical preacher stood up on the small podium behind a plain mahogany lectern and within five minutes had worked himself up into a holy fervour. His arms were firing like pistons and when he started spouting loudly, "It's not the Left wing I'm worried about, it's not the Right wing I'm worried about, it's the Bird itself," I figured he was about to tell us how to do something creative with a turkey.

Lowering my eyes to hide my amusement I couldn't help but notice, since they were right in my face, the lower garb of the powerfully loud Choir's male members, who were close to blasting us out of the room. Their black trousers were cut far too short; two inches of hairy shins, white socks and clumping black shoes with those wide unattractive American soles was, to my mind, not a great look.

After the service Nixon and his wife led the worshippers out of the room and a receiving line began to form across the lobby into the state dining room where tables were laid with lace tablecloths, silver coffee urns, slices of coffee cake and Danish pastries. The Nixons took up positions in front of a large fireplace to shake hands with several ambassadors, a few cabinet ministers and generals, wives of prisoners of war in Vietnam, journalists and ordinary citizens. When Dean's turn arrived, Richard Nixon slapped him rather too hard on the back before saying with a smirk,

"You *Time* magazine guys, you come and you go."

A veiled hope that Dean, along with most of the White House press corps, would stop probing sensitive issues surrounding the maelstrom of

Watergate, or get another posting, but it was Nixon himself who eventually had to go.

WATERGATE

The *Washington Post* was the first newspaper to break the real story following a burglary by five men of the Democratic National Committee headquarters in Washington in 1972, which rocked the city. This became known as the Watergate scandal. A cover up was authorised by the President that clearly intended to block the course of justice.

The tongue-in-cheek pseudonym 'Deep Throat' was given to the secret individual who provided information to journalist Bob Woodward, who then shared it with Carl Bernstein, both reporters for the *Post*. Key details about the involvement of Nixon's administration were uncovered. The burglars were caught and in a desperate bid to keep the net from closing round him, the offices of political opponents, activist groups and journalists' home phones, including ours, were being bugged on Nixon's orders. *Time* magazine, at that time a real family concern before it merged with Warner Brothers, was seen as sympathetic to Communism by Nixon's republican cronies.

Nixon himself, deeply suspicious by nature, and Kissinger, with whom he had a close relationship, shared a penchant for secrecy. At the time nobody in Washington talked about anything else. Around correspondents' dinner tables, the subject of Watergate was served up every evening. Forty-eight people involved were eventually found guilty, many of whom were top Nixon officials. Facing certain impeachment Nixon resigned the Presidency in August 1974, and the following month his successor, Gerald Ford, pardoned him.

PRESIDENTIAL CAMPAIGN

Dean had been off travelling with President Nixon most weeks on the 1972 Presidential campaign year so for much of that period I saw little of him. At the time the reporter and columnist Timothy Crouse travelled on both the Nixon and McGovern campaigns, which resulted in an amusing, insightful book called *The Boys on the Bus* about the chief political reporters of the campaigns, in the process witnessing the birth of modern campaign journalism. But the provocative book could bite as well. He described my dear spouse thus:

"Fischer, a tall blond, who with his horn-rimmed glasses bore a slight resemblance to the actor Michael Caine, was a silent man who occasionally flashed the tight, cryptic smile of a hatchet murderer ..."

I can't remember what Dean's take was on this; he probably just shrugged his shoulders, but I thought it was pretty nasty. Crouse slightly redeemed himself later in my eyes by writing,

"Many of *Time's* best correspondents worked in the Washington Bureau, Champ Clark, Hays Gorey, Simmons Fentress and Dean Fischer, all of whom it was said, could probably have held down front-line positions on the *New York Times*. Some of them were legends within the *Time* organization, but to the public at large they were about as well known as engineers at Cape Kennedy."

When early one morning in Mitchell, McGovern's home town in South Dakota, Dean asked a reporter what the Senator had for breakfast that day, Crouse quipped, "Not for nothing was Fischer a golden boy at *Time*."

When he was in office the affable President Gerald Ford had a mountain home, his Western White House, tucked among the aspens in Vail, Colorado. As Dean had remained *Time's* White House correspondent, we took the little ones skiing there in the winter and introduced them to the flower-filled mountain meadows in the summer. Every August we went back to England so the children could see their grandparents, most years going to Cornwall and staying at Medla, a large, much loved Victorian house overlooking the sea at Polzeath. It belonged to great friends of my parents, Peter and Fay Courtauld—their daughter Sarah is my oldest pal. In the days when we came as children from Africa, seals lay basking on the rocks by the beach and Sarah and I would hook large crabs out of the crevices and take them back for supper, but they've all gone now. If we scrabble hard enough in the shingle we can still find six or seven tiny pink cowrie shells in an old smuggler's cove—a family tradition; the unbeakable bond between our families has since happily travelled down four generations.

After a day or two relaxing in a deckchair and with a couple of whiskies warming his cockles on a summer's evening, my father's giggly sense of humour would surface. Years ago there was a particular Major who lived in a house on the opposite side of the bay whom Pa and Peter considered a snobby, pompous old bore. One moonless night they decided to creep across the beach and give him a treat. With a pair of my mother's knickers in one hand, they shimmied up the Major's flag pole, struck his flag and soon had the lacy white pants flying proudly in the wind.

Life back in Washington was a heady existence and I only wish I had kept a diary of all the fascinating people with whom I had interesting conversations over dinner. However, I made some of the best friends of my life there. Muffy Stout was a photographer with four offspring and since we lived on the same street in Georgetown our children ran in and out of each others' houses and learned to ride their bikes together. Pammy Barnes, Wendy's sister, was a talented artist, and her lawyer husband Peter, one of the funniest, wittiest men I have ever met. I really love clever American wit. They owned a charming old farmhouse in Virginia where we spent many great weekends together with our mutual friends, the poet Elizabeth Goldring, then a director and lecturer at MIT, and her doctor husband Steven, Tasmin's godfather. One simple pleasure on a Saturday morning was piling the children into the car to go to the farm—no seat belts in those days—putting on a cassette and listening to Tara sing Don MacLean's 'American Pie' which she had learnt by heart by the time she was three. That song will always remind me of her.

But with Dean so involved with Time and often gone, especially during the 1976 Presidential campaign year in which Jimmy Carter eventually emerged victorious, I began to feel increasingly alone in caring for the children, even lonely in my marriage. I became obsessed with Leonard Cohen's sad songs and would lie on the sofa playing them over and over again as if he had written the beautiful lyrics for me as well as Marianne and Suzanne. I devoured *Zen and the Art of Motorcycle Maintenance* and *Fear and Loathing in Las Vegas*, Hunter S. Thompson's *roman-à-clef* about the American Dream seen through a drug-induced haze. As I imagined frolicking with the hippies in Haight Ashbury a job with an interior designer in Georgetown came my way. In the mornings, after dropping off Tasmin on my bicycle, at school, I learned the subtle intricacies of fabrics and design. Tennis with a girlfriend on the public courts at the end of our street became part of my week, together with another group of good tennis pals at the British Embassy which we named the 'Big Bosoms' versus the 'Little Bosoms'—Carla Powell, whose husband Charles was First Secretary at the Embassy, and myself, against Muffy Stout and Liz Gibbs (a Kenya Baring) which as you can tell, we took very seriously.

Then one day on the public courts I met Jan, an extremely good player. He was tall, attractive, and invited me to knock-up while waiting for my friend to arrive. All went well until I tripped over a crack in the court's surface and broke my ankle. Jan helped me hobble to the bench where I gave him the keys to my house and asked him to bring the car down and take me to hospital. Within a few painful hours I was the proud owner of a plastercast and crutches. Jan turned out to be a Vietnam veteran who had been wounded and sent home to a country reeling from a monumentally unpopular war, with little desire to greet their Vets as returning heroes. Many Americans looked upon them with disdain and some even spat at them on their arrival home. Few Vets could find jobs, leaving them bewildered and disillusioned and turning increasingly to drugs. Who knows why these things happen when least expected or sought after but we soon fell hopelessly for each other. Within weeks, it had become irresistible and needed more strength and will than I possessed at the time to end it. Jan was six years younger, highly unsuitable, and I still loved my husband, but the affair began to rock my marriage to its foundations. Within four months I began to feel completely powerless, as fragmented as I had ever been, and unable to make any decision about the following day, let alone the future.

London Life

S O IN 1976, after living in Washington D.C. for eight years I moved to London with my girls and Dean who had been transferred to *Time's* London bureau. We got them into Queensgate, a good private girls' school where my sister Digs had gone and my father was once a governor, but within a few months Dean and I separated, which was incredibly sad, for the children in particular. It will always be a source of huge regret that our eventual divorce became an ongoing loss for both children as they made their way through adolescence and into adult life. To complicate matters Jan came over to live in London to be near me, which turned out to be another painful, unsettling time.

I was now thirty-three, very unhappy, but determined not to let things drift into complete chaos, especially as I had my precious girls to look after. I badly needed a job and was eventually successfully interviewed by Oliver, an affable public school educated Lloyd's underwriter in his early forties who worked from his house in Mayfair. Although the job offer was hardly a post for a high-flyer in the inner sanctum of MI5, he made it clear from the start that he had no interest in employing anyone with any 'baggage' as he put it. Oliver wanted no 'issues'—no marital discord, no painful romantic involve-ment nor financial impecunity, and definitely no problems concerning young children. He might just as well have added 'no criminal record', but somehow desisted.

I assured him with my most engaging smile that every aspect of my personal life was indeed in tip-top shape. I gave not an inkling that I was currently undergoing my own *Annus Horribilis*. My ten-year marriage had ended, the love-affair, something that had made my whole life spin out of control for a while, proved impossible; my father was extremely unwell and my youngest daughter had developed a frightening illness which would take many months to come to terms with. Without question it was the worst year of my life. Besides, apart from my large loving family I had few friends in London, having only lived here for nine months as an African fledgling in the 1960s.

So mine was a battered soul endeavouring to deal with a mind-bogglingly boring job but my boss and I got on well. He was urbane, cultured and a thoroughly decent sort—tall and manly in a ruddy-faced Yorkshire squire sort of way. He was a pheasant plucker and loved nothing more than going on country house shoots in Scotland to kill wee birdies. During the slaughtering season there were so many braces of pheasant hanging from the doors that I felt I was wading through some avian abattoir when I arrived each morning. After a few months it dawned on me that Oliver might be interested in more than just my typing skills. However he had a singularly unusual way of delivering his message.

One steaming July day I arrived at my desk promptly at 9am and sat down. Oliver sauntered into the light and airy office we both shared and started pacing around looking for a particular file. It was hard not to notice he was butt naked—not even the briefest hand towel covering his modesty.

'Oh well, it must be the heat', I said to myself, 'He'll soon put on some shorts.' But he didn't. After reassuring myself I wasn't going to be ravaged by some rutting stag from the Highlands I thought it best to act cool and ignore his bizarre behaviour. After all, I reasoned, it was the '70s—he would realise soon enough that he was having zero impact on any doe-eyed stirrings. Oliver was not exactly George Clooney with his clothes on, so a stark-naked underwriter prancing round the office and simultaneously dictating a letter to me was even less appealing. To make matters worse, every so often he would come over to my desk and look down at what I was writing, his dingly-dangly hanging like a bleached bat a mere foot away from me.

Putting another slant on it, perhaps I had dented his manly pride by not responding and as the hours rolled by he felt unable to back down without losing face. This had now become a stalemate, a tussle of wills as I kept a beady eye on his movements. At one o'clock sharp Oliver announced,

"As it's such a lovely sunny day I've made a delicious lunch for us on the terrace."

"Wonderful," I replied as if nothing was untoward.

We sat at the round table with me sitting comfortably in my skirt and tee-shirt and Himself in the altogether, legs akimbo, his pale perspiring body quickly turning pink in the flickering English sun. I kicked off my shoes in a vague attempt to relax, not knowing exactly who was in pole position here. After a pleasant hour chatting about 'this' but not 'that', we went back inside and let this strange day run its course. For eight hours Oliver stubbornly declined to get dressed and for eight hours I refused to remark on it. At five o'clock I said goodbye and went home by tube, wondering how many of my depressing fellow passengers had a raving loony as a boss. But I couldn't help but muse on Oliver's rather pathetic predicament. Poor guy, how desperate must he be?

I had barely stepped through the door of the office the following morning when I saw that Oliver was once again as naked as a New Guinea tribesman. That was it. It was time to whup ass. I drew myself up, taller than usual in my new snazzy high heels, and came over all Miss Jean Brodie.

"Good morning Oliver. Now look, it didn't work yesterday and it isn't going to work today. I suggest you nip off to your bedroom and put on some clothes, there's a good chap."

Off he went, meek as a hungover schoolboy, and returned fully dressed for work. Nanny had thoroughly scolded him, telling him he was a naughty boy, which was probably what he needed all along.

HIS LAST SAFARI

It was early one spring morning that year when the phone in my parents' bedroom in Wadhurst, Sussex, rang. They were both still in bed and my mother picked up the call from a Harley Street cancer specialist who had the results of my father's lung biopsy.

"If you have anything you need to discuss with your husband," he said briskly, "I suggest you do it now as he will be dead in nine months." How callous can you be? Though Mum was shocked to the core she said nothing and for the next nine months she looked after the man she had always loved with total undivided devotion. We four girls living in London went down to the family house to help, mostly at weekends.

I was staying with Ma and Pa two weeks before my father died when he called me into his bedroom. Although he had never admitted to any of us, including my mother, that he knew he was dying, we were well aware that all he longed for was the village doctor's nightly morphine shot to release his agonising cancer pain which had by now spread to his bones. I pulled up the chair beside the bed and touched his hand. It was an effort for him to talk but he managed to say,

"You must promise me, darling, you will always look after your Mother afterwards." With a lump in my throat, I replied,

"Don't worry Dad, I'll make sure she's alright." That was the last time I spoke to him, the last time I saw him.

A fortnight later my mother and sisters were at his bedside holding him as he slipped away and I was driving far too fast from Somerset with the children to get there before he died. But by the time I arrived he had already been taken away to the funeral home. At fifty-nine, he was far too young to die. Pools of tears were shed but because I had not been there at the end, I felt I had missed out on the bonding, the dying process, and was bereft at not being able to say goodbye.

It is not often one experiences both tragedy and humour within the space of a morning, but on the day my father died, there was an incident that provided a few hours' light relief on an otherwise brutal day. It was agreed that Susie and I would accompany our mother to the funeral home to discuss arrangements for his cremation. When we arrived at the building in Tunbridge Wells and pressed the gleaming brass doorbell, the door was opened by a middle-aged lady dwarf—something we hadn't really banked on. Looking down at a three foot vertically-challenged person radiating bonhomie and bustling with efficiency was bound to start us off on a wobbly foot. After greeting us with suitably sympathetic words, we found ourselves following her large, bouncy bottom down the hall and into an empty, rather soulless room. Three hard chairs neatly placed in a row faced a high wooden mantelpiece and my sister and I dutifully arranged ourselves on either side of our grieving mother. We sat there silently, like condemned men in a courtroom, while the little person squeezed her substantial *derrière* into the chair of a knee-hole desk fit for an ancestral home, her full head of teased blonde hair just managing to peak like the rays of the rising sun over the top.

However helpful the woman was at trying to keep us on an even keel, we found the next half hour excruciating. Numerous questions were fired at us as to the type of coffin and wood desired with particular emphasis being placed on the most suitable handles to use—apparently some burn more efficiently than others. The only ornament on the mantelpiece was an out-sized clock and as the lady dwarf became increasingly excited by her visions of deathly grandeur, we tried hard to concentrate on its loud 'tick-tock', 'tick-tock', in order to control ourselves. But it didn't last long.

Eventually one of us giggled rather too loudly at something she said, and the others were off. To make things worse she instantly came over all motherly understanding, obviously keen to calm us down and get the session over with.

"There, there, dears. Don't worry; this happens all the time. It's just nerves."

I am sure she was right. Somehow we managed to pull ourselves together until, still deep in discussion about the handles, she rose to her full height from behind her desk and pronounced in her best counties voice,

"I'll just go and see what I have in S-s-stock."

With that she flounced purposefully out of the door and the three of us fell on the floor, choking with laughter.

In the nick of time, like mischievous schoolgirls, we were back in our chairs when the door opened and the woman reappeared, followed by the Director of the parlour. Like every funeral director one has ever seen in a film, he was tall, thin and deathly pale with black oiled hair plastered flat on his head and a clear parting carefully drawn down the middle. With a friendly smile he nonchalantly sidled through the door like Basil Fawlty with his knees bent and his arms outstretched, and as he approached we could see every imaginable type of coffin handle hanging wistfully off them. Catastrophe! Within seconds all three of us had lost any vestige of decorum and were up on our feet, unable to contain ourselves a minute longer. My mother somehow managed to splutter to the by now speechless couple,

"I am so sorry. I don't know what's come over my daughters, but we really do have to leave. Terribly sorry."

We ran down the hall, jumped into the car and laughed, and cried, all the way home.

On a cold misty morning sometime later when I was walking in the fields around the house in Sussex where my Mother now lived alone I chanced upon a group of deer stepping silently out of a thicket into the field. In their midst I saw one that was unlike any I had ever seen before. It was pure white, luminous and exquisite. From where I stood I could almost believe it was a unicorn. I stood transfixed, staring at it until it eventually vanished into the woods, feeling somehow that it was a premonition, like an angel on my shoulder.

FOREIGN CORRESPONDENTS

One of the things that kept me going was my luck in having a number of good foreign correspondent friends, mainly American, who had been posted to London at the same time I came to live here in 1976. Many of them were among the best in the business in what were the glory days of print journalism. They reminded people why journalism mattered and of the good that it could, and should, do. Most of the men and women felt that working for their own particular newspaper, magazine, or television company, be it the *New York Times*, the *Washington Post*, *The Times*, *Los Angeles Times*, *Time* magazine, *Life* or *Newsweek*, was the most exciting job in the world. Many had covered pretty much all the main wars in the past half century. It was a different time when journalists in a far off place had a sense of freedom about what they did. They would arrive in some hellhole by plane, rapidly assess the situation, interview the big players and have time to think before composing their story at the end of the day. In those early days before email and mobile phones the most difficult part was how to file, how to get the stories back to their papers. It was also a time of long boozy lunches with gossipy journalists revealing their gory experiences from the front. A golden age in journalism and I am fortunate that through my husbands and my friends, I was part of it.

Two of my great friends at the time were Johnny Apple, the *New York Times* London bureau chief and Peter Jennings, who later became the legendary news anchor for ABC News. Dean and I already knew Johnny and first got to know Peter in Chicago when he was a twenty-seven year old fledgling TV reporter in the Middle East, looking debonnair in his bush jacket. He was urbane, movie star handsome with a good sense of humour but underneath the wordly veneer there was a real shyness and lack of confidence which was appealing. At the time he was married to his first, very attractive wife, Anoushka, who is still a friend.

I saw Peter's compassion and kindness first hand when Tasmin was six and ill at home in London. My loyal, caring mother was the only person constantly by my side and was quite simply heroic. When my beloved daughter was ensconced in Great Ormond Street Hospital for Children for a month Peter came with me to see her, which was a great comfort.

Four years later Tasmin spent the day with Peter in New York when she was ten and he took her to a splendid lunch. Once they were back at the ABC News room where he was to record, either Tasmin asked him or Peter asked her if he could be her surrogate godfather. She was particularly thrilled when he flew over to London in 1995 on Air Force One with President Clinton one cold December day to come to her wedding.

When Johnny was sent to London to be bureau chief we spent a great deal of time together. It was his huge appetite—for art and music, for politics, for a brace of partridges and a speckled trout—that made Johnny such great company. His devotion to his enthusiasms began early by being expelled twice from Princeton for spending too much time working as Chairman of the *Daily Princetonian*.

Johnny was rotund with a cheery, apple-cheeked face and dark hair and always did everything with great style. For seven summers he took me to see glorious operas at Glyndbourne, in Sussex; we were driven down by his driver, complete with silver candlesticks, champagne and a gourmet meal meticulously prepared by Johnny at his sumptuous flat in Eaton Square. In the interval we happily sat on a large rug next to a field of cows by the Opera house and tucked in. I helped him host many of his soirees at his flat, filled with politicians and writers, intellectuals and actors, the *beau monde* and numerous journalists.

His great friend, the journalist Jon Randal, said of one of his closest pals, "Johnny was smart, fast and hard-working when young. His orotund faults were as nothing compared to his immense gifts as a journalist. I first met him at Sardi's in New York in 1965 when he was just back from his first tour in Vietnam where he became famous for claiming that a bullet and not his big butt had split his trousers!"

Johnny's coverage of the Vietnam War earned him many awards. He exposed the failure of US Military, with 500,000 troops in the country, to make progress in the war after two and a half years of fighting. With his close friend, the respected American writer Ward Just, Johnny was covering the 1976 presidential campaign and found themselves in Portland, Oregon where after filing their stories, they were relaxing with a strong drink. A young man, who turned out to work for a local counter culture paper, pulled Ward's sleeves and inquired,

"Is that the great Johnny Apple?" As he kept on singing Apple's praises, his obsequiousness got up Ward's nose.

"Christ, kid, how much do you make?"

"$35 a week," said the man.

"Shit, Apple spills that much!" replied Ward.

It was during one visit to Portland that Johnny got into a slanging match with the owner of one of the Portland papers who sat on the Pulitzer committee and had continually blackballed Johnny. Jon Randal recalled, "Every year, after the Pulitzer prizes were announced, Apple, Ward and I would exchange messages to the effect that "we wuz robbed." It was a kind of private joke. Except towards the end they thought they stood a good chance. I never harboured such illusions."

Johnny eventually married his long-time girlfriend, Betsey Pinkney Brown, also a friend of mine in Washington, and I felt flattered to be their best woman at their wedding in London in 1982.

I found British politics soporifically dull after all the excitement of Washington's dramas. The Labour leader James Callaghan was in power and his tenure was characterised by widespread strikes from the powerful trade unions. Together with the coldest winter in sixteen years, 1978/79 was dubbed the Winter of Discontent, from Shakespeare's *Richard III*. Callaghan's other claim to fame was being the father of Margaret Jay, the wife of the British Ambassador to Washington when we lived there. She later became infamous in Nora Ephron's amusing book *Heartburn*, about her affair with Ephron's husband, the *Washington Post's* star reporter, Carl Bernstein. Washington's elite was naturally riveted by all the gossip. Margaret Jay came to dinner at our house during all the hoohah and was charming.

IRISH CHARM

I had a very funny Irish friend whom I had known in Washington D.C. for many years and who, in retrospect should have remained just that. I don't know why I eventually succumbed to his amorous advances in London but I had been going through a difficult time since moving here and he was amusing, determined and very persuasive. One afternoon after a particularly engaging lunch, however, I discovered there is nothing more off-putting than a naked Irishman striding round the bedroom with a fairly jovial appendage and talking to it as he would a close friend who was about to pogo across the Strait of Hormuz.

"Look at this magnificent beast. What a fine fellow he is," he crowed in boundless admiration as he narrowly missed pole-vaulting out of the second floor window. It was almost as if the two were engaged in a private conversation—one heaping praise, the other nodding sagely and agreeing. As I watched this odd peacock *pas-de-deux* I remember feeling I would rather be at Wimbledon watching a McEnroe-Connors game and hear the former utter his immortal words, so appropriate here, 'You cannot be serious!' Despite his own personal love-in, we remained good friends.

THE MAGIC OF FINDHORN

Badly in need of some emotional solace after all the recent drama I went to Findhorn on the Moray Firth in northern Scotland for three weeks. The family and my schoolfriend Hut looked after the children while I went off for a blast of spiritual, communal living at a place that emphasised personal growth and transformation, into what I wasn't quite sure.

In the 1960s, Peter and Eileen Caddy, on the brink of starvation in a rundown caravan park and surrounded by friends in the same boat, founded Findhorn. Eileen began planting a small vegetable garden on the rocky soil to sustain them all and while digging, and presumably not on the drink, she was visited by what she called 'nature divas' who begged her to plant vegetables together and talk to them; she thought she might be going a bit loco but carried on anyway. Soon word got around that something mystical was happening in Findhorn—enormous roses were flourishing in the snow, delicious forty pound cabbages were being produced and everyone now had plenty to eat. Eventually people from all over the world turned up.

When I was there we were never asked for money but I gather people since have to pay up. Findhorn was somewhat similar to a kibbutz; we took turns waiting on tables, scrubbing lavatories, building foundations, cooking three vegetarian meals a day. Drugs were not allowed and nobody drank. I was still in my hippy stage searching for answers and wore a deeply unattractive brown alpaca poncho to keep out the biting Scottish cold. But as harmony and peace prevailed, I was quickly seduced by the calm, thoughtful attitude each person had towards others. New friends were made and we became more caring people. Meditation was encouraged and the small chapel was always open.

One morning I was walking alone in the grounds and decided to sit on the grass. As I looked down I suddenly saw a tiny spot of intense colour on the tip of a blade of grass which kept changing from a piercing gold to a startlingly electric blue and back to gold again. It was so beautiful I could barely comprehend what I was seeing. I looked closer, thinking that it must be a speck of dew or a prism through a raindrop but it wasn't. It was midday, it hadn't been raining and there was no dew anywhere. Mesmerised, I gazed at the brilliance of this little image for a few minutes as it continually changed colour, trying to figure out what it could possibly be. Then I made the mistake of bending my head closer to it and as I did so it rose swiftly into the air and disappeared. Afterwards I could only think it was a fairy, not a little winged person but a minute pocket of concentrated energy. It doesn't really matter what it was. It was exquisite and gave me a feeling of great happiness and peace that day.

Findhorn's spiritual experience went a good way to healing sore hearts. But once I got home my feeling of euphoria quickly evaporated. I soon came to realise that many of those who assumed an advanced spirituality were in fact scroungers, wanting freebies and somewhere to stay in London. Plus mounds of free food until the walls of my flat were oozing sleeping bodies and lentils while I was trying to get the girls to school in the morning. A couple from Findhorn gave my name to others and devotees from Poona in India descended on me like flying bats, often wearing unfresh orange robes as fervent disciples of their batty leader Bhagwan Shree Rajneesh. Their sole contribution in providing circles of hugs and love and a bit of chanting in return really wasn't enough and so they had to go.

The children were happy at school and they made good friends. Their faltering dance steps at the famous Madame Vacani's Ballet School however, were soon given up—Tara was into drama and poetry, Tasmin preferred being a gymnast. As she was also mad about riding we bought Chippy, a pretty looking pony for her which was kept at a fairly shambolic stables near my mother's house in Wadhurst. He was a palomino, part Arab, part Welsh cob and turned out to be a headstrong creature, having been broken in too early, and was constantly careening off with Tasmin across the wilds of Sussex. She totally worshipped him. Fortunately she didn't fall off too often or break any bones as she had started modelling, once being on the cover of *Tatler*, and earning money to put towards Chippy's upkeep. Both girls adored staying with my mother. Among her many attributes was a highly infectious laugh. Once she got going, rather like a steam train gearing up and realising just how funny the situation or remark was, she couldn't stop until she was in paroxysms of laughter. Everyone else was incapable of doing anything other than join in.

THE THANE OF WESSEX

Among the first people I made friends with in England was the eccentric, sharp-witted Alexander Thynn. On a spring day in 1979 the good citizens of Shepton Mallet in Somerset were busy preparing a Spring Equinox feast fit for a king, which in essence is what the late 7th Marquess of Bath considered himself to be. Then heir to Longleat in Wiltshire, one of the grandest Elizabethan houses in the land, with a fabled safari park, Alexander wanted specifically to be known as the Thane of Wessex—the king of a once proud 11th century kingdom. He was a flamboyant man with a colourful taste in caftans, an unusual artist who had filled every inch of the private rooms of Longleat with his slightly dotty, impasto murals made out of sawdust and oil paint.

Whenever we stayed for the weekend my children were charmed by the day nursery with Alexander's cheerful murals of fairies, flowers and small woodland creatures. The night nursery was another matter entirely. Goblins, evil beasties and the dark nightmare colours frightened them when they had to sleep there with Alexander's two children, Lenka and Ceawlin and their nanny. I was given the Karma Sutra bedroom with its famously saucy fresco of rather hideous cavorting couples engaged in some curious jiggery and a good deal of pokery. Alexander's bizarre wish of wanting forty children by twenty different women, known as his 'wifelets', was something I thought utterly bonkers. Something must have gone askew for as far as I know Alexander never had any other children other than the two with his wife Anna, who had lived in France with her lover for most of their marriage.

The weekend of the Spring Equinox arrived and I drove down to Longleat after stopping off at Heathrow to pick up Lorenzo, an old Italian friend who had arrived from Kenya. He had once played the role of Jesus in the film *Ben-Hur* in which he appeared to be carrying a heavy cross, made out of the lightest balsawood, as he struggled up the hill to Golgotha. He was married to my dear friend, the well-known African photographer Mirella Ricciardi. Lorenzo was an adventurer, a sea-farer, a seducer of exotic women, who once bought a dhow with the proceeds of one reckless night at a Swiss casino, and enjoyed wearing eye-catching apparel as much as the charismatic Alexander did. He strode through Customs dressed as an Arab sheikh in a flowing white robe with a red and white *keffiyeh* over his halo of greying blonde hair. He was quite happy to stay in his outfit all day which fitted in with the generally odd-ball Longleat dress code.

For the evening's festivities I dressed as a druid maiden in a floor-length ruby velvet cape with a mass of daffodils entwined in my long hair. Alexander was dressed as a magnificent Thane, festooned in velvets and silks, lace at the cuffs and long boots, with his unruly hair tumbling down his back. The Sheikh, the Druid, the Thane and one of his former wifelets, dressed as a saucy 14th century maid, set off from Longleat in Alexander's black Range Rover, in lieu of a medieval horse and cart, for Shepton Mallet, there to join the Mayor and other revellers. The evening, however well-meaning, was excruciating. The four of us, all honoured guests, were seated at a high table on a raised platform in the town hall. A vast suckling pig with the ubiquitous orange stuffed in its mouth, was laid before us and for most of the evening all eyes were upon us. We were entertained by eight young dancers—plump, pubescent local girls dressed up as daffodils and tulips. The girls did their very best and we clapped at suitable intervals, but alas, oh dear, not one of the little flowers was cut out to be the next Margot Fonteyn. They skipped and twirled in their pretty little outfits with a definite heaviness while we stuffed our mouths with pig in an effort to control ourselves.

At midnight we thanked our hosts and the Mayor and fled back to Longleat to find the place surrounded by police. During the hours we were away, there had been a break-in in the long formal dining-room which was open to the public during daylight hours. Numerous valuable items had been stolen. Alexander wound down his window as a policeman stopped the car at the back entrance and peered in suspiciously at its odd assortment of occupants.

"And just who are you, sir?" the copper asked, looking at the dazzlingly dressed driver.

"I am the Thane of Wessex," replied the indignant heir.

"Pull the other one, sir. You are just a bunch of old hippies and I am not allowing you over this 'ere threshold."

Twenty minutes later, amidst much tossing of aristocratic locks and our laird's indisputable air of *droit de seigneur*, the disgruntled copper finally let through its four strange, bedraggled inmates.

COMMANDO MUFFY

Because the children and I missed America and our friends there, every summer for seven years I took the girls to spend August on a farm in Massachusetts. 'Timberock' belonged to one of my closest pals, Muffy Stout, and her family, and was a huge and happy part of our lives. Muffy's paternal great grandfather, a Swedish potter, had emigrated to America and made a fortune with another businessman from holding a patent for their invention, the diamond steel cutter. He bought a thousand acres around a lake near Worcester where he built a large house for himself and his wife. Part of the land was turned into a dairy farm complete with story-book red barns and two working Belgian shire horses. Properties and land, which had slowly been reduced over the years to two hundred acres, eventually trickled down to his great-grandchildren. Muffy's unconventional old farmhouse in this idyllic slice of New England, was built on a small hill overlooking an ancient pond, really more of a lake, that Native Americans had called 'Quaboag'. It was surrounded by rolling pastures and dark, unsettling woods. A hundred years previously they had been inhabited by tribes and their spirits could still be felt in every corner of the forest.

Close American friends came to the farm with their children every summer and we five mothers were known as the 'Hags', a name of which we became rather fond. As all our offspring grew up together many have remained good friends. Besides Muffy, the 'Hags' consisted of Judy Bizot, who lived in Paris and along the way had acquired four husbands, worked for UNESCO for thirty years and became a film maker of third-world women. I was very close to Judy who was also a superb diver, who produced a book of her underwater photos of rather beautiful soft-bodied molluscs, the 'nudibranch'. Jennifer Franchina was involved with documentary making in Rome's art world—her mother-in-law was the daughter of the famous Italian futurist painter, Gino Severini. Kind, creative, wildly bright Deborah Gillette made up our group.

During those crazy farm days, teenagers had fledgling crushes and the grownups generally misbehaved themselves. Laughter and tears, romances and divorces, swimming and tennis, drinking and dancing on the wide, wrap-around porch; canoeing and skiing on the lake; long Labour Day Swedish 'Aquavit' lunches by the pool singing the drinking song, "Helan Gar" at the top of our voices. It was all summer fun which Americans seem to do so effortlessly and better than anyone else. Muffy, attractive, bright and generous to a fault, had gone to the liberal arts college, Bennington, with Deborah and was loved by everyone. She had an enormous sense of humour, a deep, husky voice and was full of wise words for others, especially the young.

To feed the growing rabble Muffy employed a cook and caretaker named Eddie. He was an amiable giant, chubby with an extensive beer gut, hirsute beyond any reach of a razor, with thick tufts of hair sprouting all over his back and shoulders. Eddie was definitely a one-off but he became part of the family and looked after the house and gardens with great care. He had a penchant for wearing an unattractive and rather sweaty white vest with his shorts; he played the trombone with great gusto and had a witchy wife with rotten teeth with whom he quarrelled often and loudly. They lived on the ground floor of a house built for Muffy's four great children, Craig, Carder, Antonia and Julie, a short distance from the main house.

One night Muffy and I were sitting alone on her porch, screened off from the Kamakazi mosquitoes that invaded the woods all summer long. We noticed at one point that Eddie had abruptly stopped practicing his trombone and angry voices began to filter through the fir trees. As the noise grew louder, Muffy said,

"Come on, let's see who's doing the murdering."

"Right. Let's dress up as commandoes," I suggested.

We hurriedly put on black leggings and tops and blackened our faces. Fuelled by mischief and vodka, we crawled on our stomachs down to their house before crouching in the grass beneath their back window, trying not to giggle. After ten minutes their voices suddenly went quiet and in our fear we imagined Eddie pushing open his screen door and coming out to investigate. Muffy whispered loudly,

"Better make a run for it."

In my blind panic I rushed off into the pitch black night, forgetting, rather like Peter Rabbit, the waist-high net of chicken wire surrounding the large lettuce patch at the back of Eddie's house. I ran smack into it and every finger and toe became painfully enmeshed in the wire, cutting into two of them. Muffy had naturally gone round the perimeter and was on her back in the bushes, splitting her sides at my misfortune. Eddie never came out and once I could move again I joined her. Nursing my bleeding wounds, we lay there, whispering while we looked up at the stars in the summer night sky and thinking that, in spite of everything, life really was rather amusing.

Some years later Muffy died, far too young at the age of sixty-six. The drink did for her in the end and I miss her to this day.

After Muffy's funeral, where Judy and I gave the eulogy, her eldest daughter, my beloved godchild Antonia, and I took the canoe to her grandparent's house further round the lake. We were both paddling away, talking quietly about her mother and looking at the ripples made by the fish snatching at the dragonflies that hovered above the water. We were halfway across when a magnificent Bald Eagle flew out over the tops of the fir trees and swooped low across our boat. With its snowy-feathered head, yellow beak and white tail, the powerful bird of prey flapped its massive six foot wings as if to acknowledge us. It was a very moving sight and we both felt it was Muffy's spirit telling us that she was still with us.

Honey and Vinegar

WHEN ALAIN CATZEFLIS and I met at a Chelsea drinks party in 1983 it was one of those *coup de foudre* moments. He stood out amongst all the nattily turned out men, casually dressed in jeans and a tweed jacket and looking madly attractive. He was tall, had a sweep of thick dark hair, brown eyes and an easy smile—surely a writer or journalist, though perhaps a foreign one, I thought. When my friend Carla Powell introduced us, he turned out to be half Greek and half Polish; he had lived in England since he was fifteen, and was currently Asia Editor of the *Financial Times*.

No one could doubt that the quality and passion of our romance was highly charged—Alain admitted I became an instant obsession for him and I, just as quickly, fell wildly in love. Within two months, when we felt we simply couldn't live apart, he moved in with Tasmin and me into our flat in Earl's Court—Tara was by then at boarding school at Cobham Hall having been thrown out of Queensgate for some forgotten misdemeanour—the beginning of her rebellious years. Our courtship was swift and passionate and a month later we became engaged at the romantic Galle Face Hotel in Columbo, Sri Lanka. I hadn't felt this ecstatic in years. But both caught in a maelstrom of fevered emotions Alain, more than once, threatened to leave if I didn't agree to marry him by a certain date. Naturally this made me wary but the plunge forward seemed inevitable. We were inextricably close, I wanted to make him happy and within eleven months I had succumbed.

I was very fond of his two young children Claudia and Jules and Alain got on reasonably well with my own two girls who were thirteen and eleven when we met. Claudia and Tasmin remain the best of friends to this day and are godmothers to each other's children which is a special gift from that time. Ours was an interesting life but the best times were when we away travelling with his job as Asia editor—he later became the *FT's* news editor. Alain took me numerous times to places I had always dreamed of; India, all over the Far East and South Pacific, China and Australia. Those were exhilarating days and the countries he showed me became a fascinating part of my life. I will always be grateful to him for that.

In April 1984 Alain's father had flown over from Paris, presumably to look me over as a suitable spouse. When he arrived at my flat, I couldn't help but notice was that his blue jeans would have been too tight on a man half his age. He was a lawyer who had lived in Paris for thirty years and was obviously keen to appear older-man 'cool' in that smoky Charles Aznavour 'toss me another Gauloises' kind of way. The trouble was he was Greek and couldn't quite pull it off. His own father had been a Supreme Court Judge in Alexandria in Egypt but it soon became abundantly clear his son had not inherited the impartiality gene normally essential, I would have thought, to pursuing a career in law. I knew that Monsieur Catzeflis had spent many years competing with his clever, infinitely more attractive and successful son, Alain. But I hoped I might dazzle him with what I thought was my most charming future-daughter-in-law smile before he quickly dashed all hope of solidarity. After saying a cursory, "Allo", he stepped over the threshold of my flat, looked round the walls and promptly remarked, "Did you get zee paintings and drawings in a junk yard or did your friends paint them?"

Well, that pretty well stopped me in my pre-filial tracks. Talk about putting his own big fat Greek foot in it. He continued by being unspeakably rude to me throughout dinner until his outraged son finally lost it, plonked him in the car and rushed him back to Heathrow. Charming fellow.

Alain's mother on the other hand was a gentle, timid soul—the Greek had probably done her in. A great Polish beauty in her youth, after the war she had moved to Alexandria where King Farouk, among others, was an admirer and a smitten Lawrence Durrell felt compelled to write her poems.

After her divorce from the Greek she left Egypt with her son Alain, first for Greece, then London, but slowly over time she withdrew from the harsh realities of life. I hardly knew her before she died but my abiding memory of her was at our wedding at the Chelsea Registry Office on the Kings Road in December. We had a small gathering of family and friends and were being married by a tough, impatient registrar. None of my family wanted me to go ahead with the marriage but we were deeply in love and this commitment seemed important. I wore a silk mushroom-coloured Bruce Oldfield dress with, as was then considered the height of fashion, broad shoulder pads that would have done the American Green Bay Packers proud. My Mama was sitting next to Alain's, whom she had never met, in the front row. Alain was in the middle of saying his vows to me when his normally reticent mother suddenly rose to her feet and exclaimed loudly to the congregation,

"Is It Time To Weep Now?" before promptly sitting down again. There immediately followed a stunned silence, that excruciating kind one dreads at a church wedding with the 'does anyone know of any lawful impediment...' bit and you pray desperately nobody does. I lowered my eyes and bit my lip to hold myself together. My mother and my sister Pods, wide grins on their faces, were less successful. Alain looked utterly mortified but somehow managed to continue with his vows. Was this an omen, I wondered fleetingly?

DAYAK TRIBE, BORNEO

Alain's job soon took us to Borneo where, after he had written a raft of stories, we took off to try to find a remote Dayak tribe in eastern Kalimantan. As the tribe lived deep in the rainforest, we could almost make ourselves believe it was one of those moments when travel was still exploration; a kind of Conradian adventure that appealed to us both. We managed to hitch a ride on a rickety old German trading boat travelling up the powerful Mahakam river. The aimiable captain was happy to have us on board for a couple of nights before dropping us off at a small outpost. We would have to find our own way into the forest. The boat chugged along at a reasonable pace through the murky waters of the largest river in East Kalimantan. Each night after sharing the crews' rations of fish, rice and vegetables, Alain and I slept on hard bunks below deck. The most memorable part of the journey was the family of freshwater dolphins which swam playfully beside the boat each day. There are only five rivers in the world inhabited by these fish-eating mammals, which differ noticeably in appearance from their marine cousins. Their snouts are four times as long, their eyes far smaller, their vision poor because of the darkened world in which they live.

The Dayaks were once greatly feared for their ancient tradition of head-hunting, banned many years ago by the Dutch colonisers. They believed supernatural strength was centred in the soul and head of humans and that fresh heads gave magical powers for communal protection. When the trading boat dropped us off we scrambled up the steep banks of the river to be greeted by laughing children and a few friendly men sitting round on logs. We were trying to explain that we wanted to go deep into the road-less rainforest when two Kalimantan dudes on flimsy motorbikes rolled up. Having discussed a price we were soon on the back of their bikes heading to where the tribe lived; for the next two hours we slithered over narrow muddy tracks through the undergrowth, our arms constantly lacerated by whippy branches. After a heavy rain the sun was high in the sky and the dark green leaves glistened with raindrops. The lush primal rainforest exposed tangled lianas hanging from the treetops; exotic birds flitted through the canopy as monkeys called out to each other.

Eventually we came round a corner into a large clearing and there in front of us was our Dayak stronghold, with a reasonably sized longhouse. But what a sight met our eyes. It was too much to have expected a Chief decked out in the latest tribal outfit with a headdress of glorious birds of the forest feathers, a loin cloth and a few ropes of Indonesian beads. A shaman jug-gling a few human bones wrapped in banana leaves wouldn't have gone amiss either. But the first thing we saw was the Chief in a tatty pair of shorts sitting on a wooden stool, his long black hair in Day-Glo pink plastic curlers—he was having a perm! His lips were moving in sync with loud western music blaring from an old ghetto blaster on the ground. The head of the clan barely acknowleged us but kept looking at a broken mirror to see how his hair-do was coming along. Behind him the other adult males in the tribe were sitting in a semi-circle, undergoing the same treatment, their hair curled up as tightly in pink as their Chief. This must be the Dayaks' annual Male Hair Beautifying Day. I found it impossible to conjure up images of them in rampant warrior stance.

In the background women and children were running after the few scruffy pigs; mangy looking dogs loped around and managed a short disinterested bark in our direction. Two or three scraggly fruit trees were growing around the longhouse, looking as if they hadn't produced anything edible in fifty years. It was a depressing scene. When invited into the longhouse, we still clung to a shred of hope as we climbed a ladder onto the communal platform and went inside. It was a long, empty, souless room. No shrunken heads, no decorative Ikats or subtle earth-coloured weavings, no wooden carvings, no women threading beads. No symbols or proof of their animist beliefs. *De nada*. Modern life seemed have completely destroyed the tribal culture and it was the western way they now craved. It was tragic, really. We couldn't see much point in staying and soon left the men to their curlers. We returned to the motorbikes and their sinewy owners, found our way back to the river and onto another boat going south.

After that dispiriting encounter we went to see something altogether more stimulating. Kelimutu is one of the most extraordinary volcanoes in the world. Over five thousand feet high, it lies in central Flores, a fertile island in Indonesia. The volcano contains three large crater lakes of varying colours high up on the summit. The 'Lake of Young Men and Maidens' is bright emerald green and separated by a narrow crater wall from the intense turquoise blue of the 'Enchanted Lake.' The third one, the 'Lake of Old People', lies nearby, enclosed in its own crater wall and is a deep ox-blood red; each colour was the result of chemical reactions in the minerals of the lake.

We left our guest house in the small village of Ende early in order to be at the summit by dawn, the only time you can get a brief glimpse of all three lakes. The drive was three bone-jolting hours in a tough old 4x4 up through the bamboo groves on a slippery mountain road. It was hard to believe the rickety wooden plank bridges would hold the weight of the car particularly when the forest became trickier to navigate, but we managed to reach the top just as dawn was breaking. The lakes, glistening in the clear morning sky, were breathingly beautiful and we gazed at them in wonder. Half an hour later the mist and clouds floated down and obscured the view. It was barely long enough to fix the vision in our minds, but it was worth it.

A week later we were sitting round a fire drinking beer on the beautiful island of Vanuatu in the South Pacific with a man whose grandfather was the last white missionary to be boiled in a pot and eaten by cannibals. He seemed pretty sanguine about it.

At the beginning of our marriage Alain and I bought a pretty four bedroom house in Fulham in London. In the eight years I lived there, a strange and impoverished old woman lived in the same street about seven doors down from us towards the Kings Road. She had dank wispy hair that had patently never been on close terms with a hairbrush and thick grey whiskers sprouted like wild ferns on her dimpled chin. The woman lived in a delapidated council house, had no money for heating or elecricity and would sit outside on a hard wooden bench nearby until the light grew too dark for her to read discarded newspapers. She was totally harmless and had no desire to speak to anyone; we couldn't understand how she survived but presumably she was given boxes of eggs, or found one or two somewhere. For whenever we left our houses first thing in the morning five or six residents in the street would find an empty eggshell placed on their car's aerial antenna. We never discussed it and became used to our unusual ornaments, but we all knew the old woman put them there, probably as some sort of communal greeting.

The reaffirmation of friendships has always been important to me and I was lucky to have many girlfriends in England—Appley Hoare of course, Claire Clifton, Jean Harvey, Jacinthe Rhodes, Sarah Michie, Earlene Azzam, Ingrid van Wagner. Ali Criado-Perez. Carolyn Hadden-Paton, kind, creative and effortlessly chic, was also one of them and her handsome son Geordie is my much-loved godson. Sarah's sweet daughter Flora is another cherished godchild.

Anne Morrison, whom I frequently saw, lived round the corner from me. She was tall and attractive with a good sense of humour, needed in her long career at the Foreign Office which included code-breaking during the Cold War. Her superb efficiency earned her an O.B.E. from the Queen. Anne was once ushering around a prominent government minister from Nigeria who was so grateful for all her help that at the end of the day he said to her in a very strong accent,

"You are so beautiful and so kind, I am now going to eat you".

Slightly alarmed but managing to keep him at bay, it was only later she realised that the gentleman had in fact said, "You are so beautiful and so kind. I am now going to Heathrow."

'GRAND ILLUSIONS'

Even though we were wrapped up in the delirium of romantic love, something happened after our recent marriage which gave my life an exciting added purpose. I entered the engrossing, often difficult world of writing books which has taken up a large part of my time ever since. The research is, of course, the fun, the exciting, part. Somehow I managed to find the discipline and determination, together with a love or at least liking for each subject, before getting down to the solitary business of actually writing. Because I have also always enjoyed drawing and painting and was completing a particular mural for my friend Claire Clifton's flat in London, I began to wonder what kind of interior murals were currently being painted in the country. I couldn't find any up to date books on the subject and while driving to Heathrow one day I had the one and only 'Eureka' moment of my life. Even though I had never written a book before, I would write one myself. I managed to get a small advance from Phaidon Publishers and so *Grand Illusions* began, a book on forty of the best British and American murals and *trompe l'oeil* paintings and the wealth of talented artists who painted them. Once Tom Leighton, a superb photographer who worked for major glossy international magazines including *The World of Interiors*, came into my life, off we went all over Britain and the States, from castles to mews houses; San Franciscan churches to New York lofts. It was hugely enjoyable, hard work and the best part was that I made friends with many of the artists.

A skilful artist's attempt at illusion provides an extra dimension to our need to dream and fantasize and at its best the mural should have intrinsic as well as decorative merit. At its most inspired it is art, representing the essence of a great cultural tradition of the Italian masters, Tiepolo, Veronese and Michelangelo, in the sumptuous palaces and churches of Italy. *Grand Illusions* was published in 1988 and, much to my eternal gratitude, is still used as a reference book in art schools, libraries and by artists.

When I was introduced to Claire in London, she had recently arrived with her Australian foreign correspondent husband Tony Clifton, the *Newsweek* bureau chief from Beirut, where he covered the war in the Middle East. Claire, an American and my birthday twin, was totally unique; a witty, creative, clever girl with a mass of red hair and beautiful skin, she became one of my dearest friends. Clothes, shoes, jewellery and scarves were a shopaholic passion and she wore them together in a highly individual way. She also wrote a number of well-regarded books on food as well as amusing articles for *Tatler*. After she moved to Sussex, her second marriage to a bi-sexual having collapsed, she missed living in London for the rest of her life,

"But Sloane Square is my spiritual home! I am meant to be there!" She was also adamant when reluctantly forced to go to Islington, 'I get such a dreadful headache if I have to travel north of Hyde Park." Perhaps it brought back memories of the famous English actor living there with whom she had a steamy affair many years before her marriages and who had a habit when they were in bed of scrawling 'Slave' in black ink all over her back. As she got older Claire developed severe, painful diabetes and not long before she died, she declared, "If I have to have my feet chopped off like Ella Fitzgerald I am going straight to Manolo Blahnik and tell him he has to make a sensational pair of shoes for my stumps!"

During my research trips around Britain, Alain, now the *Financial Times's* news editor, did his best to be an involved stepfather. He held the fort at home in London with Jasper, Tasmin's adored golden retriever whom we were lucky enough to have for thirteen years. We all loved dogs in general. After all, I had named Tara partly after the Nepalese Goddess of Compassion and partly after a friend's German shepherd I adored in Kenya. But to lose a beloved dog is like a bereavement. An awful grief. One misses everything about them—their smell, their loyalty, their enthusiasm and unconditional affection—forever.

By this time the children's father Dean had taken a year off from *Time* to become press secretary to the American Secretary of State, General Alexander Haig, in Washington. When President Reagan was shot after only seventy days in office, Haig wrongly blurted out to reporters his infamous twelve words, "As of now, I am in control here, in the White House." He wasn't. I know Dean felt on safer territory once back at *Time*.

His father and Ronald Reagan had been roommates at college where they were known as Elmer and 'Dutch' and kept up a correspondence for many years. After a stint in Jerusalem which he didn't entirely enjoy, Dean moved to Cairo as bureau head of *Time* magazine in the Middle East with a new wife—Peter Jenning's Lebanese ex-sister-in-law, Marina. Tara and Tasmin naturally went to stay with them and got to explore the treasures and secret places of Egypt over the years.

EXECUTION DAY, CHINA

Memories of certain trips can be seared into the mind and so it was when Alain and I travelled to southern China where he was to write about the ethnic minorities living on the borders with Vietnam, Laos and Burma. We were heading for Yunnan province which had the largest number of the fifty-five groups, some of whom had been given regional autonomy in order to keep alive the traditions and faith of China's ethnic peoples. We flew out of Hong Kong in September 1985 to Kunming, the capital of the province. There we were met by our Chinese interpreter for the next three weeks, a tall, bespectacled, scholarly clever-clogs who, besides his translation skills was there to report our every move back to Beijing. Belonging to the Han tribe, he told us fairly quickly that his father was a People's Liberation Army (PLA) officer, the formidable military branch of the Communist Party. Fu Manchu, as I soon nicknamed him, was keen, ambitious, bossy, with not an ounce of humour. He was obviously destined for big things, studying Russian and American politics at an institute in Beijing, and mentioning that he would like nothing more than, "To give the Vietnamese another lesson."

I soon realised that our haughty companion looked down on western women and had zero time for me, treating me throughout as an inferior interloper. Meanwhile, Kunming was buzzing—people on bicycles; sitting around talking and smoking long thin pipes with their small birds kept in wooden cages beside them; others busy doing *chi-gong* exercises in leafy squares. Nearly everyone was dressed in the dull Chinese uniform of blue, grey or green tunic and trousers with men wearing flat cotton Mao caps. Rows of women squatting on the dirt roads, laid out their fresh produce in neat piles. Food in China is some of the best and freshest I have ever eaten, coming daily from nearby farms and fields.

In the old city of Kunming we ambled down streets full of traditional wooden Chinese houses, primitive and charming. All Chinese must belong to a unit and the poor were allowed to sell their produce only once their allotted amount had been given to their collective. Majong was being played by men in small tea houses. The town's thriving tea culture dates back over a thousand years when the city was a major part of the southern Silk Road. The Chinese are early risers and the next morning I had acupuncture for my painful back from a famous old Chinese professor who was quiet and dignified as he stuck eight needles in my eyelids, two in the top and two in the bottom. It was extremely painful as the needles were thick, unlike the finer Western ones we are used to. It brought tears to my eyes, a few of which trickled down my face, which was a great loss of face in front of Fu Manchu. But anyone who thinks that acupuncture in China is painless is talking through their coolly hat.

We were flying to Simao the next day and arrived early at the airport. Old versions of 'Yanky Doodle Dandy', 'Swanee River', the 'Theme from Dallas' and *Swan Lake* were being played. Our manky-looking Russian prop plane was delayed due to cloudy skies. "No radar. Pilot might not see mountain," the man at desk most helpfully informed us. Most of these old internal planes often had serious metal fatigue. As the waiting dragged on I increasingly dreaded a radar-less Chinese pilot who I was sure would hit the side of something large and I'd never see my beloved children again. Yet somehow we arrived safely in Simao and immediately started a four hour drive to Xishwan Banaa, through lush, fertile countryside. I was soon entranced by the huge groves of curling bamboo and the rich rice paddies with women in straw hats bending over busily picking. Halfway there we stopped at a State Rest House and were given a feast of fried bees and their maggots, fried ferns and sweet pea leaves. In front of our hosts I smiled at Alain, who was lapping up the creatures, and uttered, "I just can't face the maggots," but he urged me on.

"Try and manage two, just out of politeness," which I did and nearly retched.

By now Fu Manchu was becoming increasingly disdainful with an unpleasant Mandarin attitude towards peasants. Also, one night over dinner he casually remarked, "All scholars think deeply while all journalists are very superficial." Another helpful comment.

We were driven to a very basic hotel on the outskirts of town which looked across the Mekong river, the largest river in South East Asia. Banana trees, mangoes and hibiscus bushes, covered with huge red and yellow blooms, burst out of the rich red soil. Our dawn chorus the following morning was a cacophony of cockerels accompanied by the inexorable hawking of the Chinese next door. Everywhere we went we were followed and stared at; foreigners are seldom seen in this remote spot of southern China. Alain tried to buy some sneakers but as Eastern feet are much smaller; nothing fitted him, much to the amusement of our growing coterie.

The first minority we visited was the Dai. It was the rainy season and the rice fields were as green as emeralds. The women were exceptionally pretty with Thai or Burmese features, and wore graceful sarongs instead of the uniform tunic and trousers. Their houses were built on stilts with two large rooms inside, verandahs and floors made of bamboo; roofs covered in thin clay slates or thatch. We spoke to a small smiling Dai woman, well over seventy, who was weaving on her verandah and invited us up. Her family had lived in the village for many generations and she proudly showed us her sparse living room. Although you can be invited by the owner to look at the bedroom from the door, it is forbidden to go inside. Beautiful children and curious young mothers with babies swaddled on their backs came to see us. The Dai people, who are mainly Buddhist, took us to a temple where all the monks were boys; they stay there until the age of eighteen then return to their everyday lives. After taking off our shoes we went inside to find it full of people sitting on the floor scattered with silk-covered mattresses for the old. Pieces of gold and silver paper together with paper money surrounded small niches for their newly dead, along with their pillows, blankets and few belongings. There was a slim bamboo ladder up to each niche. The people at the Temple were inquisitive and the women fascinated by my brass bangles which they thought were gold until they weighed them in their delicate hands and smiled knowingly.

That night we went to have a meal with a Dai family, a young couple with a small daughter. They were obviously well off for Dais, the husband being a solid citizen with five merits. They had five bicycles, a tractor; many pigs and chickens which lived under the house. We sat on the verandah and devoured the best Chinese meal we had ever had; roughly twelve delicious dishes in all, some wrapped up in banana leaves; cooked on two fires in the one large spotlessly clean room. The wife ate with us while her young child ran around shooing out the chickens. After dinner we gave the hospitable couple gifts and went home to talk about our day as we sat looking out over the pawpaw trees to the fast flowing Mekong.

We visited other villages and wherever we went exquisite butterflies, large with long tails looking like the children's kites, fluttered in front of us. The villages were quiet as most people were busy working in the fields but the few inhabitants we met were pleasant, and curious. We travelled on to Mando to visit the Jino, an impoverished tribe recently recognized by the government, and decidedly unfriendly—they had last seen a European over two years ago. Their children were only just beginning to be educated, their houses were far smaller and in order to prevent the spoiling of the rainforests they were not allowed to grow rice themselves, instead being given it by the government. They believed strongly in wood and plant Gods and were more primitive than any African tribe I have ever seen. Killing dogs and pigs for their celebrations was natural but if there happened to be a witch in the village at the time, she also got the chop.

On the drive back to Simao we stopped at a long line of lavatories not far from a village. When I opened one of the wooden doors there were no partitions on the other side, just a fifty yard trench open to the elements where numerous people either stood or squatted. We drove on into the town for the night and spotted four barefoot women from the Hani tribe in the hills wearing striking headdresses covered with big round silver metal studs. They were shy and turned away when we asked to photograph their lovely high cheek-boned faces and eye-catching outfits. Men sat round on rickety chairs smoking thick bamboo bongs. A woman carrying a large fat duck under her arm came up and looked at us with great curiosity.

Later that afternoon, we noticed many hand painted notices and posters pinned up on the trees and walls of the main street. Some had photographs of men held fast by soldiers, others with their heads bowed in a courtroom. There were paintings and descriptions everywhere of what crime the perpetrator was supposed to have committed. It appeared these unfortunates were not necessarily murderers but thieves, rapists and hooligans. One had dealt in pornography: 'yellow literature', as the Chinese called it.

After an early breakfast of tasty Chinese dumplings Fu Manchu suggested to Alain they go for a walk down the main street as there was to be a public execution. However macabre, I was cross I wasn't allowed to go because I was a foreign woman, fully aware that every Chinese woman, man or child was allowed to witness it. Half an hour later our interpreter came back to say I had been granted permission to go. The town had an expectant air about it with hordes of excited people pouring in from the countryside and lining the streets. All schools were closed and a public holiday was declared for an Execution Day. Children were happily running around with their friends and I watched a woman having her hair done in a salon. A very primitive, practically iron-age set of curlers, each with three foot long twisted brown flex, hung from a round metal ring suspended from the ceiling.

A group of soldiers, dressed in olive green uniforms and caps with a red star and arm bands, marched past us. When we arrived at the main square we found it was filled with roughly five thousand people. The law court officials, their scribes and women sat on chairs on a platform and kept refilling their cups with jasmine tea. The whole atmosphere was one of great festivity, women sat knitting on their small chairs which many of them had brought along—Madame Defarge from Dickens' *A Tale of Two Cities* sprang to mind. In front of the platform were two rows of twenty-six men, each with an armed police guard forcing the prisoners' shaved heads down. As each man's sentence was passed he stood on a small rostrum before being frogmarched back to another line. No emotion was shown either by the prisoners or the crowds except during the sentencing of one man who had been accused of rape was given forty-four years. A rippling murmur went around the throng. It seems that rape is considered the Chinese's greatest crime. Criminals to be executed had a red tick at the bottom of their posters all over town. A large poster in the square during the sentencing proclaimed, 'Heavy punishments on criminals are not political.'

The prisoners were then put into the trucks to be paraded along the streets to add to their humiliation. The parade was led by officials in jeeps, followed by white-uniformed police, two on each motorbike and one in a sidecar—about twelve in all. Behind them trundled a truck packed full of green-uniformed soldiers, one with his machine-gun perched on the roof of the cab which he bent over in a state of readiness. Next came five lorries with the prisoners whose heads were forced down over the side of the truck so that the people and the children could jeer at them. By now the crowd along the route was about six deep. Most of the criminals were very young and looked at the ground though a few glanced briefly at the crowds nearest to them. Two of them were girls, both placed at the front of the trucks. The vehicles rumbled over the packed earthen road and the swelling throng grew noisier as they made their way to the local football field where the main event was to take place. We were pushed along with the crowd. Once there the men who were condemned to death stood silently in a line across the field while an official again read out their supposed list of crimes and grievances. Each man was shot once in the back of the head and fell instantly to the ground. I immediately left after the first one fell, feeling if these executions were happening in this small town in the middle of nowhere, it must be going on all over China. It was a sobering thought.

Two days later and much to the chagrin of Fu Manchu, we insisted on stopping off at a market village called Baitam. Peopled by the Sani it was the most colourful market I have ever been to, surrounded by houses built of mud and brick with traditional sweeping tiled roofs. The people were poor and the place was chaotic. Families arrived at the market with their wooden carts laden with produce, some of them pulled by small ponies or mules. Women carried their smallest children in panniers which they balanced on thin poles across their shoulders. Many wore simple tribal turquoise costumes edged with broad black strips and colourful, embroidered patterns. The vibrant blue on the clothes flashed everywhere, complemented by the women's coral and turquoise earrings and topped by intricate head coverings. Both men and women wore wide-brimmed straw hats and I noticed two old women leaning against a tree with bound feet in tiny, beautifully embroidered, three to four inch blue and red shoes. Men wore blue jackets and the oldest of them squatted on the ground smoking long delicately-made wooden pipes. Rows of women sat on the red murram earth selling vegetables from the surrounding countryside—ginger, spring onions, melons, kale, root vegetables and spices, heads of pigs. They smiled at us whilst chatting to each other. The sight of such vivid colour, noise and bustle was glorious. Fu Manchu became agitated when Alain began photographing the scene. He couldn't understand our curiosity for such dirt and poverty and our enthusiasm disturbed him. But we only saw colour and beauty, movement and smiling faces. I bent down to a baby bear being lead on a string by a young man he had captured in the forest. He was going to sell it to a restaurant where they would kill it for bear paw soup.

By now I could barely speak to Fu Manchu so intense was my dislike. He was continually terrified we might see something that would reflect badly on him, which is why we were only allowed ten minutes to take photos of a minority tribe or five minutes' diversion from the planned day, the official reason being 'your security' which was rubbish. But that evening back in Kunming we were taken to the best little restaurant in town, next to the University. It was owned by Mr. Tong, an ancient Burmese who had been imprisoned for seventeen years by the Chinese during the 1950s because he owned three dance halls. He was now raking in the money from his restaurant which was frequented by foreign teachers from the University. We talked to an American couple who told us a strange little story about the importance of 'face' in China:

"A professor was due to give a lecture to some students but couldn't come, so sent his assistant. It was a great loss of face for the young people who had to be told that the eminent professor was dead. Thus his face was saved for not appearing, the assistant's face was saved and the students' faces were saved. If the professor comes next year, they will just resurrect him. The Chinese have a strange concept of the truth."

In Chengdu, capital of Sichuan province, we stayed in a Stalinesque monstrosity of a hotel and were met by endless officials who smiled and bowed and scraped; who never told you the truth; who were the least interesting or informative bureaucrats. Our first official dinner on our arrival in China had gone on for so long I felt my eyelids drooping and my whole body slowly sliding under the table. No one spoke English except Fu Manchu; we spoke no Mandarin and all we did was smile weakly at each other and knock back the fermented Shaojiu, which tasted like sweaty socks. This time Alain went alone.

Early on Sunday we were taken to an energetic village near Chengdu blaring out western music where we were introduced to a woman business genius who was well on her way to becoming the province's first millionaire. She possessed the only telephone in the whole area and had made her money by making shoe soles out of waste material for the standard Chinese canvas black shoes. Two hundred peasant households worked for this lively thirty-four year old who had had her schooling abruptly stopped when she was ten because her family was Nationalist Chinese. That evening we went to a new invention in China. A small building opposite the hotel had a band playing both western and classical Chinese music, known as "Linkage of Friendship Dancing", and we managed to wangle our way in so Alain could interview the manager. Couples were trying rather cluelessly to teach each other the foxtrot and waltz. A few women were very dolled up, no doubt hoping to find true love or at least a twinkling possibility. Beer was sold and dancing stopped promptly at ten o'clock. A young Chinese man came up and politely asked Alain if he could dance with me which I found rather endearing but alas his foxtrot was all over the place and we constantly tripped over each other's feet. It was obvious the young Chinese desperately needed this type of recreational fun as their lives appeared so drab and dull. Wherever we travelled, if they spoke a smattering of English they enjoyed coming up to talk to us and I felt their enthusiasm appealing.

Our final port of call was Beijing, a city with broad avenues spilling over with a river of bicycles. Officials were busy getting ready for National Day where a big parade would take place in Tiananmen Square, this, of course, four years before it became infamous for its student blood bath. We made a quick trip to the spectacular Great Wall of China and with only few people visiting, I managed on more than one section of the steep wall to slide down the rounded banister rail and save my back from hundreds of steps. Back in Beijing we visited the exquisite Temple of Heaven and Mao's Memorial Hall where the Chairman's body lay in a crystal coffin. Originally, due to shoddy embalming and fierce heat, Mao's facial features had spread alarmingly, so he was hurriedly put in a cooler place with very dim lighting. In dazzling contrast was the exquisite sight of the Forbidden City with its five marble bridges stretching over the moat to the Gate. In the peaceful inner square, the rich terracotta red and sweeping tiled roofs of the slender-pillared buildings remain such an exquisite symbol of old China. The one that Mao wanted to tear down and destroy.

Alain and I obviously shared a passion for travelling and in all our trips together over the years, we often came across the unusual. One spring we were driving through Morocco and had arrived in the magical southern city of Ourzazat. As the sun came up undimmed by dust the following morning, we decided it would be a good day to venture further into the desert, the area where old caravan routes crossed the Sahara from Marrakesh and Fez to Timbuktu and old Sudan carrying gold, slaves and salt. We were driving over a hill when a huge black mass moved like a storm towards us, quickly covering half the sky. Within seconds of stopping the car a vast swarm of locusts tore into us, beating their wings in a futile flutter after hitting the windscreen. For forty minutes we watched them fly past in a dark cloud, leaving chaos in their wake. The Berber farmers' hard labour in their fields came to nothing as all their valuable crops were destroyed, ruined by the gobbling insects.

We drove across the shifting golden sands, passing nomads and traders with their camels plodding slowly across the land, and eventually arrived in the Draa Valley. It stretches from Ourzazat to the Sahara Desert and is home to the historic Kasbahs of the great southern caravan route. In the distance the snow-capped Atlas mountains were glowing against the late afternoon sky as Alain and I headed for a small oasis high on a hilltop. We left the car in the lee of the huge sandy dune before starting up the steep incline. As he had been born and brought up in Alexandria in Egypt, Alain spoke Arabic which proved useful when halfway up we met two Berber men dressed in black who were coming down to inspect us. Delighted to find someone new with whom to talk, they promptly invited us to share their evening meal and we soon found ourselves sitting on carpets outside a large black tent on the crest of the dune. A bonfire roared and endless cups of mint tea, poured from one of the big brass samovars, were passed round. Part of a sheep was being roasted over a crackling fire, along with broad beans and a type of couscous which had been prepared by women in their village far below in the valley. As the night settled around us, a new moon shone brightly and the sky filled with stars above the black silhouette of palm trees. While the men and Alain spoke quietly to each other, the desert silence was occasionally broken by the crowing of a single cockerel. For the next couple of hours it seemed the vast twinkling canopy above us was larger and more infinite than anywhere else on earth.

After dinner, two Berber women ventured up from the valley and when they saw me, they quickly turned on their heels and returned to their village. Half an hour later they reappeared, this time with a handful of other women carrying an embroidered white Arab dress and veil which they invited me to put on. Shyly, they arranged my hair under the delicate white veil, put kohl around my eyes with the utmost care and covered me with sparkling gold jewellery which glittered in the firelight. I was now complete as a Berber bride.

Once they had finished arranging the finery the women on either side of me, now laughing and singing, reached for my hands as we danced slowly for the men around the glowing fire. I look back on that night as an enchanted time.

Although there were times of great happiness and harmony during our marriage, there was no comfort in the memory of Alain's darker moods. These were the wild seasons. Alain's two demons—his manic depression, for which he took Lithium, his life-long medication, confused me, while his deep-rooted jealousy and possessiveness frequently upset me. Days slipped by when he was in the midst of one of his dark malaises. He found it difficult to rise early as was his usual habit. Instead he would lie back on our bed, his eyes searching the grey skies through the windows. On those troubled mornings I hoped nothing calamitous would befall him—nothing irrevocable which could change the pattern of our lives. Although he clearly appreciated even my smallest gesture of affection, like many depressives he remained apart as if musing upon an abstraction.

After one of these difficult episodes we took ourselves off on a working holiday to Sri Lanka. It was a beautiful day in Galle, the sea enticing in its sparkling blue. Alain was already swimming a short way off to my left and, taking a break from writing, I stepped into the water's edge. I floated happily over the swells and dived cleanly under the first few waves but wasn't long before I realised an undertow was building up and slowly dragging me further out. I began to find myself in a new landscape, the water rising so high that I could no longer see the shore. I tried to turn back when a huge wave broke over me before I could dive under the onrushing swell. It tossed me up and rolled me over like a seasoned crocodile, then hurled me down into its spinning turbulence on the sea bed. However hard I tried I couldn't seem to gain any purchase against the pulling of the undertow. I can still feel that panic rising as I was about to be sucked out to the horizon. I started shouting 'Alain' at the top of my voice but he couldn't hear me. Suddenly a whole cliff of water collapsed over me. I could hardly breathe as it picked me up along with cloudy sand and bits of driftwood and seaweed. Tumbling over and over beneath the surface it rushed towards the shore where I was flung unceremoniously onto the beach. The strength of the wave had completely ripped off my pretty green bikini. I lay there naked and shocked as my husband rushed along the beach to see what had happened. He covered me in a towel, put his arm round me and took me back to the house.

BOOZY BANGKOK

For Christmas 1988, Alain and I decided to take our four children plus Tara's best friend Melissa on a three week trip to Thailand and India, two countries we both felt passionate about. All went swimmingly at first. Beaches on Ko Phi Phi, the exquisite Royal Palaces and floating markets in Bangkok, riding elephants deep into the forests in Chang Mai and exotic hill tribes around Chang Rai on the border with Burma, engrossed them, thank the Lord. You never quite know with teenagers.

The trouble began when we boarded our Thai Airlines plane to Delhi, a five hour trip away. Off we flew, everyone happily ensconced in their seats with cokes and peanuts, rubbish food and films no one had ever heard of. Various exotic palace hotels in Jaipur, Jodphur and Udaipur in Rajasthan had been carefully booked months before. Alas, we had never been told that in late December and early January there is often a thick fog lying over the Indian capital. The precise time is unpredictable and it was just our luck that it was lying there like some vast malevolent creature from the swamp determined to spit us out us once we hovered over Delhi. We were not allowed to land and were ordered to fly back to Bangkok. I was at the peak of my fear of flying, convinced that each plane I was on was going to fall out of the sky.

During the outward trip the Thai air stewards and stewardesses had been liberal in pouring out drinks for the passengers and a large number of people were becoming rather too jolly. A family of Indians sat directly in front of us, a large man and his wife, a daughter and teenage son whose entire leg was in plaster. The father had been drinking non stop and once he was completely plastered, he started smacking his poor wife around the face and then demanded another drink which the by now terrified stewardess meekly brought him; we were soon convinced he had probably beaten up the poor boy as well. Instead of dealing with the man the crew turned a blind eye and carried on swaying charmingly through the cabins.

After arriving back and sitting on the tarmac in Bangkok for a couple of hours, the decision was made by the Thai equivalent of the Wright brothers to once again tackle the second leg back to Delhi. Midway we were hit by the mother of all storms. It became so bad that I was convinced I saw the wings of the plane flapping in the wind as the plane sliced sideways through the night. For hours it bucked and fell hundreds of feet at a time, leaving my heart not only in my mouth but on top of my skull. This flight was becoming just too scary and despite the fact that the Wailing Wall was back in Jerusalem, I was beating my head against the seat in front in order to control my rising panic. My younger daughter, Tasmin, was lying with her head on my lap, sick with a nasty Thai bug, but when I couldn't take it a second longer I just stood up, turned round and waved wildly to all our children to catch their attention.

"I love you all, darlings," I shouted rather dramatically before plonking myself down again and putting Tasmin's head back on my lap. I might as well have been saying goodbye. Tara and Melissa who were six rows behind us pretended I was just some deranged woman they didn't know. My stepchildren Claudie and Jules tried not to giggle. Tasmin was too sick to really care. I might have embarrassed them but at least they knew I loved them.

After a mindbogglingly frustrating five hours we arrived back in Delhi to be met with the same wretched problem. Back to Bangkok goddammit— it would be a twenty hour plane ride by then. It was fast becoming a nightmare, added to which many of the passengers were now seriously drunk. Suddenly in mid air, the most befuddled of these, the original Indian basher, obviously lost the will to live. I was just on point of shouting to the air crew, channeling Eliza Doolittle at the Races, "Move your blooming feet—tie up the rat-arsed twit ", when the man staggered over to the door of the plane and tried to pull the lever open so he could jump out, probably dragging his cowering family with him. As he was slurrily shouting in broken English, Alain and another passenger, immediately seeing the danger, leapt out of their seats and rugby-tackled him to the floor. It was like something out of a movie. He was quickly trussed up like a prize turkey and put back in his seat until we reached the tarmac back in Bangkok. Absolutely nothing was done there and the sozzled fool and the plane again sat waiting to leave yet again for Delhi in a few hours. Alain, furious, got up and demanded that the Captain take the entire Asian family off the plane otherwise we would all refuse to fly.

They were eventually booted off but by that time we were so fed up with the whole shebang we got off too and took a flight to Bombay. But we missed all our New Year stays in the palace hotels and the seven of us had to doss down in Rajasthan where we could. However India is overwhelmingly beguiling and we still managed to have a marvellous time. I still do whenever I stay with my generous friend Pippa Clarke, who I have known since my twenties, and her partner Siddhartha, in their glorious Raj-style house in Delhi, before we travel together to the four corners of Rajasthan.

A WILD RIDE

If my first marriage was easy and considered, my second was passion and obsession. I was probably not always as patient as I should have been when dealing with Alain's manic-depression, regarding some of it as self-indulgent. Looking back, I think I just found it difficult being embroiled in an affliction of which I had never had any previous experience. But it must have been equally hard for him having to hide his mental problems at work where he was considered a brilliant editor, one of the best in what was then still known as Fleet Street. Instead, it was kept for home—a pretty normal thing to do, I accept. But what made things worse was his destructive jealousy which started to blunt the freedom of my personality. In some ways I was increasingly allowing myself to become diminished, less outgoing—and so inevitably I began to feel small pangs of unhappiness.

That particular year the Chelsea Arts Club Ball was being held at the Royal Albert Hall in London. Since it was fancy dress my sister Pods and I dressed up as Swiss milkmaids looking a bit like 'Julie-Andrews-skipping-up -your-nearest-Alpine-meadow.' All that was missing was a cow and a milk pail. We thought our costumes were rather winsome—tightly nipped-in waists, puffy sleeves and square tops edged with white embroderie anglaise which showed just a hint of chest. Todd, my energetic brother-in-law, thought his wife looked very pretty and as he is one of the world's natural dancers, he soon whisked her off to the dance floor. Alain didn't like me revealing a smidgeon of cleavage to other men but it wasn't exactly as if my boobs were out on display, dancing their own pneumatic rhumba. As he and I were twirling round the floor, a slightly inebriated man, unknown to either of us, made some vaguely flirtatious remark to me and that was it. Pow! In the middle of the dance floor, in front of hundreds of people having a fabulous time, my husband socked the man straight in the kisser. As he fell to the floor Alain grabbed my arm and pulled me like some flapping goose out of the Albert Hall. Once outside he complained,

"It's all your bloody fault for wearing that outfit," and took me home. All so embarrassing and unnecessary.

Little by little I changed without even realising it as I tiptoed around Alain's fragility. Most days I wore loose sweaters up to my neck over long flowing skirts and boots, looking increasing like some poor Niqab-covered Sultana lost in the midst of Fulham. Though I often pondered upon his actions between his spoken words of love, I kept my thoughts to myself and struggled to keep hidden any welling resentment, especially as this was my second marriage and I desperately wanted it to work. Besides, I loved him.

A memory floats back to me of my sensitive and perceptive seventeen year old daughter Tasmin, whom Alain adored, occasionally asking me, "Mummy, are you happy, really?" and I would say, "Of course darling," as I walked upstairs to our bedroom. But after nearly six years I began to find myself navigating my days between the increasing divergence of our needs and the passionate love that had always bound us.

Then one fine day in early May 1989 I flew into London from San Francisco where I had been researching a new book for Phaidon on contemporary American and British portrait painting. That afternoon, riddled with jet-lag, I was having a nap. Alain arrived back early from the office, woke me up as he sat down beside me and without missing a beat said,

"I am leaving. I want my space."

His last words flung at me as he left the bedroom, which only a careless, self-absorbed man could say,

"You'll be fine. You're a strong woman."

Ten minutes later he was gone and I never saw him again.

I felt broken. Devastated. I stayed in bed for two weeks, never having been more vulnerable or helpless in my life.

Getting back on track

THE LOVE AND patience given to me by my girls was invaluable at that unhappy time. We talked of the often imperceptible times when you begin to diverge in a relationship, those tiny little moments that corrode, until I began to draw my sadness inside, not wanting to further burden my children with their mother's troubles. And as I did, a small seed of relief slowly began to sprout that no longer would I have to be the main focus of Alain's mercurial temperament.

My gorgeous Tara, a tall, intelligent girl with long blonde hair, had long been expelled from Cobham Hall. I think a bottle of wine in the woods with two other girls might have been involved. She attended a London tutorial where she got her four 'A' levels. She also met and fell in love with Marlon Richards there, the son of Keith Richards of the Rolling Stones. Within a year they would be off to New York where she was going to take an English and Drama degree at the University of New York while the charming, artistic Marlon went to Parsons School of Design. Keith very kindly lent them his huge flat in the East Village to live in which was handy. I stayed there when he and his beautiful model wife Patti Hansen threw Tara a sumptuous twenty-second birthday party.

Tasmin, also tall and beautiful with long dark hair and a quieter nature, had nearly finished a foundation course at Byam Shaw School of Art in north London and had been signed up by Models 1. Deep down she knew she wasn't really suited to the modelling world emotionally and only worked

145

intermittently. She had begun dating Rupert Norman, Melissa's eldest brother whom we had all known since he was eighteen at Eton and who now worked in the City. Three years later the two had a romantic winter wedding in a church designed by Christopher Wren, on the river at Twickenham near the large Georgian house Rupert and his siblings had been brought up in with his mother and stepfather, Rosey and Ben Goodden.

Dean flew over from America to give Tasmin away. My daughter looked ethereal, utterly glorious, in a simple white dress and floor-length veil with her long hair swept back under a tiara and veil. Rupert looked dashing with his light brown wavy hair, smiling blue eyes and a flowery waistcoat under his morning coat. I, on the other hand, was told by a guest I looked like Charles II after the hairdresser had gone tonto with the curling and blow-drying. But it was such a happy day.

Mind you, at the end of Dean's long speech he just managed to squeeze me in, saying, "... and of course we mustn't forget the (little) woman on the ground...", like I was some half-baked hunchback. Peter Jennings nudged me and whispered, "Nice one, Dean."

Alas, he had never forgiven me.

As for Tasmin's modelling, ten years later, after she won a competition out of a thousand girls and was presented at the Ritz with a prize, money and a further modelling contract, she gave the whole thing up and concentrated on the first of her four delicious boys, Cal, Jago, Zac and Fin—who all call me 'Bibi', Swahili for grandmother. Rupert is one of those rare men—kind, caring, principled and a great cook; a Wikipedian trough of knowledge about the blues, rock, pop, punk music and history; a fanatic Chelsea football fan since he was eight who still takes his equally ardent sons along to the games. I enjoy my son-in-law's dry sense of humour. We were talking about all the poor old people fading away in care homes the other day and I said to him,

"When I get too old, please will you just hit me on the head with a frying pan."

Quick as a flash Rupert said to his youngest son,

"Fin, can you just nip into the kitchen and get one, please."

Cheeky chap.

MARY ANNE—LIFE ON THE EDGE

Towards the end of my second marriage, my dear friend, Mary Anne Fitzgerald, a stunning blonde and intrepidly honest journalist in Kenya, was arrested and imprisoned in a Nairobi jail. Criminals and prostitutes shared the squalor and dirt bucket in the filthy twelve by six foot cell into which she was shoved. She was soon deported from her home in Kenya and lost everything—her house, her job, her friends and African life. She was forty-two. Through articles in the *Financial Times* and the *Sunday Times*, she had made an enemy of President Daniel arap Moi, leader of the nation and head of the armed forces. As she freely admits, she had been foolish to expose the unpalatable truths of a rotting political system, the corruption and tyranny inherent in many an African country. Playing with political fire was to change her life when the President decided he wanted her head on a platter. An astute woman, M.A. and her younger daughter Petra were driven by a friend to the Tanzanian border, a country where they would also be *persona non grata* due to its treaty with Kenya and Uganda. Once across the border the two were on the run with little money or food until they eventually arrived in England where Tara, her eldest daughter would join them.

Used to living among Samburu warriors, dodging bullets, or scrambling for cover under a canopy of trees from attacking MiG fighter jets trying to blast her convoy with high explosives and phosphorus bombs in Ethiopia's civil war, M.A. was a fearless correspondent passionately in love with Africa's magic. On arriving in grey, cold London, she found her first year of exile profoundly difficult but it was was there that M.A. wrote her book *Nomad*, an account of her journeys and political writings in sub-Saharan Africa. It is a heartfelt testament by a white African in search of her roots amid the turmoil and tragedy of modern Africa.

Ten years later, detention finally lifted and living back in Kenya, M.A. fell in love with a handsome middle-aged American named Wayne in charge of United Nations security in Somalia. He had once led a clandestine militia of Hmong to reconnoitre the Ho Chi Minh trail in the Vietnam war and was later a founding member of Delta Force, the US Army equivalent to the British SAS. Wayne might have been a gung-ho, secretive Vet but he was also a tall, silver-haired, Alpha charmer. The wedding was to take place on the beach at the coast in Galu but by mid morning on the day, M.A's outfit was still being completed on the old-fashioned Singer sewing machine on the verandah. Like many Kenyan girls, she was quite relaxed about the domestic side of life.

A small *rondavel* in the garden enclosed a shower and basin for the bride-to-be's *toilette*. Yellow geckos darted up the walls and whispering palm fronds rustled outside in the breeze. M.A. started to panic as she began washing her hair.

"I'm not sure I want to go though with this," she said to me. "Should I get on with marrying the man or trot swiftly down the beach?".

Having once gone through the same last minute doubts myself, I cluck-clucked encouragingly and told her to stick with the wedding scenario.

"It's just nerves, completely normal. I'll get you a strong cup of tea", I said and quickly darted off to the kitchen in the main house where the cook helped me liberally lace the tea with a large dose of brandy to help the blushing bride along.

Back in the rondavel I found my reluctant friend drowning in shampoo and uncertainty under the longest shower in bridal history, While she dried her thick blonde hair and fiddled with her ill-fitting gold and silver dress, I nipped off once again to the kitchen and brought back another cup of fortifying tea with its miraculous ingredient. By the third cup M.A. was definitely more mellow, glowing with a large grin spreading from cheek to cheek.

The next task was to escort the bride down the beach to where her beloved Somali friends, looking dignified and resplendent in their turbans and crisp white finery, were holding the camel she was to ride up to the ceremony. Somehow, with the help of Tara and Petra, they managed to hoist her on board. The vision that appeared up the beach was, however, magnificent: her gorgeous face showed no sign from overdoing the brandy. M.A. also managed to sit side-saddle in Manolo Blahniks without falling off which must have been quite a feat. The camel rose splendidly to the occasion; two tall branches of pink bouganvillea were tied on to the pummel and M.A., her hair blowing in the wind, held them aloft as she glided like Gertrude Bell across the desert. Behind rode her maid of honour, Orgei, a beautiful young Borana girl wearing a long black and white veil floating out like a fan over her camel's flanks.

The guests that greeted them were resplendently dressed—a Ghanaian man in emerald green robes, his wife in a voluminous yellow outfit, Kenyans in colourful traditional dress and old Kenya hands in pale linen jackets and kikois. Quite a contrast to Wayne's friends who had flown over from America, some of whom were still Marines, and called every female above twelve years old 'Ma'am'. They were very formal, very stiff, with horrible crewcuts, looking as if they had just stepped in as extras for the film An Officer and a Gentleman, without possessing an iota of Richard Gere's good looks. The ceremony was conducted by an African pastor under a baobab tree and M.A. and Wayne seemed relaxed and happy. The Marines no doubt thought they had stumbled upon a den of iniquity with louche white and black Kenyans happily mixing and dancing together through the night.

But alas, Wayne the Vet turned out to be a rotter—a chronic liar, permanently unfaithful, dishonourable and unkind. After constant trying on M.A's part to save the marriage, the couple eventually divorced. For all the memorable wedding, my dear friend is far better off without the scum-bag.

After leaving Mary Anne I flew back to London where I had the misfortune to be placed in a mixed ward of men and women in a hospital in Chelsea. This practice had been the brilliant brainchild of the Conservative Government to prevent the National Health Service having any empty beds. I was in there to have a long planned osteotomy operation. Without getting into veterinary detail, it meant slicing through the bones below the tractor accident knee and reattaching the lower leg back on at a straighter angle. That was to be followed by a full leg cast and crutches for six weeks. The only thing that took my mind off my woes was the strange assortment of bedfellows on the ward.

In the bed opposite me lay a heavy middle-aged man. He was under the illusion he was so devilishly attractive that had he been able to hop off his bed, he could have any nurse or half-comatose female patient on the floor whenever he chose. He was a *wink, wink, nudge, nudge* kind of guy and kept gazing at me as if I was a prime rib sent up from Le Gavroche. The very last thing you want when you feel wretched is some slime ball giving you the eye. Long sympathetic looks came my way as I was being sick for the umpteenth time into my grey cardboard bowl until I was tempted to throw the whole thing at him. Next to him by the window lay a young Catholic Filopina nun who was so horrified at being put in a ward with the opposite sex that she lay on top of the bedcovers and refused to take off her blue nun's outfit.

On Lothario's other side was an old dear with a severe case of Alzheimers who kept chuntering on loudly to her dead relatives in Armenia throughout the night. Beside me a Sikh gentlemen with a turban lay prone with a hospital curtain permanently round him. The only sign of life were the moans emitted at regular intervals and the occasional sounds of his bedpan results. There was the usual crazy old woman. Late at night she would skip out of bed in her fuzzy candlewick dressing gown and scamper down the corridor clutching her precious green handbag to her bony chest.

"Let me outta 'ere, let me outta 'ere," she shouted at the top of her cigarette-raddled voice.

"Well go on, you old bat, bugger off," one of the men shouted back in the dark. It was not easy to sleep.

Our strangest occupant was a young man who was supposed to be in a coma. He had a policeman on duty around his bed at all times, waiting for him to wake up so he could be arrested. He had stolen a car for a joy-ride with a friend and crashed it into a shop front in Knightsbridge, mowing down some unlucky Prada browser. The guy was obviously for the chop but some of us doubted the coma. I could swear that whenever the policeman on duty heeded the call of nature, the comatose patient would very slowly prise his right eye open just a smidgeon and sneak a quick peak to see what was up.

My only solace when not being comforted by my family and friends was a young gay nurse with pale red hair and a single silver earring. Whenever the pain became too intense, he sat on my bed and taking my hand in his long thin fingers he would talk very gently to me for a while, soothing me and telling me that every day I would improve and would be out of bed in no time. I never knew his name but I have always thought of him as my NHS angel.

Susie and Pods were, as usual, wonderful in having me to stay while I recovered and my dear Mama came to help. She was always immaculately dressed whenever she left her flat in Chelsea. She would never have worn anything 'kutchcha'- shoddy. Like many colonials my parents used quite a few Hindi words—*fundi, dhobi, chit.* She arrived one morning at my Earls Court Square flat, looking very 'Paddington Bear.' A smart red coat, her pearls, naturally, a chic navy blue hat and new black boots and bag, carrying a large bunch of flowers for me. She must have been around seventy-seven at the time. When she knocked on my door, Tasmin's skittish Weimeraner, Niven, pleased to hear her familiar voice, rushed out of the door to the landing, jumped up and knocked my mother straight over backwards. The hat fell off, her bag bounced down the stairs, the flowers hit the back wall and my daughter and I, along with Mum, went limp with laughter. It was a miracle she wasn't hurt.

Later that day my grandson Zac asked me if I was too old to have children.

"Absolutely," I replied, "besides, I had the plumbing fixed many years ago." As my grandchildren have grown up around endless dogs, he pondered my predicament before asking,

"Bibi, does that mean you have been spayed?"

Put so well, I thought!

GEORGE WEIDENFELD

In 1990 I was introduced to the highly successful publisher, Lord Weidenfeld. George was about twenty-five years older than me, extraordinarily cultured, gossipy and an avid opera lover. A Viennese Jew who fled the Nazis in 1938, George had a formidable intellect, adored being surrounded by pretty women and was a great raconteur and party-giver. He certainly managed to lure many a beautiful woman into his bed even though he was very short and very plump. I had already heard that he was known as 'the Nijinsky of *cunnilingus*' at one stage and when I mentioned it to Digs and my brother-in-law Henry, the latter asked,

"The dancer or the horse?"

George and I became friends, however, and I would go to his wonderful flat on the Chelsea Embankment overlooking the river for drinks and the occasional dinner, listen to his stories and amusing anecdotes and look at his marvellous paintings, including a large 'Screaming Pope' by Francis Bacon. One night one of his senior editors was there and suggested that since I came from Kenya I should write the first biography of Joy Adamson and her lioness Elsa. I was in the middle of a painful divorce at the time, had very little money and badly needed a new book. Since finishing my book on contemporary portraits, I had been writing pieces for magazines—the *Telegraph* on the English surrealist artist, Leonora Carrington; the *World of Interiors* on murals; *Marie Claire* on Kenya's 'Happy Valley'; the *Financial Times* on Borobudur in Java and so on. I had never written a biography but quickly cobbled together a short piece on Joy, sent it off to the editor and a within a month I had received a decent advance from Weidenfeld and Nicolson to explore the life of one of the first of Kenya's great conservationists. It was to be *Joy Adamson, Behind the Mask*, published in 1992.

George was also looking for a girlfriend, or a wife and was always dropping little hints of a flat in his building perfect for me, or weekend trips to Vienna, but there was absolutely no question of me getting involved. I simply didn't fancy him. There is something, how can I put this delicately, disconcerting about the age thing which always made me slightly queasy. When I think of the older men who have taken a shine, I cannot but help having an inward shudder as my brain goes into overdrive about things I would really rather not think about; the saggy flesh; the once bouncy protuberances which have since gravitated towards the knees; the rheumy eyes and problematic ear-hair. I realise the ancient bargain of power and wealth for relative youth and questionable beauty has ever been thus, but still, you know what I mean. Now as I creep quietly towards senility myself I am only too aware that gravitating south is a cross oldies just have to bear.

JOY ADAMSON AND ELSA

And so, thanks to George and my editor, I went back to the country I loved. A Spanish poet, whose name I have forgotten, once wrote "One's homeland is their childhood," which I completely understand. It is true that once experienced, Kenya can hold you in its thrall forever. Each time I arrive back on African soil I feel more alive. A feeling of "Here I am where I ought to be". Perhaps the aura of mystery and magic that enfolds the country has evolved slowly from a balance between the mythology of the tribes, the mass of wild animals and the haunting majesty of the landscape. Life seems more vivid, more dramatic and the senses begin to dance to the country's rhythms. The heart opens up, passion and love come easily, magnified by their nearness to constant danger and death. Whatever the tensions in the country, every year or two I am irresistibly drawn back to the coast, to Galu, south of Diani, the most beautiful beach in the world. And if all the Gods are on the same side that idyll is followed by watching wildlife, surely one of life's greatest pleasures.

Over the next year I spent weeks at a time travelling round in my sturdy

Land Rover interviewing people who knew Joy well; visiting all the places she and George had lived with their big cats—Naivasha, Meru and Shaba in the Northern Frontier District. My parents had known the Adamsons and their young lioness Elsa when I was a child and I was occasionally allowed to play with her as a cub. Within a few years of her arrival in Kenya from her native Austria in 1938, Joy's reputation as an infamous seducer with voracious carnal needs were to become legendary. Rumours abounded that more than one young officer and game warden in the Northern Frontier District failed to escape Joy's clutches. A few of them told me that on hearing via bush telegraph of her imminent arrival, they would jump into their jeeps and scarper for the hills. One District Commissioner put it to me this way,

"The fingertips didn't yearn to touch".

In her thick Austrian accent, Joy announced to anyone who listened:

"Men in Kenya are so sveet, but ze women, zey are cabbages." I also recall my parents' stories of Joy running round my father's desk trying in vain to catch him.

I soon realised that Joy, who was also a serious and talented flower and tribal painter, producing over seven hundred paintings of the Africans' fast-disappearing tribal culture, was a complex woman, not the gentle creature people imagined from the film *Born Free*. She was passionate, tempermental, controversial and married three times; first to the cultured Viktor von Klarwill, a fellow Austrian; secondly to Peter Bally, a respected Swiss botanist, then George. She admitted she never experienced happiness with any of her husbands or lovers and all her life her restless spirit searched for fulfilment and contentment which continually eluded her.

When George Adamson and Joy were first married, he took her to live in Isiolo, the dusty heart of the Northern Frontier administration where he had spent the past five years as an assistant game warden, responsible for policing an area of more than 100,000 square miles of mainly semi-arid thornbush. It was dry and windy and the land around was the colour of shifting grasses, amber, burnt yellow and ochre. Dust-devils rose out of the land like capricious dervishes. Beyond lay a boundless landscape of volcanoes and scrub, doum palms and sand, where vultures drifted on the wind over the limitless plains. Colourful Samburu, Turkana, Boran and Somali tribesmen mixed with Indian traders in the noisy market. Outside the straggling town two roads stretched away towards the horizon. One led to Ethiopia, where wandering tribes spoke of holy men who built their churches deep in the ground at Lalibela. The other road led to Somalia, the area from where the troublesome *shifta*, the poachers, would roam south of the border.

Joy was appalled by George's small spartan dwelling where he lived when not on safari. She insisted on her own bedroom as she had no intention of making love to her husband more than was absolutely necessary. George, who was madly in love with his wife, never slept in the same bedroom as her from their wedding day. Perhaps by way of compensation for a lack of close friends, Joy adopted numerous small animals, young mongoose, bushbabies, on which she lavished affection while George each evening, with a whisky by his side, filled his notebook and drafted his reports from his diary. George had a natural gift for telling a story and his amusing, descriptive reports were much in demand. These, in one DC's opinion, "Rendered them readable and understandable to the sort of clots that cluttered up the various department headquarters".

The stories of the couples' battles over George's whisky drinking at the Club and Joy's *affaires* caused much merriment in the *boma*—the village community. Joy, often in a towering rage, would let a hail of pellets from her shotgun fly at George when he came back from drinking with his cronies, forcing him to get down on all fours to avoid the flak. Once she whacked him with a dining-room chair and broke two of his ribs.

But within a year Joy was to find her life's work, the legacy which was to bring her worldwide fame and wealth. The lion cub Elsa and her two sisters were found by George as three week old orphaned cubs and her arrival was the beginning of a friendship which culminated in one of the most remarkable relationships ever recorded between human and animal. For two years the Adamsons took Elsa on safari, often to their camp on the banks of the Uaso Nyiro in Meru National Reserve, an area rich in baboon-laden doum palms, fig trees and scrawny acacia bush. At night Elsa slept in George's tent. The Adamsons showered the young animal with love, affection and daily walks. But two incidents happened with Elsa which deeply affected Joy's rapport with her.

One day, as she was sitting on a rock sketching, Elsa padded up behind her and took Joy's entire skull in her mouth. Joy froze, panic-stricken as Elsa's jaw closed around her but the lioness soon spat her out and walked away. In the second incident Joy was walking ahead of her, an unwise move. Elsa pounced on Joy, knocking the breath out of her as she hit the ground. Before George managed to beat the animal off, Elsa had clawed Joy's head and deeply lacerated her back. Joy was hysterical and was taken to hospital. She never mentioned these incidents but became afraid of her lioness. It was George who truly understood wild cats and their behaviour and although it was never acknowledged, much of the content of Joy's first book *Born Free* was taken from her husband's notes on Elsa. Writing proved an arduous task for Joy, whose English prose and speech was difficult to understand and whose typing was often unintelligible. However, with a great deal of help the book was published in 1960 and was an instant and phenomenal success. Its great achievement was that it was the initial seed that led to a harvest of concern for conservation. George, in one sense the real author, did not have an equal share in her royalties. With typical understatement, he said,

'I got all the fame but none of the fortune'.

Elsa was eventually released in the Meru National Reserve and once able to kill for herself, the Adamsons left her on her own for longer periods. From then on, Elsa managed to retain her extraordinary link between the two worlds. Possibly Joy's greatest triumph was the occasion when Elsa came back across the river to the camp with her own cubs. She opened her legs, exposing her teats to two hungry cubs, stretched herself across Joy and placed one paw round her. Joy was totally overwhelmed, claiming it was the happiest moment of her life. With her book proceeds she bought a small stone house in fifty acres on the shores of Lake Naivasha, for their old age. Named 'Elsamere', the house stood on a promontory and nestled in a small belt of primary forest. The biggest attraction of the area was its birdlife and each morning the cry of the fish eagle echoed along the carpet of water lilies fringing the shore. Elsamere is now a museum and memorial to the conservationist. George, however had already decided that he needed no house—his home was the bush.

In 1961, while Joy was in Nairobi, the five year old Elsa fell fatally ill at their camp in Meru. Cradling her head in his lap, with George wiping away his tears as he said, "In a few minutes she gave a great and terrible cry."

The couple were devastated, with Joy saying at the death of 'The one creature in my life I loved more than any other ... when Elsa died our loss and bond for her was so strong that a part of me died as well...'

All of Joy's considerable accumulated wealth was ploughed back into what eventually became The Elsa Conservation Trust. Later came royalties from the famous film of *Born Free* and her books, *Living Free*, *The Spotted Sphinx* and *Pippa's Challenge*. But Joy's choice of clothing frequently got her into trouble. She was often scantily-clad when painting African chiefs and when abroad she saw nothing incongruous in wearing her old leopard-skin coat while lecturing on conservation or posing with a leopard cub. She continued to live a tough life in the African bush with a new campsite beside the Rojewero river, ninety miles from the nearest phone and one hundred and twenty miles from the nearest tarred road where she studied cheetah behaviour through the solitary young Pippa. George moved to another part of Meru with his lions and his young and devoted assistant, the handsome and hard working Tony Fitzjohn about whom George admitted, "Tony and I had begun to enjoy the kind of reciprocal benefits that zoologists call symbiosis".

They worked together until George's death. Joy eventually moved to Shaba north of Isiolo where she lived with Penny, a nervous young leopard, in a camp framed by rocky hills and huge boulders, lava flows and mountains which had been twisted and stirred like toffee. But on the eve of her seventieth birthday and having made numerous enemies over the years, Joy met a violent end. In September 1979 on one of her walks near the camp, she was stabbed to death with a *simi*, a dagger, by a disgruntled African employee. Ten years later George, by now a sun-gnarled, greatly loved figure of eighty-three, died in a hail of bullets from Somali bandits near his camp in Kora National Park in Northern Kenya as he frantically drove to the rescue of an assistant and a young European girl.

I travelled roughly three thousand miles researching material on Joy and on one trip I took Tasmin as she adored being out in the Kenya bush. At nineteen, she was great company and added hugely to my enjoyment of the trip. Just watching her palpable excitement on seeing a leopard kill in Samburu was a joy. Isiolo was our last main town before my bumpy old Land Rover continued through the vast Northern Frontier District to Joy's former camp at Shaba.

My home away from home was the house of Peter Marrian, my generous-hearted surrogate father who lived near Karen, a pretty suburb of Nairobi. He and his adored American first wife, the beautiful Susie, became great friends of my parents when they had farmed coffee and cattle at Mweiga, near Mount Kenya. Susie took me riding in the forests during the risky days of the Mau Mau which I thought was wildly exciting. Peter was a remarkable man with boundless energy and hospitality who had won an athletics Blue at Oxford. He was President of the National Farmers' Union, a devoted supporter of the legendary Muthiaga Country Club and a respected lawyer. He became increasingly at odds with the argument that one per cent of whites should rule over the ninety-nine per cent of blacks and accompanied a freed Jomo Kenyatta to London when he was presented to the House of Commons and spoke about his policies for his country's future. Peter also became the Mzee's first white Junior Minister after Independence in 1963. After three wives, Peter now lived on his own. His bridge nights were sacrosanct and women of every age and colour remained a particular interest. They in return adored him. He once told me that Africans were far sexier and more fun, less demanding and complicated than other women.

One night I had driven all the way back from Isiolo when my Land Rover broke down on the Langata Road, three miles from Peter's house. If there's one road in Nairobi your car should never break down on at eleven at night it's this particular one. Car-jacking is rife with gangs of young men placing logs across the road before robbing or kidnapping the occupants. The only way I could get back to Peter's was to hitch a ride. Looking around in the dark, I noticed two young, smartly dressed African women in tight skirts and high heels walking along the side of the road in front of me. I jumped out of the Land Rover and rushed up to them, explained my problem and they agreed to flag down a car. Within minutes an old blue VW Beetle driven by a young African man in a smart suit and tie pulled up. I noticed he had a black brief case on the front seat so I assumed he had just left the office. The two girls had a word with him and then quickly got into the car, shut the door and drove off, leaving me stranded on the verge. I couldn't believe it and ran after them, shouting, "Hey, stop, stop!" and waving my arms. They were my only hope.

Taking pity on me the driver slowed down and when I banged hard on the back of the car he opened the passenger door and reluctantly let me in. It suddenly hit me—of course, the women were prostitutes and had just found a willing customer. Dumb, it simply hadn't occurred to me. I didn't care at all but since they were going my way I insisted they take me right to Peter's house and quickly explained the directions. It must have been quite a funny sight, four of us huddled together in a small blue Beetle in the middle of the night—one nervous moustachioed business man looking for a few minutes of passion before going home, two glamorous hookers covered in red lipstick and cheap scent, and a dishevelled lone white female traveller—arriving at the house and having Priscilla, Peter's much-loved African housekeeper, open the door of the house with a horrified look on her face and whisper fiercely, "What are you doing with these bad people, Caroline?"

"I know, I know Priscilla, but sometimes needs must," I answered as I tried to soothe her moral outrage.

The following day I went out walking on the plains next to Peter's house with his adult son David, of whom I was very fond. A tall slim Maasai holding a spear came silently towards us through the grass. He was holding something in his right hand. When he came close he spread out his palm and showed us the most perfect lion's fur ball. It was hard and the size of a ping pong ball, with a smooth downy brown covering, like worn felt. He offered it to me, telling me that the lion had coughed up the fur ball just before he died. It remains one of my favourite objects.

PETER BEARD AND TONY FITZJOHN

During my book research I flew down to Tanzania to interview Tony Fitzjohn who knew Joy Adamson better than most. Having worked with her husband George for eighteen years Tony enjoyed a close relationship with him. Before being kicked out of Kenya, Tony's continuing dedication to wildlife, after his mentor's murder, resulted in a game reserve at Mkomazi where he introduced wild dogs and in time twenty-seven black rhino. Tony was devastatingly handsome, had a wild, passionate personality, was irresistible to women and in those days more than partial to a drop of drink. I had seen him only recently at his great friend Peter Beard's 'Hog Ranch', outside Nairobi, when we sat on logs talking round a crackling fire as we watched the sparks fly up and melt into the night sky.

Peter, coined as 'Half Tarzan, half Byron' by an American writer, was also extraordinarily handsome and had women dropping at his feet. Both men, adventurers by nature, were complicated and Peter's life in particular was often reckless and chaotic. He was a wonderfully creative photographer, impassioned artist and author of the thought-provoking *The End of the Game*. Gored badly by an elephant, charged by a lion, he was a man of untamed appetites which gave him a reputation for being as wild as the animals he photographed. 'Hog Ranch' was a tented camp and the place to be, often filled around the campfire with political activists, gorgeous girls, foreign correspondents, Iman and other models, tribal leaders, artists, writers. There was a strong sense of the exotic about it, especially with the sun setting over the Ngong Hills. Situated in forty-five wild acres with roaming giraffe and warthogs, Hog Ranch was adjacent to what was once the writer Karen Blixen's coffee farm. Long ago while we were discussing Joy, George and the future of Africa's wild game, Peter reiterated his fiery, long held opinion expressed throughout his entire adult life and laid down firmly in his book::

"It's really all about the *wananchi*—the ordinary people—versus the animals. As the population explodes, the game will be pushed out until it is all gone. It is that simple.'

The mutual friend who flew me down from Nairobi to Kilimanjaro airport to see Tony was David Allen, one of the best bush pilots in Kenya. Being in his light Cessna felt like being on the wings of a swallow sailing on the breeze. One moment we were soaring over the crest of the Ngong Hills and looking at the Maasai boys below herding their goats, and the next the plane was swooping down across the immense breadth of the Great Rift Valley, where game scattered as our plane's shadow fell across them. This immersive excitement must have been what Karen Blixen and her lover, the English aristocrat Denys Finch Hatton, felt each time they soared across the skies.

I was aware that Tony's relationship with Joy had been tricky. She often accused him of leading George astray; was jealous of their closeness and detested the small whiskey bottles hanging up in the mess tent. But in our discussions Tony always remained fair: "Her contribution to conservation was huge and I always admired her steely determination to succeed. I understood her."

When the day came to leave for Nairobi Dave and I rose into the sky from Kilimanjaro airport when the heavens opened, obliterating the land. Hailstones were flung against the windscreen like stones thrown from a group of young thugs and we were flying blind in dark, thunderous clouds when the plane's altimeter broke. Our route took us directly between two massive mountains, Mount Kilimanjaro and Mount Meru and Dave needed every ounce of his expertise to judge our altitude plus the distance between them. It would be more than possible to smack straight into either one should he get it wrong.

"Do you want to go back to Kilimanjaro?', Dave shouted at me through claps of thunder. Every molecule in my body wanted to cry out, "Immediately!" But not wanting to be considered an utter wimp I managed to stutter, "I'm OK." When we finally touched down in Nairobi I staggered out of the plane, swearing "Never, ever again."

When I began writing Joy's biography back in London I became involved with a tall, dark brooding Englishman named Drew who looked like a dishy Italian filmstar—a cross between Heathcliff and Dracula had either been Italian. The hurt from the sudden break-up of my marriage gradually subsided. I managed to bury it beneath a stone slab and cover it with ferns and mosses. It peers out of a corner from time to time when the light falls on a particular memory, but then creeps back into the shadows. Drew lived near me in Fulham and was six years younger. We both had children and it turned out to be another complicated relationship. I must have been certifiable but I was quickly hooked by his handsome looks and easy intelligence. At one stage he was working in Connecticut and I was due to join him, flying with Virgin Airlines from London. For some reason, I didn't really want him to know that I was that much older and decided to alter the year of my birth in my passport. In those days there was no plastic covering the vital statistics that were handwritten directly over the tiny blue and white background pattern of the page. As I have altered and mended things all my life, fixing the numbers was child's play. Somehow it never occurred to me it was a criminal offence to change the year of one's birth in a passport, and happily went off to Heathrow.

The efficient young man at the Virgin desk checked me in. My mind was already on my furry little white Virgin socks with the red pompoms at the heel and a soothing Vodka with ice the minute we rose into the air. For some inexplicable reason just as he was about to hand me back my passport, he decided to put it under an infra-red machine. A moment's silence

Rullie, my first love.

Left: getting out of our pool in Salisbury, Rhodesia, aged 22.

Our staff in Salisbury.

Above left: relaxing, with my journalist husband Dean, Washington D.C. 1970.

Above: Dean with Tara in North Carolina.

Left: New York Times *and* Washington Post *journalists: Ward Just, Johnny Apple and Jon Randal in Martha's Vineyard.*

With Tasmin and Tara in Dumbarton Oaks Park, Georgetown, Washington DC.

Below, left: My mother at Medla, Cornwall, where we go every year; right: my father at 40.

Left: Alain Catzeflis. *Above: Tasmin and Tara.*

Above: Tasmin and Chippy.

Right: In my green burqa which I had to wear in Afghanistan, with one of Topikai's daughters.

Above: Joy Adamson and Elsa the lioness.

Below: Akmed Gul, ex-Mujahid, teaching me how to shoot a Kalashnikov.

Above:Tasmin and Rupert's wedding, December 1995. Mum is next to the bridegroom.

Below: Muffy Stout, Judy Bizot with her son Polo.

Below: Tara with Peter Jennings (ABC News Anchor, New York) at Tasmin and Rupert's wedding.

   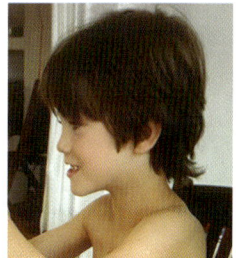

Top: With Appley in an Ethiopian shelter on the Simien Mountains at 14,000 ft.
Middle: The four sisters, Pods, Susie, Me, Rachel.
Bottom: The four grandchildren, Cal, Jago, Zac and Fin.

followed before he ordered me to follow him into his office and said, some-what testily,

"Modom, has someone been tampering with your passport?"

"Oh no," I said, my eyes opening in *ingenue* amazement.

"Have you yourself done anything to it?"

"Absolutely not."

"Well then," he continued in an increasingly cold voice, "I will have to ring up the Home Office and see if this is the your real birth date," and turned to talk to his superior. I immediately began to panic and blurted out,

"Oh alright, alright, I did, but only by two years, so it's really not that bad, surely?"

"Modom, you are now a felon and America does not allow felons into the country. You cannot therefore travel with our airline." Not a shred of humour or forgiveness, that one.

He retrieved my suitcase from the rubber flippy-fringed black hole and I sat steaming on the train all the way back to London. Once home, I rang Drew and confessed to my crime which amused him since he had known my real age all along and couldn't have cared less about it. The next morning I stomped off to Petty France Street in London to get a new passport and bought another ticket to New York for the next day. Useless vanity!

SOTHEBY'S AUCTIONEER

As well as writing Joy's biography I was working with my brother-in-law, Henry, at his successful St. James' Art Gallery in Jermyn Street and for a while my sister Digs was also involved. Henry is six foot eight inches tall with a mop of grey curly hair and has a penchant for red socks. He possesses a huge sense of humour, much enjoyed by his artworld friends who call him the 'Hamster'. For behind the geniality, the crinkly blue eyes and joke telling, his mind is fairly tearing round, like a hamster on a wheel.

We had a large number of talented portrait artists on our books and were running 'Portrait Commissions' from the gallery. It was fun, interest-ing and worked well for a number of years until Henry was headhunted to be Chairman of Sotheby's Europe, becoming the best auctioneer in the busi-ness over the next twenty-two years.

I have watched him giving sales which were always done with the perfect blend of humour, seriousness in focusing on bidders and just the right amount of bluff. He said to me once, "Selling Rubens' *The Massacre of the Innocents* was the greatest painting I ever sold in my forty years and was my favourite moment." The Rubens sold for £45 million and was the most expensive Old Master painting ever sold at auction.

While at Sotheby's Henry gave Christmas lunches that were tremendous fun. I was once seated between the diminutive, adorable comedian Ronnie Corbett and the very witty writer, A.A. Gill, which I couldn't have enjoyed more. Every year Ronnie would rise to his full height of five feet, one inch, and deliver an extremely funny, very naughty poem that had everyone giggling. It was written by Ronnie Barker, his comedic partner, in the 1960s and was considered so spicy it had been locked up by the television company for forty years. How lucky we were!

LOST IN LUCCA

One winter's day around the time of the portrait peddling, Tara and I flew out with a planeload of guests to a swish three day wedding extravaganza in Lucca. The famous Tuscan town is an almost perfectly preserved jewel of medieval architecture surrounded by a high wall and lies in a lush green valley near Florence. The groom was a good looking Old Etonian whom our family had known since childhood and he was marrying an Italian publishing heiress in the magnificent Lucca Cathedral. Some people were staying outside the walls of the ancient city but we wanted to stay inside as Lucca was old and beautiful and we hoped to find time to explore. It had been arranged that all the guests were to be transported to each shimmering venue in private buses.

After the nuptials, we changed into our glad rags for the evening shindig. My blonde daughter looked lovely in a long slinky halter neck dress made of silver sequins. I wore a black floor-length dress by Amanda Wakeley and my much cherished pearl and diamond choker, alas since sold. As the glittering party raged on into a new day, those of us who left trotted back to our respective wedding buses to be dropped off at our *porta*, one of the six famous gates of the walled city. Tara and I stupidly got off at the wrong stop with not a single light left on in the town to guide us. The further we travelled down its narrow winding streets the further lost we became, until we felt like Alice falling down the rabbit hole. The night was bitterly cold and snowflakes were settling on the pavements. We walked for half an hour, our feet hurting so much we had to take our high heels off. Our hair, no longer magnificently coiffed, dripped in sodden rivulets down our backs and we looked like a couple of dubious *babushkas* stumbling about, our scrunching steps in the snow sounding as loud as thieves as we crept around. Even the stray cats had given up scrounging for discarded fishtails and had slunk away to curl up in a dry nook somewhere.

At one point Tara, who had forgotten to bring a coat with her and was shivering uncontrollably, gave up and cried, "I can't go on any further. I just can't," and promptly sat down on a doorstep, refusing to budge.

"Don't be ridiculous, darling," I replied, "You'll die of hypothermia."

I simply wasn't going to have our two frozen bodies found in an obscure cobbled alley by the dustbin men first thing in the morning. I looked round frantically for help as I didn't relish the thought of carrying my grown-up daughter on my back like some forlorn mother turtle. I nearly shouted with joy when I eventually saw the faintest light coming from a small building at the far end of a street. I dragged my daughter to her feet and pulled her along, feeling like Shackleton striving against massive odds to reach the South Pole. When we got to the window with the beckoning light, I pulled the door open and staggered in, leaving Tara by the door.

Our Holy Shrine turned out to be a small bakery where four men were busy kneading dough and making bread and buns for the morning delivery in a few hours' time. A mist of fine white flour hung in the air like a stubborn sirocco wind and the floor was an inch thick in the stuff. As I stood there shivering, with my feet bare and the hem of my lovely dress melting into the whiteness, the men looked up in amazement, their eyes not quite believing what they were seeing. I could practically hear their thoughts,

"*Madre di Gesu*, what is this *signora inglese* in a ballgown and flashy jewels and no shoes on her feet in mid-winter doing here. Is she *pazzo*—crazy? Is she so hungry for bread?"

My dripping daughter was now right behind me and they sighed at the thought of another bedraggled unfortunate to deal with.

"*Scusi senore*," I said to the largest baker who seemed to be in charge, as if I had just swept in from the Ritz, "*Per favore*, where Hotel Romano?" Within seconds the man became our veritable shining knight.

"But *signora*, it is near. Hop in van. I take you there." Relieved beyond belief, we tripped outside to the small white delivery van parked by the curb and our Italian saviour quickly opened the back doors. The floor was covered with the dregs of his last delivery and Tara and I, grateful to still be alive, disappeared into the white cloud within and collapsed on top of them. Gone were the glamour puss's of a few hours earlier; we wouldn't have been out of place in a Spielberg ghost movie. The baker shut the doors firmly, drove for precisely three minutes round the corner and delivered us safely at the large wooden doors of our elusive hotel. We scrambled out, looking particularly frightening, and thanked him profusely, "*Grazie mille, gracie mille senore, buonanotte.*"

He gave us a beaming smile and drove off down the snowy street back to the only little light in town to meet his doughy deadline. What a man!

Earth Dancing

LEONORA CARRINGTON, MEXICO

WHILE DREW STAYED at his family house in Dorset with his two boys, I went off for six weeks to San Miguel de Allende, a beautiful 16th century Mexican town full of cobbled streets, church bells, music and vivid fiestas. It was an exciting time as I had signed a book contract with Bloomsbury to write a biography of Leonora Carrington, the surrealist painter who was then in her eighties. Tara came too, which made me happy. She was twenty-two, recently returned to London from New York University and needed a break.

In a land where magic is part of daily reality, it did not seem unusual that Mexico's most celebrated living female artist was a *gringa*. A slender, dark-eyed English beauty with long black hair and skin like alabaster, Leonora Carrington was born to a textile tycoon in Lancashire and the family had a retinue of footmen, gardeners, French governesses and maids. Leonora was introduced at a London dinner party to Max Ernst in 1936 when Surrealism was all the rage. He was 46, devastatingly handsome with white hair, startling blue eyes and a beak-like nose, a renowned ladies' man and married. It was love at first sight, *amour fou* as the surrealists called it, tempestuous and irresistible. The couple soon eloped to Paris and Leonora's father disowned her. Although Max continued having a turbulent time between his understandably furious wife and Leonora, she regarded their creative life together in a Provence farmhouse where she wrote stories and painted, "As a kind of paradise time of my life."

Their idyll ended abruptly when war was declared. Max was denounced by the Nazis as an undesirable. He was interned as an enemy alien for the second time in May 1940.

Traumatised and alone in Provence, Leonora's mental health grew increasingly fragile. She fled to Spain where her breakdown in Madrid was rapid. She was incarcerated in an asylum for six months, given powerful psychoactive drugs and subjected to horrific physical and mental torture. Her downward spiral into lunacy subsequently established her as a surrealist heroine. Leonora was finally released into the care of her trusty old nanny whom her parents had sent over by submarine to rescue her. Many surrealists had fled to Mexico and taking up the Government's offer of citizenship to political refugees, Leonora marched on the Mexican Embassy and soon married a Mexican diplomat,

"It was the only way of getting out" Leonora admitted,.

Peggy Guggenheim promptly came to Max's rescue and into his bed.

"Still deeply in love with Leonora, Max begged her to return to him but she refused," recalled Peggy.

Months of anguish and turmoil followed and both Leonora and Max continued to remain tormenting inspirations to each other. Once in Mexico Leonora ditched her diplomat husband, before marrying and having a family with Chiqui Weisz, a Hungarian photographer who worked with Robert Capa, legendary founder of Magnum Photos.

After corresponding with her from England and talking on the phone, I sent her my biography of Joy Adamson, which she enjoyed, so I flew out to spend time together at her home in Mexico City. I found the eighty year old artist of dreams and demons, spirits and myths, fascinating and formidable, charming, eccentric and marvellously intelligent. Wavy grey hair loosely collected in a small knot on top of her head set off fine, powdered cheekbones. Like most sorceresses, Leonora remained pragmatic at heart. With her cat purring quietly on her lap, the rebel was restrained.

"I'm an old woman, living in Mexico", she told me, "and I don't give a damn if my painting endures or not". Such no-nonsense declarations only added lustre to the legend, mystique to the muse.

But it turned out she had decided never to engage in a biography while she was alive, which came as a bit of a shock. We had got on very well and felt completely as ease with each other. But in the end it proved impossible. I gave the advance back to Bloomsbury and promptly gave in to the delights of San Miguel.

Apart from Leonora, my strongest memories of Mexico was a surreal Good Friday re-enactment of Golgotha in Atotilinico, outside San Miguel. This poor rural community set in a landscape of dry grassland and desert studded with sweet acacia and mesquite trees was reminiscent of the Holy Land. Vendors, anticipating huge crowds, set out their booths along the only street—pottery and rosaries, whips for self-flagellation and cold drinks. My friend Jean Harvey, now living and painting in San Miguel, and I joined others in the shade of a thorny tree outside the village waiting for the young man from Atotilinico who had been chosen that year to represent Jesus. It was considered a huge honour and families vied for the role. Christ was at that very moment still dragging his heavy cross down the Via Dolorosa of San Miguel. We had been invited by two charming Dutch men, who had a swish villa and garden at the base of the hill, to drop in and have a Bloody Mary and a swim to fortify ourselves for the gruelling climb in the broiling sun to watch the Crucifixion. As we swam, crowds outside the bougainvillea-covered walls watched Pontius Pilate conducting Jesus' trial; his painful whipping by Roman soldiers was real as was his crowning with a living crown of thorns. It was like a medieval miracle play. Little children began to cry as the scourging began while unconcerned dogs wandered amongst the players in the spectacle. Jesus, with his hands tied behind him, and the two robbers setting off on the long walk up to Golgotha, soon struggled past us with blood on their bodies. The crowds had swelled to up to a few thousand and we began walking beside them up the hill. At the top the two thieves and Jesus were tied to the crosses with rope before being hauled upright. They remained still and soundless in the heat for many hours which must have required enormous inner strength. At the end of the day and illuminated by the setting sun their ropes were untied and they were finally taken down. The three of them were covered in white shrouds and carried on the shoulders of the villagers down the hill, accompanied by the now laughing children. Images of the macabre afternoon have long stayed with me.

The following Saturday Jean and I were invited by a Mexican friend to an afternoon party in the countryside—the main attraction being a cockfight. It was to be a birthday celebration for a local landowner and popular San Miguel guitar player, Ben Jamin, whom we had never met. After driving through miles of farmed artichokes, dotted with cacti and peyote plants, we arrived at the dusty yard outside a small farmhouse. When our host came out to greet us I nearly dropped my maracas. Ben Jamin was tall, impossibly handsome, about fifty-five, with a dazzling smile which must have melted many a senorita's heart. He was also the spitting image of Sean Connery which is what we nicknamed him. It was such a pleasure to see a tall Mexican, one who didn't need to wear built up heels on his cowboy boots. The birthday boy was followed out by a very beautiful wife with long flowing black hair, wearing a red flamenco dress. Brightly dressed women arrived carrying baskets and plates of delicious Mexican food; *tamales*, *chilaquiles*, corn, beans, chillies; and men clutched fine-feathered cockerels under their arms.

Soon everyone began drinking wine in an arc from leather holders before gravitating towards the cockpit, a small earthen ring under a tree which the men sat round in a circle, their silver money clips holding the bills fastened to their belt. Cockfighting was a serious business and they were prepared to gamble large sums of money. They soothed the feathers of their valuable birds and made sure the brutal spur, a three inch long curved ice-pick, was tied securely onto the back of one foot. Ben Jamin turned to me and asked me to open the cockfight. Naturally, being a *gringa*, I felt honoured. The first two gamecocks went for each other in a furious whirlwind; the fight was violent, feathers flew and a good deal of blood was spilt. It lasted for a few minutes and then suddenly it was over. Whenever possible, fighting was stopped before their prized birds got killed. The victor was claimed, wads of bills were exchanged and the fights continued throughout the afternoon. When the men finally finished, glasses of tequila were handed round and we tucked into sumptuous Mexican food.

At twilight a *Mariachi* band, dressed in black and silver, appeared miraculously out of the desert. They strode into the arena strumming their guitars to everyone's delight. After a while an attractive singer put down his stringed instrument and asked me to dance. Everyone joined in; mothers holding their babies, children, old men and women, teenage boys and girls. I remember feeling a moment of pure happiness as we all danced under the starlit skies. Afterwards my new friend sang a poignant Mexican love song on his guitar to me, none of which I understood though the sentiments were clear enough. Mexican songs of love must be amongst the most plaintive and heart-rending, especially when they are sung by a handsome stranger. Even though theirs is a poor country, Mexicans find such joy in celebrating and it is hard not to fall in love with the country and its people.

THE DALAI LAMA, DHARAMSALA

Looking back, I think I have been able to travel so frequently, not only for work and researching books, but because, for a number of years in between lovers, husbands and boyfriends, I have been unattached, footloose and unencumbered. This was the case when my long held ambition to visit Dharamsala, home to Tenzin Gyatso, the fourteenth Dalai Lama, finally came to fruition in 1998. After staying in Delhi with my old friend Pippa Clarke, my Paris pal, Judy Bizot, and I spent a sleepless fifteen hour train journey followed by a jolting truck ride, to reach McLeod Ganj, a small hamlet which sits on a spindle-like ridge above Dharamsala. Surrounded by pine trees, this has been the permanent home of the Tibetan spiritual leader since fleeing his homeland in Tibet in 1959. The following year the Indian Prime Minister Jawaharlal Nehru offered him and over one hundred thousand destitute exiles, the small former British hill station, now affectionately called 'Little Lhasa'.

Judy and I had come to be near His Holiness and to witness the ancient Buddhist religious ceremony celebrating the Tibetan New Year and Hotel Tibet, a primitive dwelling, was to be our home for the week. Our first bone-achingly cold night was abruptly ended at four in the morning, the day of the ceremony. From the Dalai Lama's personal monastery, adjoining his modest yellow cottage, came the sudden boom of a large gong being beaten which reverberated across the steep hills of Dharamsala. The low chanting from the two hundred Gyuto monks followed each thudding beat, enfolding the village as the people readied themselves for this auspicious day. After meditation and prayers with his monks, at sunrise His Holiness would be presiding over a four-hour religious ceremony in the Central Cathedral to celebrate Losar. The three story lemon-yellow temple which the Dalai Lama had designed exuded peace and tranquillity.

We had arranged to meet the Dalai Lama's sister Jetsun Pema, whom Judy knew, and her husband Tempa, before dawn at the entrance to the temple. Without their considerable help in obtaining us passes we could never have attended the ceremony. The sky was still dark as we followed a flotilla of figures towards the Cathedral, waiting with growing excitement as the square began to fill with Tibetans of all ages. Although most of the inhabitants of Macleod Ganj and Dharamsala lived in poverty, those who could dressed up for the occasion. Men wore colourful embroidered hats lined in fur, women showed off their precious turquoise, coral and amber jewellery; children put on brightly coloured jackets to ward off the biting cold. Most would have to wait patiently until after the service to catch a glimpse of their spiritual and temporal leader. Having been thoroughly frisked, we proceeded to a small, private religious ceremony in the upper temple. Smiling Tibetans gave us white silk *khatas* (scarves) as offerings, which symbolise the pure heart of the giver. Besides a small posse of press photographers, only eight other Westerners were permitted to watch the private ceremony. The roof of the upper temple was open—a rectangle of roughly thirty by twenty feet—and out of the darkness shone the majestic peaks of the Dhauladhar Range, glistening with new-fallen snow. We sat cross-legged at the very edge of the roof, facing the gold pinnacles which topped a covered portion of the temple. In front of us and divided by a carpet leading up to the Dalai Lama's east facing brocade-draped throne, sat abbots, lamas and six rows of elite monks dressed in maroon robes, who had come to join the Dalai Lama in chanting and meditation, recitations and singing. About sixty people were present in all. Behind the monks on the far side two large painted cone-shaped banners with colourful religious symbols and mandalas representing an image of the cosmos, dominated the small ceremonial setting. Beneath them conical dough offerings, grains, rolls of bread, fruit, butter tea and blessed saffron water, were stacked.

At the appointed time the monks, led by the *umze*, the chant master, quietly began their mellifluous chanting and the mournful boom of ten foot Tibetan long horns resounded like ships in the fog. His Holiness entered from a door on the right of the temple. Bare headed and bespectacled, he wore his burgundy and gold monk's robes. His arms were bare and on the right one four large distinct vaccination marks were visible. Silent, bowed, and occasionally stooping to greet a particular monk or relative, he proceeded to walk to his golden throne on the west side of the small roof. It was perched on a dais against a simple backdrop of yellow cotton cloth bordered on the top with a ruffle of blue, red and yellow. The table in front was covered in multi-coloured embroidered brocade silk, over which lay a plain white silk cloth. Once seated, the Dalai Lama, a tantric lama, held a small tantric drum in his right hand and a crown-shaped bell in his left. On the table lay two intricately carved gold spirit boxes, a large square brass bowl, a small tea bowl and various receptacles. On a smaller table to his right sat his lama's crescent shaped yellow hat with its distinctive fringe and red trim, a tea pot of peacock feathers and a flask of hot butter tea.

Over the next two hours, as the dawn gathered in the stars and the sun appeared over the mountain peaks, his Holiness immersed himself in the rituals of one of the Buddhist calendar's most important ceremonies. He chanted and intoned prayers along with the monks who sat with bowed heads and eyes closed when following their spiritual master in meditation. At intervals the Dalai Lama's graceful, delicate hand movements, which are part of the tantric rituals, included ringing the bell and flicking the small drum so that the wooden balls on the end of two strings beat against each side. He donned his lama's hat and held the peacock feathers to his lips before pouring the liquid from the teapot into the brass pan. During the ceremony he often looked towards the mountains in the east and at other times he went so deeply into his meditation that he seemed oblivious to the world around him. Occasionally he would recognise a face in the rows of people near him and smile with delight. He is a modest man, without vanity or pomposity. Throughout the ceremony, the long horns were interspersed with the shrill notes of silver short horns, the boom of large green and gold embroidered drums being beaten and turquoise-coloured cymbals clashed.

Young monks with the lower part of their faces covered by white scarves, brought offerings of food and bowls of tea to the Dalai Lama's throne. A red conical shaped cake of *tsampa* covered in intricate pink and white icing and crowned by a solar disc was carried by the first monk as he walked slowly up the aisle. Another stood patiently holding a large red silk parasol to hide the Dalai Lama's face from the rising sun, shading his face in a half-moon, like a scallop shell. At times during the ceremony the abbots and lamas placed their curved ceremonial yellow hats on their shaven heads. The awe-inspiring panorama that unfolded before me was remarkably moving. I felt I was floating between heaven and earth, having stepped into an enchanted realm, a visual feast where all was colour and mysterious ritual.

While we sat there we were offered rice and tea by solicitous monks who managed to squeeze deftly between the cramped rows. Indian secret service men watched vigilantly over the small crowd while directly behind us stood a sole Indian soldier with a Kalashnikov, our only reminder in this exotic prayer festival that danger constantly followed His Holiness—there have been many attempts on his life and each year the day of the ceremony is moved.

Once the first part of the ceremony came to an end, his Holiness walked downstairs to the hallowed quarters of the main temple. All who entered were given small red ceremonial *khatas* and once again we were given privileged seating on the floor, this time surrounded by many more monks and ordinary Tibetans who obviously felt as fortunate as we did at being there—a constant stream of devotees had been turning the vast brass prayer wheels as they entered the temple. The Dalai Lama changed his hat for a tall pointed golden yellow one with sides lined in yellow silk which curved round and elegantly crossed over at the back. The outer part of his robes were now golden instead of burgundy. He sat serene and cross-legged on his high throne in front of a giant gilded statue of Sakyamuni Buddha, holding manuscripts and scriptures in his hands.

On either side in front of his throne two young monks held brass pots and intermittently threw handfuls of yellow barley seeds into the air. Monks chanted melodically throughout the ceremony and two articulate monks became involved in an intricate dialectic debate which at times became heated. The adversaries paced vigorously up and down the aisle in front of the Dalai Lama, who sat motionless throughout the ceremony. Four young Tibetan musicians in beautifully embroidered silk outfits and red ribbons floating down from their hats played small drums and a short horn. As they were playing their vibrant music, pretty young orphan girls from the Tibetan Children's Village, run by Jetsun Pema, a charming and highly organised woman, danced and sang in the aisle for his Holiness. In their traditional Tibetan costumes, and with their sweet smiles and high clear voices filling the temple, they were an exuberant contrast to the serenity of the monks. As soon as the four hour religious ceremony ended, his Holiness walked onto the balcony, palms pressed together at his chest, nodding and smiling broadly as he went. The crowd was electrified as they tried to cram into the courtyard to hear their living Buddha of Compassion give a short speech welcoming in the New Year. Being privileged to witness this most sacred of ceremonies is a treasured experience never to be forgotten.

CAL, JAGO, ZAC, FIN

When reflecting upon the vagaries of the human heart I have always held the view that happiness is mostly momentary, a rare and fleeting instant like retaining upon awakening the face of a past love seen in a dream. But when Tasmin's first son Cal was born prematurely, my heart was completely taken by this tiny little being. He became a beautiful, gentle child, happy with life and the adoration heaped upon him. Clever and diligent, he has the same *Kikuyu* sense of humour as I do and we laugh at the same things. These few pages are not long enough to include the boys' various virtues and sensibilities, differing dreams and aspirations, suffice to say that watching them grow up is a fascinating, never ending trip. I totally adore all of them. Jago, the second son, looked like a fallen angel as a child, tall, blonde with a gorgeously-shaped mouth. He was decidedly vocal and simply adored his eldest brother. When he wasn't running around in the summer happily shouting, "I in the sun", he had a tendency to fall asleep anywhere, even inside his Scalextrics car racing track by the front door. Jago was shiny bright, had a passion for Percy Jackson books and aged five, told me kindly, "You are not as old as Jesus, who went to Devon."

One summer day when Cal was four he was walking with his grandmother Rosey in the magical Lost Gardens of Heligan in Cornwall and suddenly ran into an empty maze, becoming lost. He kept walking deeper into the greenery, eventually coming across a little girl with blonde hair in a white dress. He talked to her for a while before saying goodbye and finding his way back out of the maze to find Rosey. Rosey told us later many years ago a little girl had been murdered in that maze. Cal follows his mother Tasmin in having a strong psychic streak; although she seldom talks about it unless asked, she also sees people's auras and events in the future which is both intriguing and alarming.

Zac, the third handsome guitar-playing brother, is naturally funny, a passionate lover of the 1994 television sitcom *Friends* and can repeat every word of each episode. One of its stars, Matthew Perry, arrived in London a few years ago with his play *The End of Longing* and Zac begged me to take him. I really didn't know much about the actor and for some reason I had mistakenly thought the play would be a latter day imitation of Friends. Alas, the star had lost the cute looks that women once swooned over. He had turned into an overweight imitation of sweet-faced Chandler Bing from the series but it didn't really matter as Zac was entranced by him. I had no inkling that

Perry had been an alcoholic, ferocious drug user, sex addict and that the play would concentrate on this particular side of his life. This was made clear as soon as we got through the theatre doors.

First the manager came up and said,

"Madam, you do realise that this play is highly unsuitable for this young gentleman. What age is he?"

"Fourteen," I lied smoothly and carried on; having paid a vast amount for the two tickets, I was not prepared to disappoint Zac. The next person to confront us was a programme seller.

"Really, I don't think the boy should see the play," she said rather huffily.

"It's ok, don't worry," I said, by now beginning to feel like some awkward granny-pervert. We grabbed a programme and walked swiftly down the aisle, Zac looking slightly bewildered by my blatant lying to the manager. Great example, I thought. I finally slightly lost it with the nice man taking our tickets and showing us to our row of seats.

"I must tell you this is not a children's play," he said.

"It's quite alright," I responded firmly, "Matthew Perry is his godfather and he says it's fine." Another porky.

There wasn't a single child in the theatre and I sank low into my seat, pulling my coat collar right up and hiding my face with my hair. I had visions of people turning round and throwing rotten tomatoes at me but hoped most of the play would go over Zac's head. It didn't—he loved every minute of it. When we finally escaped into the London night I asked him,

"Darling, have I corrupted you for life?"

"Bibi, I have two older brothers and they've told me everything already."

"Oh thank God," I said, heaving a sigh of relief as we stepped into a taxi.

Fin, the youngest, was a child with a huge imagination and sense of creativity, writing whole books from the age of five. He loved listening to my stories about encounters with lion and rhino and one day, rather perplexed, asked, "Bibi, did you really grow up in a bush?" He learnt to be quite savvy with his elder brothers to escape their wrath, shouting aged two and a half, to Zac, "Don't kill me, I'm just a baby, kill him!" pointing to Cal, who was twelve.

At three Fin was a chatty child, fond of saying, "I just dropped by to have a word," and also became a imaginative little artist, full of curiosity and questions.

I seemed to have spent half my life at the Natural History and Science

Museums with all of the children, plus the Victoria and Albert Museum, all of which are near my house And of course there's the theatre, which I greatly enjoy taking them to.

WILLIAM GOLDMAN, SCREENWRITER

Sometimes its easier to recall the pecadilloes of one's lovers rather than husbands but perhaps when the heart is not totally involved they are just simpler to relate. Besides, marriage and its long-tolerated habits and foibles are off-limits, especially when you have children together, but the occasional snippet on famous lovers is sometimes too tempting to resist.

In 1992 while I was working on a portrait exhibition at the gallery I began a romance with the American Oscar-winning screenwriter and novelist William Goldman in the forlorn hope of pushing a long-term lover out of the nest. Although I was still semi-cuckoo about Mad Max I needed to start thinking with my head and not my heart.

When the silver-haired American and I met over drinks with friends, my Joy Adamson book had recently been published which luckily he had read and enjoyed. He was charming, brilliant, extremely handsome in a seasoned Paul Newman way (my absolute number one pin up), quite a lot older and had a tendency towards melancholy—probably the result of a childhood injury when he was deliberately pushed, falling heavily on his back onto a large metal doorstop. He had been plagued by pain ever since. Three times a week a small, sleek-haired Japanese woman came up to his Manhattan penthouse and with firm, miniscule feet, trotted up and down his back for an hour to relieve his pain. I never saw her but for some reason I always imagined her to be like Cato, Clouseau's deranged manservant from the Pink Panther films, flinging open the front door and launching like one possessed onto his wonky coxis.

In many ways Bill was entirely right for me. I was full of admiration for his huge talent in being able to write superb screenplays and win Oscars for *Butch Cassidy and the Sundance Kid* and *All the Presidents Men*. His book *Adventurers in the Screen Trade* became a classic and my children adored his film, *The Princess Bride*. I could have led a fascinating and very agreeable life with this interesting man—travelled everywhere and shared adventures with his equally well-known actor friends, John Cleese, Peter Cook and Stephen Fry whom I met over dinner on several occasions. Bill had a flat in Knightsbridge near Harrods and another in The Caryle in New York, where Muffy's great friend Bobby Short often played the piano. Concorde tickets regularly arrived from Bill to go and join him which was kind of him but for all his devilish good looks and virtuoso ability, I just didn't fall in love. I tried. I tried so hard but alas it seemed my heart continued to rule my head. Far too late I have learnt that being a dyed-in-the-wool romantic is an unfortunate trait which can rob you of a perfectly decent long lasting relationship.

My screenwriter friend had one particular, very generous habit. He took great delight in giving me silk lingerie, mostly lacy Janet Reger teddies, then the height of intimate fashion as I recall. Whenever he came to London or I arrived in New York, a large expensive-looking box wrapped in a luscious ribbon lay on the bed for me. Inside, nestling in pale mauve tissue paper, was invariably an exquisite little creamy or black silk and lace number. I would gush appreciatively even though, no longer in the first flush of middle-age, I thought I might look slightly ridiculous; ageing mutton dressed as lamb cutlet. Once donned, I'm sure he secretly hoped that I would swing breezily from the chandelier or ooze seductively round the candle-lit room like some taunting Turkish temptress—anything to spur him on to ever greater heights and triumphs. Turning my inner reluctance into the amorous flame of Aphrodite should have been a slam dunk, but the pretty apparel did nothing to enrich the pastures of true love. I felt I was drowning in silk and lace as I racked my brain to conjuer up some new scantily-clad take on Goya's *Naked Maja*. After nine months when I knew I must leave for good and catch my plane to London, I said goodbye to the last of the pretty Janet Regers. I gave Bill back his Concorde ticket to his best friend's wedding in Sandy Lane in Barbados and deserted my glam suite in the Carlyle all because I still carried a torch for Mad Max. Oh, what a compulsive fool I was!

DEVON RAINBOW

Down by the sea in Devon there is a much used and loved summer house owned by my sister Susie and her kind, thoughtful husband Roddy Hill, a successful businessman who is generally adored by all his friends. Their charming children, Casper and Chloe, have grown up playing endless rounds of golf and sets of tennis, nestled in the green grass above the beach. I am lucky enough to be invited down two or three times a year. My caring sister, a fine botanical artist, has been pretty since childhood, with brown wavy hair and blue eyes in a fine-boned face. As well as being a brilliant cook, Susie has a huge reservoir of energy and we spend hours combing the pebbly beach for cowrie shells.

Last year I was driving back to London with Chloe when, a mile from the house the morning sky darkened and, as if by magic, a magnificent rainbow pulled itself out of the heavens. Within minutes the curve of the arc appeared to be drifting there directly above, waiting to enfold us. For a few extraordinary moments the glorious colours swirled numinously around us like a mist as we slowly passed through the sea-shades at the end of the rainbow. I didn't know it was possible but it certainly happened to us that day. Our pot of gold was never found but as a memory it is priceless.

A month after the magical rainbow Tara and I were booked in to stay at a rambling old Cornish house near Padstow for the christening of my grandson Fin. My daughter Tasmin and all her sons have been christened in a tiny 12th century church, St Enedoc, which is built by the sand dunes of Daymer Bay near Rock. It lies on the site of a cave where St Enedoc lived as a hermit and is one of the most romantic small churches in England. John Betjeman, the former Poet Laureate who also dearly loved the little church, lies in a grave in the small flower filled churchyard, cocooned by a thick tamarind hedge. Over time the wind-driven sand formed banks around the church and for nearly three hundred years the church was almost completely buried by the dunes. Only the steeple, like a witch's hat, managed to peep out of the sand. To maintain the tithes required by the church and to keep it consecrated, a service had to be held once a year when the Vicar and one or two parishioners were lowered down on a rope through a hole in the roof. Eventually, in 1864, the church, known locally as 'Sinking Eddy'

was dug out of the sand. As there was no road the only way for us to get to St Enedoc was to walk for ten minutes up through the fields and over a golf course. We have done this trip many times, often carrying a baby in the old family Christening robe and lace shawl blowing in the wind. We carried with us a full hotwater bottle to pour into the font to prevent the baby screaming with fright. These days the Vicar brings his own Thermos flask.

The centuries old house we were to stay in belonged to the Doppeldorfs, old friends of Roddy's, who ran a B&B business. Before we left London Roddy took me aside and said in a conspiritorial voice,

"Dal, I think I should warn you that the Doppeldorfs are swingers. Their favourite playmates are the Ponsonby-Gores who live nearby but I'm sure Tara and you are liberal enough to deal with that."

"I had absolutely no idea you cavorted with with such a racy lot, Roddy," I replied in astonishment.

The house had a stunning position high on the cliffs looking out to sea. Since we were Roddy's relations the Doppeldorfs met us with a friendly kiss. Our host put his arm round my shoulder as he took us up to our room and once alone I said to Tara,

"I cant believe they are really swingers, can you? They look so terribly unlikely."

She agreed. He was short with not much hair and she was a rather homely woman, possibly happiest living as far away as possible from the bright lights; mind you, if she had gone any further she would have been swimming half way to Caracas by now. It was hard to imagine them in the throes of Cornish passion but perhaps things could get a bit lonely living in perpetual sea mist. That evening we joined them for a drink. They were sitting cosily by a roaring fire in their navy blue Cornish fishermen's jerseys and sensible corduroy trews, sipping a glass of wine.

Of course the next day at the Christening I spilled the beans about our hosts' swinging antics to Tasmin's mother-in-law, Rosey, her sister and their mother, who had all owned summer houses in that part of Cornwall for many years. They had known the Doppeldorfs forever and were, quite frankly, amazed. Tara and I had wound ourselves up into a minor frenzy by the time we got back to the B&B. As we fully expected, our host invited us to have a nightcap with him which we regretfully declined as we discreetly oiled our way up the bannisters and bolted our door against any nocturnal prowlings. God forbid them flouncing into our room and declaring themselves ready for action.

All was quiet on the Western front when we said goodbye to our hosts in the morning, their sexy shenanigans clearly hidden under a bushel for more malleable visitors. A week later Roddy sheepishly admitted,

"The whole thing was a joke, Dal. There is absolutely nothing fruity or unfresh about the poor old Doppeldorfs."

Once I admitted I had amused others in Cornwall with my tittle-tattle, Roddy, nervous they might hear from someone else, promptly rang up the Doppeldorfs to apologize in advance. Big mistake. They were furious and after calling him "silly, silly Roddy," a couple of times, they refused to talk to him for a while. Roddy has always had a fine sense of the ridiculous and playing pranks no doubt stretched back to his old schooldays at Harrow, but occasionally it backfires and gets him into deep doo-doo.

ALWAYS THERE

My longest-lasting, dearest and most caring of all my male friends has been the American foreign correspondent, Jon Randal. His bright intelligence still shines through at eighty-eight; his kindness is legendary. Still living in Paris, having started off there as a foreign correspondent during the mid-1950s, he worked for many years for the New York Times and the Washington Post, primarily focusing on war zones. Not only is he a highly regarded foreign correspondent with a long and distinguished career, he is an extraordinary man, passionate about truth and reason, right and wrong, a loyal support to friends and takes a great interest in the lives and achievements of their children. Besides the numerous tins of caviar he sent me while reporting on Iran in 1981, his best present was a watch with Ayatollah Khomeini's face on it. When it struck on the hour, the Ayatollah beamed out like some sort of demonic bear.

Jon's book, *Going All the Way: Christian warlords, Israeli adventurers and the War in Lebanon*, met with wide acclaim and he is still closely involved with the Kurds, many of whom are dear friends. He has always been a great listener and comfort to me and although he lives in France with Genevieve, his French wife of many years, we are constantly in touch. He often ends his emails with "I kiss your feet" or 'May your shadow never diminish', two of his favourite Oriental proverbs.

Jon and I were both extremely fond of Bill Tuohy, the London Bureau Chief of the *Los Angeles Times* who was another supportive friend. The son of a Chicago judge and a Pulitzer prize winner for his reporting in Vietnam, Bill was wonderful company and like his friend Johnny Apple, a *bon viveur*. A great storyteller, he also loved dancing and would swirl my mother round the floor at parties given in my flat in Earl's Court Square, despite an injured leg from a train crash when he was twenty-one which never seemed to bother him much. Bill and his charming Vietnamese wife Rose Marie had their wedding party at my flat.

He was a reporter's reporter, a wonderful writer, adept at 'hitting the ground running' and knowing intuitively how to work under extremely high pressure. I agree with Jon who first met him in Vietnam, that Bill epitomised the romantic image of a foreign correspondent: "Most journalists look like slobs, but Bill looked like what most people think a foreign correspondent ought to look like. He was tall, had this beautiful shock of white hair and was always impeccably dressed."

When Tuohy was Rome bureau chief, he and another journalist commisioned Gucci to make cases for their lightweight typewriters, which seemed to me the height of sophistication.

PRECARIOUS PAKISTAN

Having finished my biography on Joy Adamson, I agreed to travel into Afghanistan to help Drew in his newly formed Non Governmental Organisation (NGO) outfit in Jalalabad, the 'Emergency Relief Unit'. Initially we were going to take a short trip to northern Pakistan. After collecting me in Islamabad we were driven off down the Grand Trunk Road by Qasem, a quiet, goodlooking Afghan *Mujahid* and former pharmacist, to Peshawar, capital of the North West Frontier on the border with Afghanistan. From there we would travel to Hunza, once a small kingdom, bordering the Xinjiang region of China. One of the most lethal roads in the world, the Grand Trunk was manic. Huge painted, overloaded lorries tilted dangerously as they thundered past us like belching dragons. I was hypnotised by the metal trinkets swinging off their sides, brightly coloured fish, flowers and naughty ladies painted on every surface, with 'Highly in Falammable' scrawled on the back; they were the pride and joy of Pakistani lorry drivers. With no rules of the road, we mixed haphazardly with cows and tongas, bullocks, buses with wonky axles and camels trotting down the wrong side of the dual carriage way. Peshawar turned out to be a dusty, one-horse town but it was once a beautiful city, laid out with tree lined boulevards filled with flowers and exquisite Moghul architecture. It was taken over by Sikhs in 1818 who cut down the trees for firewood and razed most of the buildings to the ground.

Peshawar was flush with guns and drugs, mainly opium, and the Khyber Pass was considered one of the most dangerous areas on earth. Women in tentfuls of blue or green burqas glided unobserved down the narrow streets. At night men drank tea in 'chai' shops, eating chunks of mutton and rice, while their women stayed at home. The next day, after exploring the noisy bazaar, we had lunch in Peshawar's main hotel which had a large notice leaning against the front door, 'Please do not bring your guns into the hotel and tell your bodyguards to leave their Kalashnikovs outside.' I rather liked the word 'please'.

We continued on to the lush Swat valley which lies in the monsoon belt and is fertile with wheat, fruit and lucerne. It was surrounded by green pine forests where, beside the road, the trunks of the pines grew out in an upward curve from the slopes. The high hills were scattered with small houses built of stones and beams, covered with mud and straw. I was by now permanently dressed in a *chador* to hide my hair and a yellow nylon *shalwar* kameez bought in the bazaar that made me look like Babar the Elephant. We passed Churchill picquet where Winston Churchill had served in 1897 and led his men against a Pathan skirmish, and eventually arrived at the White Palace Hotel to spend the night. A lovely old pillared house with a large verandah, it nestled at the end of a valley next to a small river hurrying on its way. It was once the summer palace of the Wali of Swat, made infamous partly by Lewis Carroll's many-versed nonsense limerick:

> Who, or why, or which, or what,
> Is the Wali of Swat?
> Is he tall or short, dark or fair?
> Does he sit on a stool or a sofa or chair?

Does he beat his wife with a gold-topped pipe
When she lets the gooseberries grow too ripe?

Before drifting off to sleep beneath the wobbly ceiling punka, Drew told me stories of his recent life in Jalalabad—this one among them: "Last month, the rich foreign women in Islamabad decided to help the Jalalabad refugees by giving them their cast-off clothes. How strange the Afghans looked and how they all laughed as they tried on pin-striped suits, ties and cocktail dresses!"

The next morning we set off for the Karakoram Highway, one of the highest paved roads in the world and a long-held dream of mine. It connects Pakistan to China, twisting through three great mountain ranges, the Himalayas, Karakorams and the Pamirs and follows one of the ancient silk routes along the Indus, Gilgit and Hunza rivers. I imagined all the caravans of camels, horses and mules which transported goods for fifteen centuries— from jade and gunpowder to ivory, ceramics and spices, gold, silk and glass— between China and eastern Asia to the edge of Europe and the Levant. The Highway was cut out of towering cliffs on one side, which promised to fall away and send us hurtling into the Indus, a swirling mass the colour of wet cement. Earth tremors can happen every three minutes; Karakoram means 'crumbling rock' in Turkish. Rockslides wiped out villages, large parts of the Silk Road have disappeared, and huge boulders sit in orchards and fields like large uninvited guests. Unbeknownst to us we were trundling through the middle of a geological collison belt at the most dangerous time of the year and after being held up by a spectacular landslide which blocked the road with a number of Pakistani buses bound for Kashgar in front of us, we were told we were lucky to get through.

We spent the night in Dasu in ninety degree heat—a place full of surly looking ruffians wearing *Chitrali* hats who looked as though they would just as soon knife one for a few rupees. Not a woman in sight which made me very conscious of being a Western female. The next morning there was a sudden commotion in the bazaar when three western dudes in shiny black leather and red bandanas roared into town on Harley Davidsons, each determined to look more like Dennis Hopper in *Easy Rider* than his companions. It was an odd sight but besides being a source of fascination to the excited children, they brought some pizzaz to the dull and drab colour of Islamic clothing. How I sometimes longed for the colourful saris of India—the saffrons, pinks and reds.

We left the depressing little town early and forged ahead to Gilgit. Beyond, near the border with China, lay Hunza. Isolated and majestic. An hour's drive away, we found ourselves surrounded on all sides by a labyrinth of mountains, their folds concertinaed in the afternoon light. It was a wondrous place. To the east lay ridge upon ridge of white peaks like a tented world suspended in ice. Soaring from its centre was Rakaposhi, a snow-covered mountain of such ethereal grandeur that I felt certain I had arrived at the most beautiful place on earth. Once famous for its ruby mines and red garnets, when snow leopards roamed the land, Hunza was best known for its perfect small, round apricots, the sweetest in the world. As we neared the capital Karimabad, we glanced up at Baltit Fort, a stone and timber fortress plastered over with sun-dried mud and once the palace of the Mirs, perched like an eagle's nest high on the mountain. The people of the area have been ruled by the same family for eleven centuries, and six hundred Himalayan winters have battered the old palace from whose carved portals the old Mir rode out each day on his horse.

As late as the nineteenth century the Hunzakuts were involved in slave trading, caravan raids, plunder. When British forces stormed into Hunza in January 1892 after "a splendid little fight", they ransacked what was left of the spoils in the fort. They found antique suits of chain amour, a Parisian music box, bottles of quicksilver, Dutch engravings and an extensive library, a cache of guns, powder and bullets fashioned out of large garnets.

Huge numbers of apricot trees were grown on precarious terraced slopes and in the spring they were covered in swaying blossom of such profusion it seemed as if clouds of white butterflies had settled on each bough. When we arrived the fruit were being carefully dried, like a golden-orange carpet, on the flat roofs of the houses.

Once an important staging post on the silk route, Hunza was full of handsome men with green eyes, who live to be well over one hundred. Such friendly children everywhere. The Hunzakut women wear their hair in long thin plaits framing their faces and when young they are pretty, not yet affected by the harsh climate. The strict laws of Islam seem relaxed as they did not hide behind veils. Instead they wore colourfully embroidered caps covered by a shawl. Of all the Ismailis to whom Prince Karim Aga Khan is the glorious Imam he is said to love Hunza and its people the best. (When I was thirteen and he was young and handsome he came to Government House, where I developed a huge crush on him.) It is also thought that Hunza might be the mysterious kingdom of Shangri-La in James Hilton's book *The Lost Horizon*.

FALL OF THE WALL

Two years previously, in November 1989, the Cold War had ended forty years of division between the capitalist West and the gruesome regime of the Communist East. In January Drew and I arrived in the buzzing German city to see ordinary citizens hacking away with hammers and pick-axes at segments of the polarizing Berlin Wall. With hundreds of others we stormed through Checkpoint Charlie into East Berlin. West Berliners were dancing on the Wall with excitement, and the shouts of relieved citizens hurrying through from the East rang through the air. Right beside the Wall a tall, amusing Scot in a kilt had seized the moment and was doing a brisk trade in small graffited chunks of wall which he had placed in a neat pile beside him.

"Walk up, walk up. Look at these lovely rocks. Only £1 a piece," he shouted in his lilting Highlands burr.

He effortlessly seduced passing punters who found his cheerful chutzpah impossible to resist. My own piece has blue graffiti on it and is the size of my palm. I keep it on a special shelf next to my lion's fur ball and other treasured possessions. To remember.

AFGHANISTAN AND KALASHNIKOVS

Once we got back from Hunza to the dusty frontier town of Peshawar and before setting off for Afghanistan, Drew and I hear bad news. All hell had broken loose in Jalalabad; one thousand dead just outside the town as a result of a *Mujahideen* commander being killed by another faction. I was not allowed into the country. Fortunately we had just been to the United Nations post stores and stocked up for the month with wine, cases of beer, vodka and food for everyone in the ERU, Drew's organisation in Afghanistan. Meanwhile we stayed in its Peshawar guest house. The next day, wearing my voluminous *chador* I visited the bazaar bursting with people and noise, where old textiles, carpets and Afghan silver jewellery—'everything very old'—were going for a song. I was looking for a not-too-hideous burqa to cover myself from head to foot during my stay in Afghanistan. Once bought we left for the border, passing the Tribal areas—a no-man's land of tall mud towers and forts, lawlessness and opium factories where only the drug barons rule. We were told that any one of them would be happy for us to visit and enjoy a cup of tea together in his compound. We politely declined. As we travelled west the scrubby landscape and pink and beige hills gave way to the dramatic barren hillsides of the Hindu Kush.

The Khyber Pass and the border post at Torkham were chaotic, filled with gun-toting men. It was easy to buy a weapon in a country with a glut of gun-shops. Hundreds of trucks were lurching into Afghanistan with many more trying to get over to Pakistan. Men with sticks beat our cars while Pakistani police and soldiers with thin, stinging lathes beat back the hordes of desperate Afghan refugees who were trying to push through on foot. My visa to get into Afghanistan stated I was a nurse, alas something I have never been. The Immigration officer looked at me for longer than necessary as if I was Nurse Ratched herself, the heartless battle axe in *One Flew Over The Cuckoo's Nest*. We then headed for the gate which was being pushed close by the guards and soldiers, some of whom were shooting their Kalashnikovs into the air in frustration. I knew going into the country might be about as risky as bungee-jumping from the top of the Ritz-Carlton in Riyadh, but as usual I felt a surge of excitement at my new adventure.

The road from Torkham stretched away towards the horizon until it was just a pale blue ribbon fluttering between the earth and sky. The wind was still and the sun beat down on a land seemingly without life. We began driving past small villages nestling beside expansive fields of pale mauve opium poppies. Burnt out Russian tanks and deserted garrisons scattered and scarred the hills. Only the olive trees remained. White stones along the side of the road marked fields which had been de-mined and red stones indicated those in which some of the ten million land mines left by Russians were still lying in wait. Along the road people walked alone on crutches, one young man with a single leg. How far did he have to hobble when there was no sign of a village or homestead?

We sped into Jalalabad, ramshackle, dusty and dirty, filled with rough looking men and not a woman in sight. In a country dominated by warlords, the town is sixty miles from the fraught fighting in Kabul, or ten seconds by rocket. We arrived at the ERU compound wall with graffiti scrawled on it— No Wife Without a Life—which seemed plausible enough. I was pleasantly surprised to find a compact bungalow with an airy living room opening onto a verandah. A small garden with orange trees and basil, pots of bourganvillea and yellow zinnias added a touch of colour, an oasis in the barren landscape. It was August and over 100 degrees.

We were met by Topikai, a handsome thirty-five year old Afghan woman who had nine children and was head of the Women's Health Care. She welcomed me with a large hug and a kiss on each cheek. Although she looked fifty, when I asked her later why she did not hide her face, she said in excellent English, "If I was younger I would hide my face, but I am old now and it no longer matters. I will never wear it, even though the Koran says women should." The only exception was when a non-family male came into her house.

Topikai was feisty and tough in this all male world. That night in our compound, amid the sounds of gunfire, we shared a dinner of stewed meats, dal, rice and vegetables. Drew and I slept on a thin mattress on the cement floor in the bedroom and awoke early to be told not to go into the bazaar as there had been a skirmish and ten *Mujahideen* had been shot. Good timing on my part. The next day Akmed Gul, a big handsome bear of an Afghan and once a seasoned *Mujahid*, took us with Topikai to the Widow's Camp. As he knew everyone in the bazaar it was doubtful anyone would take a pot shot at us today.

A long avenue of palm trees led to what used to be a palatial winter house belonging to a rich Kabuli. There was a magnificent view from this once beautiful house across green fields and the Kabul River to the Hindu Kush. The Hizbi-i-Slaami party, headed by Gulbaddin Hekmatyar ruled this poorest part of town which was endemic with typhoid and raw sewage running into the ditches, on which the ducks alone thrived. The sociopath and biggest baddy among the Afghan warlords of seven different *Mujahideen* factions, all of whom loathed each other, Hekmatyar used the large house above the camp as his headquarters when in town. Two female Hizbi-i-Slaami commandants in charge of the widows greeted us. One of them, tall, burly and probably weighing in at two hundred and sixty pounds, had amber eyes and black curling whiskers sprouting vigorously. Her pride and joy was an enormous pair of brown western men's shoes, probably off a dead Russian soldier, in which she clomped around the compound. Having seen eleven of her extended family killed, she had joined the *Mujahideen* and fought ferociously alongside her brothers and cousins. With Akmed Gul haltingly translating, she admitted, "I have killed many peoples myself. When I scalp Russian, I take notebooks out of uniform pockets and keep them under mattress on floor to remind me." A sort of literary scalping which she proudly showed me.

This formidable woman still had her Kalashnikov and was prepared to fight any foreign intruder should it be deemed necessary. The widows and children' food and water was provided by the ERU and funded by Norway. Topikai and I passed smelly latrines and into a series of small, dark, fly-blown rooms, each of which housed up to five families. Small children were lying asleep on the floor, women were weaving baskets, new born babies were tightly swaddled in a small blanket wrapped securely with strips of material. The refugees had nothing and had lost all their families, homes and possessions. Their situation was very distressing.

A week later we passed through town and saw hundreds of fired-up *Muj* jumping into trucks full of rocket propelled grenades and guns. Something was up. Tanks were soon rumbling down the main drag. They looked angry and unpredictable so I pulled my *chador* further round my face. We quickly returned home and listened to the old gardener digging the earth at the back of the house for a bunker in case rockets really began to fly. Since he had only managed to dig down six inches, Jalalabad would probably be obliterated by the time he finished. Within a week, a deep, ominous grave had been built with numerous wooden planks on top covered with sandbags. He had left a huge gaping hole in the front for us to crawl through so if the house was blown up, it would collapse neatly down the steps of the bunker and bury us all. Even the *Muj* commander who had become our new security guard told us,

"This bunker no good. If rocket fall, it kill you peoples."

Drew admitted he was worried about me being here and decided to find another escape plan in case the Torkham road to Pakistan was blocked. I didn't exactly relish the idea of dying at the hands of the desperadoes at either end of our road. That night I sat on the verandah, looking out at the moon hanging over the lemon trees. Geckos darted up the wall and small bats flew out from a hole in the roof as I wondered if I would ever get out alive.

Akmed Gul, big, mischievous and always grinning, was friends with all the other *Mujahideen* and tried to sell us Gandahari buddhas for a fortune. The next morning he drove Drew, Topikai and myself to Sar-Shahi, the huge, sprawling refugee camp situated on stony, still-mined desert twenty miles east of Jalalabad. One hundred and thirty thousand refugees from Kabul lived there on the barren thousand-tented plain. I felt safe with Akmed Gul in charge as we passed all the *Muj* militia posts in our white ERU jeep with its large flag flying, marking us out as an NGO and friendly Indians. The most deeply buried mines were the anti-tank ones and a family in the camp was blown up the previous day while they were collecting scraps of firewood. Having lost her husband and three children with only a single baby left, the devastated young mother would now return to her parent's home and live in purdah. There were many people with missing limbs everywhere. Landlines remain a endless, continuing scar, with lives ruined and lives lost.

Drew's organised health education meetings and water chlorination for the refugees plus the widow's camp, and I was there to help as much as I could. The people, although desperately poor, seemed cheerful and one small pretty girl with an infected eye tried to give me two of her four plastic bangles as a present—probably her most cherished possessions besides her blue plastic flip flops with a silver buckle. I joined Topikai, a nurse, midwife and a born teacher, in one of canopied tents and watched as she gave a health education lesson on the prevention of diahorrea to the young health educator women. They were so young and giggly in their *chadors*, bright and able, and had been educated up to the age of twelve. Afghans are very polite and the children stand up promptly when you go into their tented classroom. The teacher reads repeatedly from the Koran in Arabic and they parrot her words.

Later I sat outside in the shade of a tree in our compound and started a sketch of the house as a present for Drew. It was odd to be here drawing and listening to gunfire and rocket propelled grenades blazing away outside our gates. It still made me jump if it was too near. Stana, our old broken down Yugoslavian refugee cook who had had the most difficult of lives, came up and asked me what we wanted for dinner that night.

"A whole chicken to roast, please," I said. A big drama and misunderstanding until Gutan Rasul, the courtly old interpreter joined us. He must have learnt his English from the British East India Company when they thrust through the Khyber Pass in 1807.

"Stana thinks you want big chicken, alive, in a cage to keep in the garden?" I shake my head. "Then you want chicken in a plastic bag to kill here?"

"Not exactly."

"No chickens in the bazaar. Very old. So sorry. Will try again tomorrow."

Before Stana arrived we had lost three cooks in three weeks. They just couldn't cope in the smoky, brain-sizzlingly hot mud kitchen with no ventilation other than the small door. I told Drew that every cook would leave unless we got them a fan. Within a week one arrived. It sat outside the kitchen fanning the air in the courtyard.

*

One August night Drew got up from the floor mattress to get some water and in my sleep I flung my left arm over to his side. I suddenly felt a pain so excruciating I screamed and leapt to my feet. I looked for a snake but instead found a pale scorpion with a long translucent tail crawling swiftly into the corner of our room. Within moments of being stung I felt a river of molten lava raging through the veins and muscles of my left arm; I felt the precise moment that the poison seeped into and captured each joint, quickly paralysing my fingers, my wrist, my elbow joint before rapidly creeping up my shoulder and down my left side. After staggering to the bathroom and swigging the remains of my vodka to try to ease the pain, I collapsed moaning on a bed and surrendered to the rhythmic waves throbbing through my body. We could not get to the nearby hospital as the two *Mujahideen* factions on our road were busy trying to kill each other so Drew gave me a shot of novocaine. By dawn the fighting had died down, allowing the *chowkidar* to run and get a doctor from the hospital.

I soon learnt that Afghans are wary of this most dangerous of scorpions, the sting of which feels like someone is holding down a red-hot iron on your skin. I was wearing a skimpy sleeveless tee-shirt but kept a sheet on me with only my bare arms visible to the Moslem men. Topikai and various ex-*Muj* ERU staff stood around my bed while she translated the incident to the fat, jolly doctor who looked as if she would enjoy sticking a submachine gun up a buffalo's backside. The dead scorpion on the floor was the subject of much speculation as to its size and toxicity, which often kills babies and the elderly.

The doc used the same huge needle Drew had and stuck it intra-muscularly a couple of times. Nothing made any difference—injections, barbiturates, paracetamol. The pain just increased and by lunchtime I was climbing the walls. Apparently you can get kidney failure and Jalalabad had no dialysis machine. The only slight relief was ice. Bibi, our small *halla*, our cleaning woman with eyes the colour of topaz, one of which kept turning in towards her nose, sat by my bed all day, gently soothing me by putting ice on my burning arm. I spent the next fifteen hours knocking my knee against the wall in rhythm with the pulsating pain, before it began to subside. Drew sat on the floor beside me and did his work in the room all day so he could keep an eye on me. As always in a crisis he was amazing, wishing the scorpion had stung him instead so he could take my pain away. Afghans believe strongly in magic and myth and wanted to go and get the scorpion *Mullah*, telling us, "He draws circle around sting with finger and chants verse from Koran and pain stops."

Alas, we didn't get him as I was being violently sick. Three days later we went off to see a British doctor at *Medicine Sans Frontiers*, who seemed so brusque compared to all the Afghan warmth given to me. A laboratory technician in the room said in a nasal voice,

"This is a funny sort of place to come for a holiday. Beats Spain I suppose."

After two weeks Drew and I left for a three day sojourn in Kama, about thirty miles from Jalalabad. In my three months in Afghanistan we were never able to travel to Kabul for fear of being shot by bandits on the road and couldn't travel at all unless our own *Muj* had cleared permission with the next faction along the road and so on for the entire journey. I was told that if they didn't kill us they were liable to kidnap me and ask for $10,000, plus take the jeeps. Our posse consisted of two white jeeps, our ex-*Muj* driver Qasem, and Kakul our guard, with whose family and tribe we were going to stay. We drove across the Kabul river where the Hindu Kush mountains appeared out of the haze and the green fertile fields hugged the river. Various militia posts were passed, one on the bridge with four *Muj* sitting around smoking, their Kalashnikovs hanging neatly on hooks, below which were rows of pots planted with colourful flowers. After an hour we reached Kamar, an area once called 'Little America' for its abundance of apricots, of cotton, wheat,

maize, rice and walnuts, and now a wasteland. The Russians had systemati-
cally blown to smithereens every village, every house in the area, their fallen
honeycomb of rooms scattered among the hillocks, before demolishing the
irrigation system. Russian tanks turned upside down like stricken dugongs
were dotted around, attesting to the Afghans determination. Eventually we
came to Kakul's village. Experiencing these adventures would have been
impossible without people like Akmed Gul and Qasem who knew the area,
plus an armed guide who could pave the way. We left the cars with a *Muj* commander and his men who knew Kakul. He had an intelligent face with warm
brown eyes and was very much the quiet commander. Sitting on *charpoys*
under a thatched shelter, he and his men held their guns strapped onto their
shoulders, while we took off on foot for Kakul's family compound, arriving
just before dusk. His family was one of the few who have returned to their
devastated village from Kabul.

When we arrived, the men and boys were silently sitting cross-legged on
long mats and cushions on the hard baked earth, eating their rice and meat.
Each shook our hands and said *A-Salaam Alakum* in greeting as we gave them
three large watermelons as a gift. We sat on empty *charpoys* and talked in the
moonlight; no other light was needed as the night was so clear. The young
boys cleared away the finished meal which had been laid by the men; the
women didn't come out of the compound. Then every man walked silently
over to the small mud mosque nearby where a *Mullah* read from the Koran
while the men prayed, a ritual they undertook five times a day. The silence
was only broken by one man's melodic voice. It was simple and rather moving.
The hills of the Hindu Kush stood out like solitary elephants against the sky
and the moon caught the tops of the maize plants in a shimmering silver line.

The men then prepared the ground for a meal for their guests and Kakul.
They brought out many different dishes, one of which was the fat from
one of the unattractive fat-tailed sheep. This lump at the rear of the sheep
wobbles like a lady at a freak show and is considered a much loved delicacy
by Afghans. With it went yoghurt, tomatoes, chicken, rice, nan and mutton.
This time the others sat on their *charpoys* and watched. I was intrigued by
two old bearded men in turbans—Kakul's father and father in law—who
had known each other all their lives and were chatting away like old men
the world over. Once we had eaten, Drew and myself on one side, the men
on the other as no Afghan Muslim can sit next to an infidel woman, not even
in a jeep. Although they seemed to be treating me most of the time as an

honorary man. Our kind hosts put white sheets on our charpoys which were set head to head, for the night. As we lay in our beds we gazed up at the clear sky filled with a thousand stars. The shrill clickety-click of cicadas in the heat of the day had given way to ribbitting frogs which lulled us to sleep. Is there anything better than sleeping outside? At sunrise I sat up, turned away from the men and brushed my hair in the early morning light, hoping this did not offend my kind Afghan hosts in some way. The sun was already hot as we sat having a filling breakfast of *paretta*—a delicious fried nan, accompanied by fried egg and sweets. As soon as we finished Kakul and Qasam took us up to meet the women behind the compound walls. Apart from the families the huge compound was empty except for a large number of turkeys sitting motionless on branches spread over a well, looking like buzzards-in-waiting. I took many photos of the smiling women and curious children and after saying goodbye to our rather exceptional hosts, we traced our steps down the dusty tracks to our cars.

All of the *Muj*, including Drew, were crack shots. On our way home from seeing Bhuddist ruins they took it upon themselves to teach me how to shoot a Kalashnikov in case things got worse in Jalalabad. Akmed Gul lent me his, and crouching down beside me he explained how to use it. With the first shot I managed to hit a wall about two foot from the target and found the kick back and noise in my ears intense. I was allowed roughly ten shots before Akmed Gul smiled and said it was time to hit the road back to town. The following day Drew and I went to the public hospital where eager young doctors showed us round orthopaedic wards full of mine victims missing arms and legs, or both. Some were peppered with powder burns, one young man seemed in shock with a missing eye, a leg, an arm and part of his nose. He had been looking for firewood when it happened. Burned babies, suffering women surrounded by their children and families who fed them and soothed their foreheads. Limbless men lay on charpoys outside the hospital waiting patiently for days until prostheses arrived from Sandy Gall's Afghan Refugee appeal, an essential organisation. Afterwards we went to Topikai's house. I was, of course, dressed in my hideous green burqa when I went out. It was a mud house with three rooms, in a compound. Her eldest girl of fourteen could not come out of the house with men around as she had reached puberty, so I went in and talked to her.

"Topikai how do you manage your job, all your children and the cooking?"

She replied, "I hate cooking, my eldest daughter does it. She is like the mother of the house and looks after all the other children."

My last night in Jalalabad was something that will stay with me forever. Kakul, Qasam, Akmed Gul and another ex-*Muj*, Pushtun who worked there, got stoned. We joined in and soon found ourselves laughing through a delicious dinner cooked by the ever-stoic Stana. Later Kakul played his flute beautifully, Pushtun the drum and an old *Mullah*, who had recently become the new gardener, played the rubab, a traditional stringed musical instrument similar to a guitar. We had to shut all the windows and doors to keep out the forbidden sound of music. He was the most benign, twinkling old *Mullah* one could imagine. With music and drugs pulsing through our bodies, the men got up to dance—a slow Afghan dance going round and round on one foot which Akmed Gul did with great panache. Islam here of course frowns on any Muslim enjoying himself but the usually reticent Qasam became totally uninhibited. He proved to be a great dancer, going round faster and faster as the music picked up. Stana and I were dragged up and did our best. The *Mullah* was looking slightly bemused at women dancing in his presence, but continued to strum away. Pushtun lifted his glass of tea, remarking,

"This is our farewell evening to Caroline as she is leaving tomorrow and we will miss her." We continued to dance for many hours in a forbidden swirl of love and friendship.

I felt sad the next morning saying goodbye to all my charming, good-looking and extremely polite Afghan friends at the compound with whom I had spent many weeks. The border post at Torkum was as usual chaotic with Pakistani lathes whipping people and Afghans shooting their guns over people's heads. Pushtun and Akmed Gul were with us, trying to direct traffic, and we said a forlorn farewell to them before crossing the border.

The next day at the guest house in Peshawar Drew and I were enjoying a quiet drink on the verandah, and extremely relieved to have got out unscathed. Just as we were talking about it a Pakistani Air Force F6 fighter jet flown by a trainee pilot, crashed through four houses just behind ours, missing us by a few seconds. Apparently these planes often flew far too low over Peshawar. Something was telling me it was definitely time to go home.

The next day I found myself driving an enormous truck down the lethal Grand Trunk Road to Islamabad for the first time with an extremely sick Drew beside me. I needed to get him to a doctor. For someone who had seldom driven a large lorry and certainly never down one of most dangerous roads in the world, it proved a nerve wracking experience. Drew was given strong pills by the doctor who told him to rest. I hated leaving him lying in a hotel bed but there was no alternative so I kissed him goodbye and rushed off to the airport to catch my plane for London. He would be joining me as soon as he was well enough.

THE OLD MAN IN CUBA

One of the things my helpful mother was more than happy to do was drive her children to the airport to catch a flight. This time I was on my way to join twelve American friends in Cuba, but half way to Gatwick her groaning car died. It was Sod's Law but it left us in a frantic quandary. As I couldn't possibly afford to miss my flight we decided to flag down a passing car. The first to stop was a white van driven by a Cockney plumber and his mate, their broad smiles suggesting,"'Ere we go again—women drivers, whad can yer say!" Without a moments hesitation they agreed to give me a lift, even though the airport was miles out of their way. "Op in luv, we'll getcha there in toime". The problem was the back of the van was piled high with pipes, plumbing tools and other unfathomable equipment and my only hope was a narrow horizontal shelf above this mayhem with a tiny pane of glass allowing me to see a sliver of sky. To fit in to the small cramped space I would have to lie flat on my tummy but at that point I couldn't be fussy.

Her brow furrowed with suspicion, my mother was convinced the men would take me off into the woods, rape or murder me and she would never see me again. I had a few doubts myself but time was of the essence. She took their names and registration number, clasped me to her bosom with strict instructions to ring her from the airport. After tossing my suitcase in the back, I clambered up onto the shelf and surrounded by four tons of clanking metal beneath me, off we went. I felt like a giant sardine freshly hauled in off the beach, trussed up with fins pressed firmly to sides, and being haplessly taken to market. Every bone felt as though it had been shaken around in a witchdoctor's bag by the time we arrived at the airport but the two men couldn't have been kinder or more helpful. Whoever you two were, thank you. I made the plane.

❉

We were in Cuba to celebrate our friend Judy's sixtieth birthday. Four of the five Hags—Muffy, Judy, Jennifer, Deborah and most of the men were American citizens who were not strictly allowed into the country. However, the Immigrations officers turned a blind eye when asked not to stamp their passports and the Americans sailed through. Havana was a hot, sexy city and its streets throbbed with loud music, dancing being a national passion. While crumbling Andalusian Baroque architecture and funky 1950s cars conjured up a long gone era of mojitos, cigars, Ernest and Che, they spoke more of the grinding poverty among the people. But to the outside world the disastrous Cuban revolution, the killings, imprisonment and torturing of so many of its citizens somehow never managed to eclipse the rock-star aura of a defiant Fidel Castro—he slept in a different safe-house each night at the time we were there. All of us were parked out in separate lodgings—Jennifer and I shared digs in a dubious alleyway next to a brothel. Sleep eluded us and for two whole nights we had to endure the sounds of carnal caterwauling on the other side of the flimsy wall.

Judy, who spoke fluent Spanish, travelled with me to Cojimar, a dozy fishing village east of Havana. I was to write a piece on Gregorio Fuentes, Ernest Hemingway's confidant and faithful companion for nearly thirty years, He was the model for one of Hemingway's most indelible characters—Santiago, the indomitable fisherman in his novel *The Old Man and the Sea*, written in 1952. Once fishing for marlin had replaced bullfighting as Hemingway's favourite manly pursuit, he bought a thirty-eight foot custom made fishing boat, the 'Pilar'- his second wife's nickname—and appointed Fuentes as first mate.

We arrived at Fuentes' humble home to be greeted by a lean, sprightly ninety-nine year old man with a craggy, weather-beaten face and warm, lively eyes that didn't miss a trick. Hemingway described Santiago's eyes as, 'blue like the sea and undefeated'. Fuentes, a lifelong cigar smoker, was happy to talk to any visitor wanting to connect with the Hemingway legend, explaining that their trips alone at sea together were particularly important.

"I was with Papa when he caught a 1,542 pound sailfish off Peru which took three hours to haul in. He was so excited."

As we walked up to Finca Vigia, the Pulitzer prize winner's attractive house which he shared with his third wife Martha Gellhorn which is now the Hemingway Museum, we stopped while the old sailor stood proudly next to his beloved 'Pilar'. He recalled how the two men became as close as brothers, particularly after Fuentes saved the life of the writer's six year old son, named Gregory, by shooting a shark with a machine gun.

I asked him, "What gave Hemingway the idea for *The Old Man and the Sea*?" Fuentes explained,

"We once came across an old man in a skiff fighting a big swordfish. He was surrounded by sharks and was in the middle of a fierce battle. We stopped and offered to help, but the old man shouted for us to go away. Later we heard the old man had died which upset Papa. I am sure that is why he wrote the book."

When Hemingway committed suicide in 1961 he willed the 'Pilar' and all his fishing tackle to Fuentes but it was quickly requisitioned by Castro. The ancient mariner lived to be 104 without having read *The Old Man and the Sea*.

Kaleidescope

ELTON JOHN

I HAPPILY RECEIVED an advance from Weidenfeld and Nicolson in 1997 to write a book on the great Oscar-winning singer Elton John. I was thrilled as I had always been mad about his songs. *Elton's Flower Fantasies* was only possible because my sister Susie had been arranging 250 flower arrangements every week for the past twelve years in Elton's two houses, one in London, and the other, 'Woodside' in the country, with a view of Windsor Castle. Henry VIII's physician had once lived in a house on the same spot before it was rebuilt in the 18th century. Whenever the King's gout flared up, a fire on the Castle's hill was lit high enough for the physician to see and he would leap on his horse and gallop up to aid his afflicted sovereign.

A child prodigy, Elton had been accepted at the Royal College of Music at the tender age of eleven. He had by now given up drink and drugs and was enjoying a clean life with his partner David Furnish. I had the idea of creating a book filled with some of the things he loved most, flowers being at the top of his list, especially roses, and so we asked him. Elton agreed, "Fine, as long as it's beautiful and not gimmicky."

I wove the history, legends and myths of flowers into my sister's lavish arrangements, about which Elton told me, "Susie has never done the same arrangement twice in all this time, which is quite extraordinary." Along with Elton's passion for his houses and country garden, designed by Rosemary Verey and Sir Roy Strong, he cares deeply for beautiful things: antiques, *objets d'art* and, among other treasures, a superb collection of paintings by Henry

Scott Tuke, a talented 19th century English artist best known for his depictions of young men. Elton owns one of the most important collections of his work in the world. Many of Elton's trademark possessions—jewellery, clothes and shoes are also in the book, helping to make each photo a personal affair.

Humour is a large part of Elton's make-up. My own introduction to his singular repartee occurred at seven o'clock in the morning at Woodside when he was about to start a brisk game of tennis with his coach. Dressed in crisp white shorts and carrying a tennis racket and balls, Elton cheerily greeted three of us standing in the courtyard, bent down to pat one of his nine dogs and promptly dropped one of the tennis balls.

"Not the first time I've dropped me balls," he cracked with a wink, without missing a beat.

It was highly enjoyable doing the book with Elton as he was interested and knowledgeable about many things: art, photography, architecture, music of course, and his charities. He was entertaining and so easy to be with; when we sat down to talk for the first time I felt I had known him all my life.

FRIEND OF THOMAS HARDY

I like to think back to encounters in my life, however brief, that have particularly touched me. Soon after my time spent with Elton I met a remarkable woman from Dorset called Norrie Woodhall who was one hundred and two. She is thought to have been the last surviving person to have known the writer Thomas Hardy, and was an original member of his Hardy Players. In 1924 the famous author of *Tess of the D'Urbervilles* cast Norrie, then just 18, as Tess's sister, Liza Lu in a stage version of his masterpiece, produced at the Corn Exchange in Dorchester.

A friend of mine, Harry Hook, had directed a beautifully photographed film, *The Heart of Thomas Hardy* for the BBC and invited her as a special guest to the premier in London. She had a twinkle in her eye and was still treading the boards as an amateur actress in Dorset. She was an extraordinary character, full of enthusiasm and humour.

"It is all wonderful, so exciting. I am enjoying myself hugely, especially as I havent been to London for forty years!", she said to me as we sat together. She was as bubbly as a young girl.

Norrie's beautiful mother, a local dairymaid, is believed to have inspired the character 'Tess' when she was milking a cow. Hardy passed by her daily on his regular walks. Norrie's sister Gertrude Bugler, a young married mother, having inherited their mother's dark, alluring looks, was later given the title role of 'Tess.' Chroniclers of Hardy's life have asserted that the novelist with the roving eye became infatuated with Gertrude, an outstanding amateur actress. His friend the painter Augustus John remembered that Gertrude was 'flushed with success' and 'dreamed of taking to the stage professionally' but her chance to play 'Tess' on the London stage was almost certainly killed off by the violent jealousy of Hardy's wife Florence. Norrie later wrote about the painful memories of how her sister was treated by Mrs. Hardy. She shared Hardy's deep affection for Dorset and at the fine old age of one hundred and one returned to the stage in Dorchester and read his poem 'The Ruined Maid' in a thick Dorset accent of a much earlier time. Harry Hook's brother Simon, a supremely talented artist and his witty, creative wife Andrea, are also two of my most favourite people.

JAMES BOND MOMENT, GREECE

Four summers ago found most of my immediate family in Paxos, the most beautiful, unspoiled Greek island of them all. A speedboat was an occasional perk for my four grandsons, all of them excellent swimmers. The first time out neither of my girls wanted to be skipper so although I had never steered a boat on my own before, I volunteered. Soon we were racing alongside our friends in their own boat. Our outward journey went smoothly and within an hour we were all snorkelling and picnicking on white island beaches.

All went well until our return trip to the harbour in Gaios. Spiros the young boat owner had firmly instructed me to dock in a certain bay next to similar small boats. As we approached the port I could see that the space had been taken and wasn't quite sure where to go. I was conscious other boats were coming into the harbour, fairly tearing around the place. A large ferry setting out for Corfu was also definitely something to avoid. I was starting to get nervous, veering unsteadily from post to post as I searched frantically for a spot. Most of my precious passengers were in high spirits, but I have to admit I had lost confidence in my novice skippering. At one point I looked round in terror and glimpsed a huge black Oligarch *fornicatorium*-boat bearing down on us, blaring its horn and warning us to get out of the way pronto. Looking like a deadly, sleek torpedo. I muttered to myself,

"This is it, it's definitely going to slice us in two and we're all going to die," but as luck would have it I had my one and only James Bond moment. I stepped on the gas and tore away in a vast semi-circle, the front of the boat leaping out of the water in a great swathe of power and white foam which delighted the grandchildren. That probably saved our lives.

I had no idea where I should go but aware I was heading for the end of the port where we would hit a wall and that would be that. Spiros meanwhile had been watching the whole episode from the opposite side of the quay in abject horror. Realising his boat might soon end up as firewood, he hurriedly jumped onto his friend's boat and they tore across the harbour after us. Still concentrating on keeping my brood alive and begging for divine intervention, I didn't really listen to the wild shouts on the wind behind us, thinking it was just more furious sailors yelling expletives. Within a few minutes, the young Greek owner caught up with the back of our boat and Spiros leapt at speed, like a flying figure from the Sistine Chapel ceiling, off his friend's boat onto ours, grabbed the steering wheel from me and saved the day. Thank God for our handsome man of the sea!

THE GARLIC BULB

I have always had a penchant for American men. After all, I married one. They are easy to talk to, treat women as equals, have a better understanding than the British of how the fairer sex tick and are often good lovers. In my early fifties, while I was writing the book on Elton, I met an older Robert Redford look-alike at a dinner party given by our mutual friends Carla and Charles Powell at Annabel's in London. Charles had been Margaret Thatcher's Private Secretary and key foreign policy adviser and I had remained good friends with them since our Washington days. Carla was a gorgeous Italian, highly amusing, a superb cook and a truly spectacular hostess.

My fellow invitee and I both had knees that needed replacing which we discovered after falling over as he twirled me too fast round the dance floor. That obviously did the trick and he became a long term boyfriend of whom

I became very fond. He was also an oil and gas millionaire many times over which was highly unusual for me. Jeff was kind and extremely generous. He lived between a large airy, wood and glass-filled house high up a mountain in Colorado with a panoramic view of the snow capped Rockies, and an artist's studio in London which I found and did up from scratch for him. In many ways Jeff was an interesting man, creative and artistic, and certainly a man of varied passions—architecture, sculpture, design and all things Chinese including, however much I argued to the contrary, the wildly inaccurate notion that the killing and wounding of thousands of innocent protesters in Tiannamen Square was pure hokum—just Western propaganda. He could not find one thing wrong with the Chinese, neither politically nor historically. Not surprisingly, in time I found his intransigent political beliefs difficult to deal with. But Jeff's varied interests led to unusual trips and treats. Flying down to Montana State University in Bozeman where I had the rare privilege of holding a real dinosaur's egg, was one of them. Or being with his friends next door on the mountain every New Year's Eve when the singer Roberta Flack and her band flew in and sang, for just twenty of us. 'The First Time Ever I Saw Your Face' is one of my very favourite songs.

Jeff had his virtues, not the least of which was a deep sense of devotion to his dog, a Jack Russell, with whom he often sang in excruciating unison. The wildflower meadow behind his house in the mountains was filled every year with poppies and the bluest cornflowers, daisies and Indian paintbrushes, which gave him and everyone else immense pleasure. But his greatest passion was reserved for exercise. At sixty-five and more than partial to a drop of tequila, I doubt if he was aware of Herodotus' writings on the 'Fountain of Youth' but even so, he was a man determined to live to be a youthful one hundred and forty. He exercised in one form or another for around six hours a day, starting with yoga at the ungodly hour of five thirty in the morning, something I flatly refused to do. And so I slept on while the pounding feet and tortured body on macho machines and buckling bicycles pumped on for hours. This gruelling marathon included two hours of martial arts twice a day with a dedicated Frenchman who must have been the richest martial arts teacher in the world as Jeff paid him the handsome sum of $1000 a day for his expertise. No fool he, old Frenchie was busily buying up cosy condominiums in California. A couple of hours of oil dealings on the phone for Jeff, then back to being martially challenged in order to achieve his longed for black belt, after which he collapsed with a soothing massage at twilight. It makes me quite exhausted just remembering it all. Each evening I took to a strong drink to soothe the effects of pilates, lap-swimming and walking. Jeff plying his own insides with tequila was most likely the reason he never achieved the flat stomach all his exercise should have bestowed.

Jeff also firmly believed in restorative natural medicines to boost his health and maintain his virility. Stored in a long stone tunnel, rows of vats and glass bottles holding strange looking potions were carefully labelled. They were dark and viscous and although it was possible some might have contained the juice of a newt or a few vipers' tongues, he assured me they were indeed all Chinese herbs. They obviously worked and kept him as fit as a fiddle. The other thing he swore by was garlic and the quicker it got into his blood stream the better. One September we flew down to Texas in his jet for an important exhibition of the work of Chinese portrait artists he had discovered on a trip to their country. He had flown over all thirty of them, plus their wives, from their small villages and towns. For many of them it was their first time outside their vicinity and they had never dreamed of travelling on a plane. As I said, Jeff was a financially generous man.

But I digress. We were getting dressed for the swish occasion in our hotel bedroom. I was lying on the bed after my bath when I happened to peer over at the shower area at the end of the room. As Jeff bent over to dry himself, I saw a large white protuberance sticking out of the least attractive part of his anatomy. At first glance I thought a crocus bulb must have fallen off the window sill and got caught.

"What on earth is that?" I exclaimed in horror.

"Oh it's just a large garlic clove," he said, rather sheepishly. "Peeled, it's great for the system."

"Oh my God, Jeff", I continued, "How utterly revolting. That could put a woman off you for life". Why hadn't I seen this before, I wondered. Had he always done it in secret? Why hadn't I noticed the pungent smell of garlic around him? He obviously took my total horror to heart as he never repeated that particular peccadillo when I was around, thank the Lord.

Every August for five years from the mid-nineties a group of us were invited by Jeff to go riding with cowboys in Colorado for a week, something I always greatly looked forward to. We all had various names given to us by Jeff, the

'Bandit'. Among them was a raffish stetson-wearing, moustachioed Texan. He had a shock of silver hair, was catnip to women, and known as the 'Silver Stallion'. Our trail boss was his wife, a cute blonde champion dressage rider called 'Rambling Rosie'. They brought with them the Texan's teenage daughter, 'Blue Ribbon Girl', named after her recent win in a major horse jumping competition. 'Dingo' (Jeff's best friend) was a well-known Australian sculptor, many of whose complex works dealing with quantum physics, were scattered around Jeff's estate. 'Dingo' lived in England and Jeff had donated one of his sculptures to the Centre for Theoretical Cosmology at Cambridge University of which Stephen Hawkins was the Director of Research. When the sculpture arrived, the three of us were lucky enough to be invited by the great man to tea at his house in Cambridge. He sat in his wheelchair and talked to us through his speech-generating device. I found him quite extraordinary and remember feeling honoured to be there.

Among the other riders was 'Flipper', an amusing middle-aged English baronet who had never been on a horse before and was in a dreadfully nervous state about the trip. My name was 'Lady Creede', the name of an old abandoned mining town deep in the Rockies where we were flying to start our trip.

In the first week of August, full of high spirits, the Creede Gang loaded up Jeff's plane at Aspen airport and set off. We flew due west for an hour as the early morning sun glinted off the snow scattered mountains and down into the deep green valley where the miners once thrived. The first thing I noticed on landing was a cell from Creede's first jail, a public telephone-sized cage of rusty bars big enough to hold one person. We were met by a raft of smiling working cowboys, the head of whom was Tom, a rangy man with a weathered face, a salt and pepper beard and crinkly blue, smiling eyes. He was sixty years old and wore a brown leather cowboy hat, a worn-in blue jeans jacket, leather chaps over his jeans. The real deal. We piled our few belongings into his chuckwagon and, drawn by two large chestnut horses, set off through the forest pines for Emerald Mountain ranch. This really was a taste of the Wild West. Titter ye not, I half expected Bill Cody on his horse Brigham to come haring round the corner singing 'Buffalo Bill' at full throttle. As the horses clip-clopped along we relaxed into the beginning of our adventure, instantly captured by the spirit of Emerald Mountain far above us.

'Dingo' had brought with him two Australian saddles as a present for Jeff and I was lucky enough to have one of them for my own horse. To my mind they are the best and most comfortable saddles invented—more like a slim version of a Western saddle seat but with English stirrups which don't pull as heavily on the legs as American ones. We were all given chaps to put on over our jeans and slowly morphed into authentic cowboys and girls. I noticed that the 'Silver Stallion' wore spurs on his boots and had a pistol hanging from a wide leather holster below his belt with its silver and turquoise buckle, looking very much as if he was setting out to defend the Alamo. Willard the mule was loaded up with bags and our posse of twelve set off through the woods, climbing higher above the beaver ponds until the trees were left far behind. Rosie, a lovely rider on her handsome bay, led us briskly upwards through spectacular scenery. After a four hour ride we stopped to stretch our legs and devour the delicious picnic lunch made by the cowboys' wives. After our break we continued climbing up into the high country and rode over the dangerously narrow pass at 14,000ft, where the air was cold and the wind blew fiercely. The faithful Willard followed us closely as our horses stepped carefully over the rocky crest, the sound of their hooves clipping sharply against the shale. Down, down we rode into the Jumper Lake crater where we were to spend our first night in tents.

Surrounded by tall dark pines, 'Dingo' and the 'Bandit' prepared the days collection of mushrooms for dinner and a goat was roasted in a pit under canvas. A night of revellery drinking tequila in coffee mugs round a blazing bonfire produced some happy campers. Cowboys sat on logs playing guitars and sang while we danced til midnight beneath a spray of stars. Jeff and I loved to dance. A local Creede girl sang country and western songs in a beautiful clear voice while high above us the mountain's summit glistened under the moon. Sleep was instant once our heads hit the pillow. As the sun came up to greet us the next morning we tucked into a full Western cowboy breakfast of eggs, beans, bacon and pancakes. After saddling up our horses we continued our second day with Tom and his band of merry men, and rode out of the valley.

LOVE OF TREES

I have always loved being out in the wilderness among trees. To my mind a magnificent tree is the finest of all nature's achievements. I have great affection for the mango tree, its ripe fruit dripping through the green leaves like fattened raindrops. The pale eucalyptus is another favourite; random washes of light and dark dissolving round its belly and the delicious smell of thin blue-grey leaves when crushed; bark sloughing off like an unwanted skin. I am also very fond of the giant baobabs that dot the parched yellow grasses of the savannah like rooted elephants, serene in their solitude.

But it is the noble beech which is an almost perfect creation and which I entirely love. The native broad-leaf possesses a natural, elegant dignity. Whenever I stand beneath one I feel in awe of the architectural beauty of its silver-green trunk rising effortlessly upwards into a mass of branches which slither over each other like careless snakes before cascading downwards in a languid confusion of leaves. The whole shape a perfect symmetry. Whenever the need comes upon me I press my palms into the tree's smooth bark, as if the process of communication might reassure me that all is right between both man and nature.

My novel *The Plant Hunter's Tale* highlights many of the beautiful exotic plants we now admire, discovered by intrepid plant hunters who travelled the world in search of new species. Lured to a remote Himalayan kingdom by the persistent rumour of a unique flowering plant, Rullie Montrose, a young botanist and plant hunter, sets off for India in 1856. I based the book around Hunza, the place I fell in love with in the Himalayas. While researching I discovered an interesting fact. The Wardian Case, a sealed glass case invented around 1829 by a London physician with a passion for botany, had forever changed the face of plant collecting abroad. The good doctor had been studying a hawk moth chrysalis on a leaf mold in a glass jar and sealed the lid. No moth emerged but instead a tiny fern and a few seedlings sprouted on the damp leaf. On a grander scale the glass case preserved plants in earth and water, from wind and salt spray, rats and dehydration during their hazardous voyages home across the ocean. Plant hunters could heave a sigh of relief; that is, assuming their plants survived their inland journey to the coast and the boats did not sink.

THE CHARLESTON LITERARY FESTIVAL

I enjoy doing separate things with different sisters—the ballet and theatre with Susie, exhibitions and adventures with Pods. Something I especially enjoy doing with Digs is going to the Charleston Literary Festival in May, one of the highlights of our year. It is a cultural event of great interest to many and over the years Digs has made friends with many of the writers and artists in the area, which has greatly enriched her life. The Festival takes place in a breezy tent in a glorious East Sussex garden at Charleston, once home from the First World War to artists Vanessa Bell, sister of Virginia Woolf, her husband Clive Bell and Duncan Grant who, on deciding to take a rare break from his rampant homosexuality, conceived a child with Vanessa. The colourful Bloomsbury group, which included among others the writer and critic Lytton Strachey, novelist E.M. Forster and the economist John Maynard Keynes, used the house as an enchanted retreat from London life. The small venue is the most charming of all literary festivals bringing writers, thinkers, artists and performers to explore art, literature and society just as the Bloomsbury group did round the Charleston Farmhouse dining table one hundred years ago. The walled garden, next to cow fields, is brimming with roses, cowslips, large pink and white peonies. To my mind it is England at its very best. As the inspiring painter Vanessa Bell wrote in 1936, "the house seems full of young people in very high spirits, laughing a great deal at their own jokes ... lying about in the garden which is simply a dithering blaze of flowers and butterflies and apples."

Digs is an extremely good painter herself, of striking, vigorous landscapes and sympathetic portraits, Jeremy Hutchinson, the barrister who defended Christine Keeler, and Olivia Bell, wife of Quentin Bell, Vanessa's son, being two of her very best. My sister's house, The Old Rectory with its own lovely garden, is not far away from Charleston and we both bubble with anticipation as the Festival date creeps nearer. The great playwrite Tom Stoppard, Vanessa Redgrave, Alan Bennett, Jeanette Winterson, Sir David Attenborough and Ann Patchett are among those who have spoken there. The illustrious guests are often interviewed by the perceptive writer and journalist, Digs' great friend Juliet Nicolson. Occasionally my lovely nephews, Ned, Leo and Wilby, the first two who have their own successful rock bands and the third, a talented artist, accompany us.

CREATIVE WOMEN

Throughout the years Kenya has also produced extraordinary women in the arts unbothered by convention, who often led creative, passionate and fulfilling lives; the Danish author Karen Blixen, with her unforgettable memoir *Out of Africa*; the sexy Beryl Markham who, among numerous lovers, bedded both the Prince of Wales and his brother Prince Henry, Duke of Gloucester, in the late 1920s. Her riveting autobiography, *West with the Night* has enthralled many. I must also mention the brilliant activist and politician, Wangari Maathai. Although her field was not in the arts, she was the first African woman to win the Nobel Peace prize for planting many thousands of trees through the formation of her Green Belt Movement.

Mirella Ricciardi, the Kenya-born half French and half Italian photographer is another such woman. She is a loyal friend, immensely articulate, and her seminal photography book, *Vanishing Africa*, about the disappearing tribes of the continent, was the first and finest of its kind. Now 92, Mirella is an extraordinary woman, curious, wildly creative. She is still writing and photographing, having inherited her creativity from her talented French mother Giselle who studied sculpture in Paris under an ageing Auguste Rodin. Giselle's uncle was the owner of the French newspaper *Le Matin*. She persuaded him that together they could start the Rodin Museum in Paris and in time managed to collect together much of the artist's work. Another relative, Mirella's uncle Jean de Brunhoff, wrote the Babar the Elephant books. And although they lived apart for years, for most of her long, temptestuous marriage to Lorenzo, Mirella referred to her philandering husband as, "my magnificent obsession". But a few years ago at his funeral, she gave a short eulogy and said to a distinctly amazed congregation, "Lorenzo's father once told me that the only pleasure he ever got out of his son was nine months before his birth!"

A GREAT LOSS

Having lead a mainly healthy life, my mother was eighty-five before she became ill. Susie and I were sitting on either side of her in the consultant's office in London when he told her she had terminal pancreatic cancer. She remained remarkably dignified about it, refused any treatment and never once complained. The dying process took exactly ten weeks and was a deeply distressing, sad and painful time. Her four girls, sons-in-law and ten adored grandchildren surrounded her with love, and caring Marie Curie nurses helped us look after her while her body and her mind gently prepared themselves for their final days.

She died in her own bed in Chelsea with the four of us sitting beside her, holding her hands. We opened the window to set free her spirit, lit candles and spread flowers all around her. For a long time afterwards we talked quietly amongst ourselves and whispered small endearments to Mum to show her how much we loved her. But I still cannot face listening to the tape of her moving memorial as it makes her loss too painful, even now more than twenty years later.

Carpe Diem

I AM LUCKY and eternally grateful to have close relationships with my sisters who have been there for me through the good times and some of the difficult. Of course we have had our differences along the way and petty quarrels when we were teenagers. There are far fewer, though perhaps felt more keenly as adults, but the core holds fast, as strong as ever. We can talk to each other in the easy patois of sisters, one step before anyone else figures out quite what we are on about. Plus our humour is the same which is a bonus. I am also extremely fond of my brothers-in-law who have always been incredibly kind to me, wise and helpful.

My sister Pods is a fine sculptor. Her excellent works of art in alabaster and stone, mainly of abstract subjects, are mainly taken from nature, while others are based on the theme of mother and child. She has had a number of exhibitions over the years where her sculptures are much admired.

A few years ago she and Todd invited me to join them and their children, Jake, my handsome godson, and his pretty sisters, Sophie and Amber, on holiday in Zanzibar. Lots of swimming and diving was the order of the day.

The elements have always seemed to conspire against me as I struggled to get my own scuba diving certificate. In my first open water dive at Swanage in the freezing Dorset sea, I only avoided being drowned in a sudden force eight gale by clinging precariously with one hand to the pier's barnacle-encrusted ladder, like an abandoned gibbon swinging forlornly from a branch. My next attempt was on the Kenyan island of Lamu where the latest hurricane had munched up the sea and sand to such a degree it was impossible to see my flippers, let alone my diving 'buddy' which all novices must have—in my case an obese American. Within five minutes he had rapidly disappeared into the murky depths and was, I assumed, floating happily down to Durban. But the sea gods had obviously decided that snorting in vast quantities of air from an oxygen tank just to stay alive underwater was not for me, and alas, I remain unqualified.

One boiling hot afternoon in Zanzibar, Todd and Jake, both deeply tanned and with newly-acquired diving certificates, went off for their second dive of the day while I lay on the crystal white beach in a deeply envious sulk. Next to me lay a golden-brown Pods who was convinced she would die of claustrophobia once under the waves. On their return Todd told us a strange story: "This large octopus swam up and tried to grab Jake's goggles off his face but Jake held on like mad, absolutely refusing to give in. So I frantically shook my octopus rattle, a sound they loathe, and eventually the creature let go."

"Wow," said Sophie and I, as jealous as two old hairdressers. It took us three months to realise the men had us totally fooled. No octopus, no tussle, no rattle.

I am lucky to have a few men friends still ticking along, most of them younger I must admit. Kinsey Marable and I met in Washington many years ago and we have been dear friends ever since. He is funny, generous to a fault with a dazzling, ultra-white smile. He ran a successful bookshop in Georgetown dealing in rare and out of print books and specialises in private library collections. He counts Oprah Winfrey, who is partial to first edition Pulitzer prize-winners, among his clients. A few years ago my pal Jean and I were staying with Kinsey, an excellent rider, and his boyfriend in Virginia where he lived and stabled his hunters.

On the way back from a lunch one day we passed dozens of shops on the road selling guns and for all we knew mortar bombs and rocket-propelled grenades. Kinsey pulled into a gas station to fill up. As we walked towards the small shop, we noticed a black pick-up truck with a large skull and crossbones emblem fixed to the front, pull in behind us. Two wiry hillbillies, looking like the main players in the film *Deliverance* got out, filled up and came in, followed by their young and extremely fat girlfriends in sloppy, sleeveless tee-shirts. They looked like the kind of guys who might bring an AK-47 and blast you for fun before they bought their steaming cups of Joe. As we waited for our milkshakes and cheeseburgers to mollify our hangover from the previous night, we sensed the hostility oozing from the truckers towards our men friends. Kinsey instintively felt these dolts, as he later said, "No doubt the result of three hundred years of inbreeding", were more than capable of hurting them. As the tension around us rose he put his arm round my waist as if I were his girlfriend and we all quickly left with our order, ran to the car and sped off.

Kinsey rang me some months ago to say he had just been passing the infamous gas station which had long since been closed. Desperate to relieve himself he drove round to the back where he found a pile of rusty old cars stacked haphazardly on top of one another. A perfect spot. Just as he was quietly doing his business, he told me, "This brute of a man, as big as The Hulk, came tearing out of the building which he had obviously adopted, like some aquisitive hermit crab, as his own." The crazed hillbilly, puce with fury, screamed obscenities at the interloper. "He told me in no uncertain terms to 'get the f… off my property.' I nearly had a heart attack. He was such a terrifying sight I had no time to zip up my trousers before I ran off."

OLD BEAU

Some years ago an old boyfriend found me again. He had managed, mostly, to retain his handsome looks and, although married for many years, he declared that he had long held a candle for me, which was flattering. However, despite the fact he lived in Devon, he was completely terrified, to the point of paranoia, that his wife and daughter, the butcher, mutual friends, the cobbler, the dog and his squash buddies might find out we had quite innocently met up.

Of course, all ages are susceptible to romance but we both knew, despite the surprisingly enduring attraction, a romantic interlude might unsettle his comfortable home life. It was clear that his was a pure soul not really cut out for extra marital affairs and besides, being single for a number of years, I have never thought it particularly wise or promising to have a married *inamorato*. Involvement, however tenuous, can seldom flourish in a vacuum. Then one fine spring day he came to lunch in my garden. A few hours of nostalgic reminiscences of our salad days together, helped along by a decent bottle of champagne and the die was cast.

But lordy, lordy I laughed for hours after my old friend left that afternoon which was naughty of me, I know. Midway through our tryst, before you could say 'Viagra', he fell off the side of the bed slap onto his back, bumping his head on the knobs of my chest of drawers on the way down. Cometh the hour, goeth the man. He lay there stunned for a minute or two seemingly helpless, like a six foot beetle turned onto its shell, long thin legs scrabbling desperately in the air. It looked so funny I just burst out laughing. Somehow I managed to help him back up and, although he didn't say anything, I think he might have put his back out. With his pride severely dented, I doubt he found it quite as amusing as I did, though he has since forgiven me. Later that day, I found myself walking down the Kings Road openly giggling, but as the writer Anais Nin has pointed out, sex has always had its absurd moments.

LORD SHAWCROSS' MEMORIAL

The writer and journalist Willie Shawcross and I have been good friends for forty years and for many of them he was there for me, in good times and bad, throughout our various marriages, divorces and hiccups with our children. He has great charm, is basically kind with a naughty sense of humour and is married to his third wife, the charming and clever Olga Polizzi. The first of his books to bring Willie to international attention was the bestselling *Sideshow: Kissinger, Nixon and the Destruction of Cambodia*, in 1979, later made into a moving and persuasive film *The Killing Fields*. I remember well a day in 1980 when he left his finished manuscript of another lengthy political book on the roof of his car while he unlocked it, promptly forgetting about it as we drove off. Writers' knowledge of computers was far less sophisticated in those days; Willie had no copies and had to rewrite the entire book, about which he maintained a surprising equanimity. But gradually over the years my dear old friend has radically changed his political views of the 1970s and is no longer the left-wing critic of the establishment he once was.

A number of years ago Willie's father, Lord Shawcross, was given a grand memorial at St Mary le Strand, a fine baroque Church standing for the last three hundred years in the middle of the Strand in London. Hartley Shawcross had been the brilliant chief British prosecutor at the Nuremberg Trial of the Nazi Leadership in 1945 and as befitting such an illustrious man, the great and good were at his Service. I was sitting with my sister Digs somewhere in the middle, pretending not to look at all the famous faces. On the steps of the chancel in front of the altar there were two vast vases on tall oak pedestals filled with the most enormous arrangement of flowers I have ever seen. Blue delphiniums, long stemmed roses, white lilies, baby's breath, the lot. They were ten foot wonders to behold, reaching, suitably, to the heavens. The beautifully chosen organ music soared round the coffered ceiling as the church began to fill up. But when my old publisher, Lord Weidenfeld and his wife Annabelle walked down the isle, the vase on the left suddenly toppled over and broke noisily on the stone floor, scattering flowers everywhere. Immediately a small curate in a crisp white belted cassock appeared out of nowhere with a broom to hurriedly sweep the water and debris away to the side. Poor Willie was mortified, rushing up and down. Of course it was a bit of a shock and I nudged Digs in the ribs; we only managed to control ourselves by concentrating fiercely on our service sheets.

Fifteen minutes later it was an ageing Margaret Thatcher's turn to make her triumphal march down the aisle to her seat in the front. Three quarters of the way, the right hand vase, not wishing to be outdone, also toppled over and smashed to the floor with another loud crack. Flowers thrown far and wide, petals swimming in water. The by now flustered little curate rushed out once again and began vigorously brushing away.

"Can you believe it?" I whispered to Digs. She shook her head in astonishment. At that moment the poor florist could take it no longer and ran out of the back of the church, but we were convulsed and it was all we could do to get through the beginning of what turned out to be a wonderfully moving service.

THE CHINESE MASSEUR

After long flights back from Africa or America I often found it soothing to have a massage with Johnny Wang, the best masseur in London. He was Chinese, short, incredibly strong and toned from his daily *Qigong* exercises and there was nothing he didn't know about the body. There existed an easy friendship between my family and Johnny, occasionally accompanying him to the best restaurants in Chinatown. The only thing I was not desperately keen on was his enormous pet python which lay happily on the sofa beneath the window during my sessions at his house. However much I admired its pale patterned skin, it was only three feet away from the massage table. Snakes hold no terror for me but every so often I would give it the beady eye to make sure there wasn't any arching sign of 'slithering-onto-table-for-a-cuddle-with-Caroline-before-I-crush-her-to-death.'

This particular massage was in the basement of an empty holistic centre near Chelsea which Johnny sometimes used. I stripped off as usual down to my knickers and lay on my front on the table for my blissful hour of relaxation. When it was time to turn over he gently massaged my head and shoulders and I was soon drifting off into LaLaland. But I came to with a jolt to find Johnny Wang's mouth, quick as a Mexican lightening beetle, firmly clasped to my right breast.

"What on earth are you doing, Johnny?", I exclaimed, horrified, as I sat bolt upright.

"Oh, Caroline, I have always wanted to do this, I would like to do it to your other one too," pleaded the masseur. I leapt off the table and quickly got dressed.

"No, no. Absolutely not. We are just friends," I said coldly. By then he was barricading the door with his arms.

"Please don't go, Caroline. Stay here with me."

My predicament was dire. Lonely basement, strong man, empty building so no one to hear me scream. Besides, I was not young. I thought the best thing to do was what so many women have had to do at some point in their lives. Keep smiling, talk normally and tell him 'of course I will come back another time.' Eventually he opened the door and I walked nonchalantly up the concrete stairs to the front door. Once through it I fled but not before noticing the new cake shop on the right was called 'The Cherry on Top'. I said to myself, 'Oh, Johnny Wang, you've lost the whole family for one quick nibble. Foolish, foolish man."

NIGHT MANOEUVERS, ZIMBABWE

In February the following year, Jacinthe and I spent ten days tearing round in a Land Rover over the vast emptiness of Namibia on our way to see the country's spectacular desert dunes, the highest and oldest in the world. As herds of long horned oryx cantered away from the road, we felt as free as two enlightened oldies can but we were really there so she could scatter her late husband's ashes. He had served his National Service in the South African Army and had chosen an unknown spot in some granite rocks with a small ficus tree shading it. I thought this would be as likely as finding a bushbaby in Belgravia but after ferretting around for an hour, she thought she had found it. We returned to the car and I sat on a nearby rock watching Jacinthe climb back up the rocks, this time clutching her precious box of ashes. She seemed at that moment the loneliest person in the world.

At the end of our trip we were invited up to a farm in Zimbabwe for a few days. Nick was an old Rhodesian friend I had known since I was 18 but saw infrequently and he had dearly loved my father, for whom he once worked. I had not been back to the country since I got married there in 1966 and although we were apprehensive about the trip, we were ultimately swayed by a few extra days of adventure. But by all accounts Nick was a pretty bad boy. He was reputed to have been an arms dealer, a gun runner and an arms-for-diamonds trader involved in numerous African wars. All I knew for certain was that he had broken sanctions for Ian Smith in the 1960s, but for the past five years he had not been allowed into Britain, Europe or America which was a pretty damning indictment and spoke of serious misdemeanours. Once, bolstered by a couple of drinks at dinner in London, I asked him with a seemingly innocent air about his nefarious activities, "Nick, what exactly is it you do when you go to Angola or the Congo to see their Presidents?," he became an instant clam.

His had been a complicated life, marred by a family tragedy. When he was fifteen years old, he cycled home from school in Salisbury one day to discover his father had shot his mother and sister before killing himself. His sister survived but Nick never talked about the incident. I am pretty sure that his emotions had been shut down from that traumatic day.

He picked us up at Johannesburg in his sleek jet, smooth as butter as we rose and sliced through the fluffy clouds before landing at the private plane terminal in Harare. Unlike most modern African airports which are colourful and chaotic this one was eerily quiet. It was expensive-looking, apparently built with the help of Mugabe's dishonest nephew, and a prime example of corruption in the country. As we approached the plump, smiling Immigration woman sitting behind her desk, I noticed Nick, with the lightening speed of a Croatian conjurer, slip her a few hundred US dollar bills. His passport had been confiscated by Mugabe a year previously and the pair appeared to know each other well. While we waited for the African porters to collect our luggage, four young Zimbabwean thugs in fedora hats, dark shades and cheap, shiny shoes, sauntered confidently up to Nick, whom they also obviously knew. It seemed clear that these guys were Mugabe's henchmen.

"Hello, Mr. T. How are you today?" the creepy chief honcho said with an ingratiating smile. The air crackled with tension—a few machine gun rounds rat-a-tatting off the walls would not have seemed out of place. Once again, Nick quickly greased their sweaty palms with handfuls of dollars. I had never witnessed this kind of blatant *baksheesh* before and Jas and I, quite mesmerised, figured out that so far he had probably parted with well over a thousand bucks. It was then the turn of a sexy young African chancer, in a red bum-hugging dress and tottering high heels, to sidle up to him. All white teeth and scarlet lipstick, she smiled expectantly before also demanding her share. At this point Nick, exasperated, smiled thinly and told her,

"Go and get a cut from your friends—I've paid them plenty."

All this did not bode well for us. We knew that Nick was not popular with the majority of whites, and a number of blacks in the country were baying for his blood. It was definitely a possibility that one day someone might take a pot shot at him and it would be in our best interests to be a few thousand miles away when they did.

A long white limousine with blacked out windows was waiting outside and Nick's driver took us speedily through the deserted roads of Harare and out into the countryside. An hour and a half later we saw a tall hill surrounded by rings of small lights circling upwards towards the summit where Nick had built his sumptuous house. As the car snaked its way up the incline, armed guards in cubicles at various checkpoints leapt to their feet and saluted smartly.

'Evening, Boss,' they said with a beaming smile.

When we reached the top there was a thick iron electric gate which would have done Guantanamo Bay proud, operated by yet another guard.

Twenty feet from it a second metal gate would open once the car was safely through.

As the first gate closed behind us all the lights went out. We were firmly stuck between two massive gates—perfect target practice for a roaming gang who had it in for Nick and, as collateral damage, his two foolhardy female companions.

"What's happened?" demanded Nick coldly, every muscle in his neck alert to danger, while Jas and I had practically passed out with terror.

"Sorry, Boss, the generators have gone off," answered the polite African guard.

"What, all three of them?"

"Yes, Boss."

Silence. We continued to sit there like rabbits frozen in a snowstorm for what seemed like an eternity until the generators came back on. Huge relief all round. Somehow we managed to drive safely through the second gate without being slaughtered and reached the house to be greeted by Nick's friendly, welcoming, Gucci-belted staff.

'FARU THE LITTLE RHINO'

These days many private game reserves, including Nick's, have a few rhinos grazing on their pastures in order to help save the endangered species. I have always loved these animals and a few years ago decided to write a children's book on the subject. There are less than 5,000 black rhino left and I felt it was crucial to help children everywhere to become more aware of the dangers and the uncertain future facing this very special creature. *Faru* is Swahili for rhino and the game reserves I visited in East Africa guard their precious rhinos round the clock. It was moving to see just how caringly Tony Fitzjohn and his game wardens looked after their twenty seven black rhinos in Mkomazi.

My friend Adrienne Kennaway did the charming illustrations for *Faru the Little Rhino* who goes on a quest to discover why there are so few rhinos left on the African plains.

ONWARDS AND SIDEWAYS

If I am absolutely candid, I have never thought I would stay this long in England. I didn't feel it was where I truly belonged. The fact that I was neither brought up nor went to school here and only came to live in London permanently at the age of thirty-three, added to my sense of rootlessness, my certainty that I didn't fit in. Not that it really matters in the long run. I will always feel lucky for having an unusually colourful, loving and adventurous life growing up in Africa and although I have always thought of Kenya as my home, the country I grew up in no longer exists. As Neil Diamond's song goes: 'L.A.'s fine, but it ain't home. New York's home, but it ain't mine no more.'

My dilemma solved itself with time; I have never lost the thrill of travel but I am happiest living near my children and grandchildren. They are my roots, my heart, my momentum and we draw strength and succour from each other. The boys are growing up fast, known amongst family and friends for their football skills, and all extremely handsome, bright and amusing. Cal has his university history degree, a job working on a complicated coding project, and a pretty, longterm girlfriend named Minna. Jago, now six foot three inches, is curious, open-minded and spreading his wings in distant lands. Zac plays a mean guitar with his band and is off to Bristol University, while Fin is an academically-driven sixteen year old and still involved in his singularly imaginative art.

Ever since boarding at the age of seven, I learnt to be fine with my own company. And as I get older and spend more time alone, I have managed to cope with the pangs of loneliness. It occasionally grips me, such a solitary kind of pain, like depression or grief. But my generation learnt to keep most things to themselves long ago and not complain. Now many of my greatest friends are gone and a few more are well on their way. But sooner or later my mind drifts back to how fortunate I have been in having my beloved girls and adored grandsons. I reminisce about my many adventures in unusual places—riding skinny little ponies with Appley across the roof of Ethiopia in the Simien Mountains as we slowly made our way to the ancient, holy town of Lalibela. Or seeing, up close and personal, the rare sight of two massive tigers mating in the wilds of India.

Apart from the eight years living in Fulham where my girls spent their teens, I have always lived in Earl's Court; back to Kangaroo Alley where my friends and I hung out in the 1960s. For fifteen years I had a flat in Earls Court Square with a huge elegant room on the first floor, the piano nobile of an old house. Three floor to ceiling windows opened onto a long balcony overlooking a glorious tree-filled square. Known as the 'party flat' for the numerous *soireés* given there, it was greatly loved and admired and I never wanted to leave. But needs must sometimes as the years increase and the money runs out. I now have a small house with a little garden in the prettiest part of the area, Earl's Court village, surrounded by pastel coloured houses built in the mid-1800s.

These days the simplest things in life give me increasing pleasure. Bluebells and lilies-of-the-valley in my garden; blackbirds singing in the spring. When the night skies are clear, I can see the moon sail over the cherry tree hanging over my garden wall. The author Vita Sackville-West, who designed the fabulous gardens at Sissinghurst Castle, insisted that one must 'cram, cram, cram' the garden with plants. Not an inch of earth should be seen, so mine is lavishly overflowing. Tucked in at the back there is a small studio where I indulge my hobby of painting and in my tiny slice of a conservatory I can read again some of my favourites novels—among them French novelist Romain Gary's *The Kites*, a Second World War resistance story, and *On the Black Hill*, about the lives of twin brothers growing up on a farm in Wales, by travel writer and story-teller *extraordinaire*, Bruce Chatwin. I have finally learned to be content and will live here until I am either carried out feet first or a handsome stranger whisks me off in his classic, open-topped Mercedes sportscar, to catch the sun.

FINIS

Acknowledgements

My thanks to everyone who gave me encouragement and support with this book. It goes especially to Tara Fischer, my elder daughter, who pored over and edited the manuscript, firmly penciling things out; and Tasmin Norman, my younger daughter, who read the penultimate draft and made constructive suggestions. My sister Anne Civardi helped hugely with producing decent prints of old photographs and my other two sisters, Susie Hill and Rachel Wyndham, joined her in sharing their own letters, photos and childhood memories. The late Claire Clifton was there for me from the very beginning, full of excitement and humorous ideas. My close Kenya pals, Appley Hoare, Mary Anne Fitzgerald, Mirella Ricciardi and Jacinthe Rhodes were always at the end of a phone if I needed them. Jon Randal had great recall of mutual journalist friends and Wendy Larsen, the first treasured friend I made in America, had vivid memories of our turbulent time together in Chicago during the 1968 anti-Vietnam war protests. Some of my most enthusiastic support has come from my grandchildren and my love goes out to them.

There are others whom I must thank for their encouraging and often essential help, including some who are no longer around: Imogen Lycett Green, Anthony Eyre (for his tremendous help and patience!), Rupert Norman, Lord and Lady Powell, Alasdair and Carolyn Hadden-Paton, the late Tony Fitzjohn and the late John Rendall, Roderic Hill, Henry Wyndham, Todd Civardi, Deborah Gillette and Eddie Mears.